AF726091

Steve Heller

Retirement Life Insurance

Steve Heller

Retirement Life Insurance

How Much is Needed to Optimize Retirement Spending

DE G PRESS

ISBN 978-1-5015-1512-5
e-ISBN (PDF) 978-1-5015-0618-5
e-ISBN (EPUB) 978-1-5015-0630-7

Library of Congress Cataloging-in-Publication Data
A CIP catalog record for this book has been applied for at the Library of Congress.

Bibliographic information published by the Deutsche Nationalbibliothek
The Deutsche Nationalbibliothek lists this publication in the Deutsche Nationalbibliografie; detailed bibliographic data are available on the Internet at http://dnb.dnb.de.

Published by Walter de Gruyter Inc., Boston/Berlin
Printing and binding: CPI books GmbH, Leck
♾ Printed on acid-free paper
Printed in Germany

www.degruyter.com

Advance Praise

I think your book is great. It will be a great tool for those who are in insurance sales because this tool shows the reality of what the insured's retirement will look like with/without insurance, and how to increase and sustain their retirement income using insurance or annuities. It should increase sales especially to women who are worried about what will happen to them if their husbands die early, because it walks you through every eventuality of what may happen and how that will affect post retirement income. It gives couples the ability to plan for the "what ifs" in life and to become prepared by just buying an insurance policy or an annuity.

As a lay person and a woman, this points out the reality of what my retirement would be without my husband's social security and how having an insurance policy can make my retirement future more secure. Because I am expected to live longer, this tool will help me to reduce stress and anxiety about money when I am older and unable to work. I have learned quite a few things by reading this book.

—Andromeda Hans,
Former stockbroker at TD Waterhouse

Finally! If you are retired and want to model increasing sustainable spending with insurance products, this is the book you have been looking for. As an early retiree in my forties, I have been looking for this type of information for several years–without success. I have met with a dozen insurance advisors–without success. This book provides the background, information, and method of analyzing and modeling various scenarios–and it does so in a brilliantly engaging manner.

—David Milligan,
Milligan Patent Law Group (Omaha, Nebraska, USA)

As someone who "thought" they had a decent understanding of all the variables that could contribute to a long, successful retirement, this book and program were real eye-openers. I would never have given a second thought to how insurance could help a surviving spouse make up for the loss of social security income.

And I am exploring annuities in a new light. Until reading this book, I never considered how annuities could factor into a retirement plan, having been a person who always managed my own investments. This book and program helped show me that annuities can play a significant role in keeping income steady in retirement and eliminating stock market stress.

—Mike Cortopassi,
Principal Staff Engineer at Digital Design Corporation

This book is dedicated to my beloved wife, Susan Heller, who was happy not to be my test reader this time.

Acknowledgments

Dennis Conlon, for his friendship and support of this project through all of its twists and turns.

My mother, Sali Heller Neff, who never doubted that it would come to fruition one day. Here is the proof that she was right.

Contents

Preface

Even though life insurance is an old, established financial product, and annuities are even older, there is one enormous market that has been overlooked: the market for term life insurance to protect a surviving spouse against the loss of Social Security payments after the death of the first spouse. This book explains how to address this market, and includes instructions for and access to the software that illustrates how term insurance and annuities can increase sustainable spending in retirement.

It is an unfortunate fact that most people have no idea how much they can really spend in retirement. Many are living frugal lives spending their social security while "saving for a rainy day". If they buy life insurance at all, they do so in small amounts because they think that's all they can afford. Almost no one would believe that buying a significant amount of term life insurance after age 60 actually can free them to spend more money on a monthly basis. Furthermore, even if they did consider that possibility, no one could show them exactly how that might work in their individual cases.

Until now.

This book and its accompanying software were created to provide a superior sales tool for United States life insurance agents, financial and retirement planners, and others interested in analyzing the retirement income status of customers and suggesting solutions to optimize their sustainable retirement spending. You no longer have to rely on guesswork or rules of thumb; instead you can show your clients specific solutions to their major retirement issues. You can show them exactly what they need to purchase, and the sales process provides an automatic follow-up opportunity each year to update the assumptions and financial picture of the client.

The author, a very experienced programmer and author of several books, set out to create a program to look at financial aspects of retirement and in particular to analyze how much money could be safely spent. Not unexpectedly, he was able to analyze the impact of annuities on retirement. What was something of a surprise was the impact of life insurance on what could safely be spent. Once he discovered that effect, he decided to develop a tool that would allow others, especially life insurance agents and financial planners, to find client-specific answers to questions common to anyone facing retirement. He refined the program to be able to accept a client's financial data and calculate answers to questions like these:

- How much money can your clients spend in retirement without having to worry about running out of money, given their current financial picture?
- What should they do to optimize their retirement spending?
- How can a surviving spouse be protected from the drop in Social Security benefits after the death of the first spouse?
- Why is it likely that buying insurance or buying a fixed annuity can dramatically increase the level of your client's sustainable spending—even if your customer is already retired?
- How much can sustainable spending be improved, and what level of term insurance or annuity purchase will achieve that optimal level of spending?
- How do US federal income taxes affect your clients' spending, and how can these effects be minimized?
- When should your clients start taking social security?

All the above questions and more are answered by the software that accompanies this book. The software, called Rhino Retirement Analyzer, though more complex than most end users would care to learn, offers you the opportunity to load in customer financial data and illustrate options for improving sustainable spending. The amazing and counter-intuitive part is that it is highly likely that most individuals can see their monthly spending capability go up significantly by buying insurance and/or buying a fixed annuity. The software enables you to zero in on the level of each of these products that optimizes their spending.

That explains the software, but why is a book necessary? The book shows you how to use the program and how to explain the results to your clients using a fictional dialog between an insurance agent and his clients. It shows what goes into making these calculations and why they work the way they do. The book also includes detailed instructions on how to use the software, with walk-throughs that you can use. The solutions that the Rhino program illustrates will allow you to offer a market for term insurance that your competitors who aren't using this program won't be able to sell into.

About the Software

The author, a published programming author and skilled programmer, has spent years developing the Rhino Retirement Analyzer software. Programmers who have reviewed the software are struck by the enormous amount of work and time evidenced by the capabilities of this program. But you don't have to pay the high price it would cost to develop such a program for your business. Instead, the program is available for free download at:

rhino-retirement-analyzers.com
or
www.degruyter.com/view/product/486326

The software will be updated periodically to fix any issues found by users and to handle changes in regulations, tax codes and so on. The updated version will be available at the above addresses. In the appendices to this book, you will find user manuals for the program's various modes of operation.

For modifications to the program, including company-specific terms, rates, or rating classes, contact Steve Heller via steve@rhino-retirement-analyzers.com for a quote.

Chapter 1
The Retirement Crisis in Brief

A Tale of Two Widows

Jane and June Smith are sisters, Jane turning 58 years old in 2017, while June turns 60 in that same year. They are married to two brothers, Jim and John Smith, who turn 61 and 63, respectively, in 2017. Jim and John work for the same company.

Each Smith family has the following financial profile:

1. $200K in investible assets, comprising $30K cash, $100K in traditional retirement accounts, and $70K in a taxable brokerage account with a tax basis of $50K. All the assets but the cash are in index funds that are expected to provide a 7% pretax return before expected inflation of 2%, whereas the cash is expected to return 2% pretax before inflation.
2. The husband works as a contractor, with no benefits other than his salary of $50,000 and plans to retire at age 65 (2021 and 2019 for Jim and John, respectively); the wife has already retired from her corporate job.
3. Projected Social Security benefits, starting when the husband retires: $2,300 for the husband, $1,800 for the wife.
4. No pensions for either spouse.
5. They have no children at home and don't need to leave a legacy to anyone.
6. Both spouses are in excellent health.

One day the call comes in to both Mrs. Smiths telling them that their husbands have been killed in a freak accident at work.

After Jane recovers a bit from the shock of the news, she asks June to come over so they can discuss their new financial situation. When she arrives, Jane says, "What will I do now? I don't have any idea how I will pay my bills or how much I can spend!" June says, "Didn't you get that retirement analysis that Bob, our new financial planner, wanted to do for us?" Jane replies, "No, what are you talking about? We never talked with him because we got too busy."

June says, "Bob showed us how, with one small change in how we handle our money, we would be able to increase our sustainable retirement spending by about $14,000 a year, after federal income taxes, even in the event of a tragedy like this. So, we did it."

"I wish I had made time to see him."

"You can fix that."

DOI 10.1515/9781501506185-001

"How? It's too late now!"

"No, it isn't. Wake up. WAKE UP!!!"

Jane bolts upright in bed. "What a terrible nightmare!" She looks across the room to the bathroom door and sees light under the door, along with the sound of the shower that Jim is taking before work. So much for her plan of sleeping in today....

After kissing Jim goodbye and sitting down to a raisin muffin for breakfast, she texts June:

Jane: "Hi, got an hour to talk this morning?"

June: "Sure, your place or mine?"

Jane: "Mine."

June: "I'll be over at 9."

When June arrives, Jane says, "Remember when you explained what that new financial planner did for you? Well, I just had a nightmare about our husbands being killed in a freak accident and my not having done whatever it was that he told you to do. The only detail I remember is that you were able to increase your projected sustainable retirement spending by about $15,000 a year (after federal income taxes) by following his suggestions. Obviously, my unconscious was trying to tell me I should have paid more attention to what you were telling me. Please explain it to me again, and this time I promise I'll listen carefully."

"Sure, glad to. He has a new kind of financial planning software that takes assets, salary, pensions, age, sex, any existing life insurance, and health into consideration when making a conservative projection of how much after-tax spending you can afford to do per year in retirement, even if one spouse dies at the worst possible time. It takes about 15 minutes to gather the data, then he runs some 'optimizers' to see if there's a way to improve the results by making some changes in your insurance and/or annuities. In our case, with the assumptions he put in for expected returns on our investment portfolio and our cash holdings, it turned out that we had to make only one change to the way we were handling our money to get a big improvement in the worst-case scenario, as you correctly remembered."

"Ok, I'll call him today to make an appointment for him to show me exactly how it works."

...

We'll pick up this conversation a bit later. But first we need to look at one of the most important sources of retirement income for many Americans.

Social Security as a Mainstay of Retirement Income

As with current retirees, one of the largest sources of retirement income for the Baby Boomer generation will be from Social Security payments, as explained in an article in the "Social Security Bulletin":

> "Similar to current retirees, Social Security will account for about two-fifths of the projected family income at age 67 and will be received by almost all baby-boomer retirees. Supplemental Security Income will be received by 5 percent of current retirees and only 2 percent of baby-boomer retirees. **The projections also suggest that baby boomers are less likely than current retirees to have enough postretirement income to maintain their preretirement living standards.** The financial planning literature often recommends having enough postretirement income to replace 70 percent to 80 percent of preretirement income; however, over two-fifths of baby-boomer retirees will replace less than three-quarters of their preretirement earnings and almost a fifth will replace less than half of their preretirement earnings."
>
> (From https://www.ssa.gov/policy/docs/ssb/v65n3/v65n3p1.html, emphasis added by author)

However, even this insufficient income is subject to a risk of loss that is currently uninsured in most cases. This is the risk of premature death of one spouse of a married couple; when one spouse dies, the remaining spouse's income is reduced by the loss of one payment. The exact proportion of income lost by this event varies but is generally in the range of one-third to one-half of the original income.

This problem is widely recognized by personal financial advisers, and was discussed in detail in a 2012 GAO publication entitled "RETIREMENT SECURITY: Women Still Face Challenges" (http://www.gao.gov/assets/600/592726.pdf). Here is a passage entitled "Widowed After Age 50" (pp. 30–31):

> "Not only did women's total household assets and income decline substantially with widowhood, but the effects were more pronounced for women than for men. For example, while men's income fell 22 percent after widowerhood, women's income fell by an even greater amount – 37 percent. The effects were larger for women living in younger households than women living in older households. Specifically, women in households where all members were age 64 or younger experienced a 31 percent decrease in assets and a 47 percent decrease in income. Adding to these effects, widowhood was a much more common experience for women than men in our sample. In fact, women were at least twice as likely as men to become widowed between any two survey periods. Consequently, 70 percent of women age 85 and over were widowed compared to only 24 percent of men age 85 and over."

However, just realizing that the problem exists, while necessary, is not sufficient. What we need is a *solution* to the problem of the "significant financial decline" at widowhood. Fortunately, there is a method to prevent this disaster in many cases. Let's see what it is and how it works.

Chapter 2
A New Use for Life Insurance

In this chapter, we are going to use a slightly oversimplified example to give you an understanding of how Social Security and life insurance can impact retirement spending. In particular, we will see how the correct amount of life insurance may enable people to safely spend more than they could without that insurance. It is important for you to understand the dynamics of the impact of life events on the retiree's level of spending and, hopefully, at the end, you will get a sense of why the variables involved work the way they do. In succeeding chapters, we will go into more detail about the exact impact of changes to life insurance and other variables.

Retirement Income Security and Life Insurance

We will start with a new example and return to the Smiths later in the chapter.

Richard and Mary Doe are a married couple, both aged 66 in 2017. Each of them qualifies for a $2,000-a-month Social Security payment at full retirement age (FRA), which is 66 in their cases because they were born in 1951. Of course, this means that when one of them dies, the survivor will be able to collect only one Social Security payment, which means a severe reduction in family income of 50% compared with the situation where both are still alive and collecting their Social Security payments.

In such a situation, it shouldn't be too surprising that the worst-case scenario is that one of the spouses (the one with the shorter life expectancy) dies immediately, whereas the other spouse lives to the end of their reasonable life expectancy. This cuts off the second Social Security payment as early as possible while the survivor requires retirement income to continue for the longest possible time.

In this particular case, the worst-case scenario is that Richard dies in 2017, whereas Mary lives a long time on just one Social Security payment that amounts to $24,000 a year. Thus, it is possible that Mary will have to live on about $24,000 a year for the rest of her life.[i]

That is a severe drop in income. Is there any way that she can mitigate this without going back to work?

Yes, there is; and the answer is surprising—life insurance. The truth is that most people, at best, look at what they have and how long they might live, divide the first number by the second number, add their Social Security or other retirement income sources, and decide that is the amount they can spend. Sadly, they

DOI 10.1515/9781501506185-002

do not take advantage of the opportunity afforded by life insurance to enable what in many cases is a significantly higher level of spending; or to realize that in already having insurance, they have more spending power than they know. Even worse, many people assume that they can spend all their current Social Security income without considering the significant drop in income if one of them dies early.

Furthermore, until now, there has been no way to calculate the amount they can safely spend. Without that knowledge, it does little good to know that you can spend a bit more. The remainder of this chapter will explain why life insurance can increase the level that can be safely spent and make it clear that the level of insurance required to fit a given situation can be determined.

Let's go back to Richard and Mary and see what an optimal amount of life insurance could do for them. If we were to add $250K of 15-year term life insurance on each of them, at an estimated yearly premium of $1,763 for Richard and $1,127 for Mary,[ii] the worst-case scenario is still that Richard dies in 2017. But with the life insurance in force, Mary can spend about $31,000 a year for the rest of her life, an improvement of about $6,500 a year, *after* paying the insurance premiums, even if Richard dies in the worst year (2017)![iii] How is this possible?

The answer is that the life insurance payout of $250K after Richard dies in 2017 allows Mary to fund her retirement at a higher level of spending. We are assuming that she lives to her 90th percentile life expectancy, which is the year 2052, so that extra $250K has to be spread out over all of those remaining years. Since Richard's dying in 2017 is the worst case, assuming no other factors change significantly, she can expect to be able to spend at that $31,000 level.

But I'm sure some of you are already saying "What good does term life insurance do if they both live beyond the term of the insurance?" The answer is that if they both live that long, then they have had a long time to collect both Social Security payments and should have been saving some of that Social Security money to sustain the survivor after one of them dies; this is why the maximum safe spending level with the recommended insurance is only about $31,000 even though their two Social Security payments total $48,000. We'll get into that in more detail later.

Of course, this analysis is a gross oversimplification of the nature of Social Security, especially as it applies to married couples. It is no exaggeration to say that Social Security is *complicated*. The ages of both spouses, both when starting to take payments and at the death of the first spouse, the tax implications of Social Security payments and how they interact with other sources of income, the special rules for widow's benefits, and a number of other factors make calculations regarding Social Security payments difficult. This is why there is an entire industry devoted to helping people decide when and how to take Social Security. Yet none of the services I have investigated mention the applicability of life insurance to the severe hazard to living standards of early death of one spouse.

Let's get back to our example of Richard and Mary Doe, but now we will assume that he still qualifies for a $2,000 benefit at FRA in 2017, but she qualifies for a spouse's benefit of only $1,000 at FRA in 2017. In this case, they should buy $150K of 15-year term apiece, at estimated premiums of $1,347 for Richard and $870 for Mary.[iv] In this case, the worst-case scenario is that Richard dies right after the insurance expires, so there is no insurance payout. However, the maximum sustainable spending in the worst case is still improved from about $24,000 a year without insurance to about $28,000 with insurance, after paying the insurance premiums. This is still a worthwhile result of about $350 a month higher sustainable spending for the widow if her husband dies in the worst possible year, 2032.

Now let's add the same assets that each Smith family had in the first chapter, namely $200K in investible assets, comprising $30K cash, $100K in traditional retirement accounts, and $70K in a taxable brokerage account with a tax basis of $50K. The results are obviously going to be better than with the previous scenario due to the additional assets, but the improvement from buying insurance is the same, about $4,000, as the contribution of Social Security is the same in both cases, and the Does stay in the 0% tax bracket with less than $34,000 of family income.

At this point, we are ready to look back at the Smith scenario itself to see how June's financial adviser could show her a far bigger $15,000 improvement in sustainable after-tax spending. In their case, the biggest problem is what would happen if John died in 2017, in which case June would have to wait until 2026 to reach her full retirement age. If she took her survivor's Social Security benefit before 2026, it would be reduced substantially due to her taking it early.[v] As a result, the amount of life insurance needed to make up for the lost Social Security income until she gets to that full retirement age is far greater, coming out to $550,000 for each spouse. This results in an estimated yearly premium of $2,088 for John and $1,124 for Jane.

The obvious question at this point is how we (or the financial planner in our story) could figure out how much insurance is needed to optimize sustainable after-tax spending, so let's look at that next.

Prerequisites for Calculating Sustainable After-Tax Spending

First, let's discuss what we would need to know in order to do such a calculation. Let's assume that we have a program that can do all the calculations for us as long as we have the correct data to enter.[vi]

The input data can be divided into a number of segments:
1. Personal: Birthdate, sex, and life insurance rating of each spouse.[vii]
2. Assets: How much each spouse has in cash, traditional (pretax) retirement accounts, Roth retirement accounts, and taxable accounts. For the taxable accounts, we also need to know the tax basis to compute capital gains taxes.
3. Income: For each spouse, the salary, retirement date, qualified dividends, Social Security start date, Social Security Primary Insurance Amount, and estimated SS benefit, if that is known.[viii]
4. Expected additional expenses: If the client knows that he or she will have a specific expense at some specific date in the future, this must be taken into account as a draw on his or her capital at that time, which will reduce sustainable income.
5. Annuities or pensions: For each spouse, the parameters of any 'single-life' or 'joint & 100% to survivor' annuity, including starting date, annuity cost, annuity basis,[ix] monthly payment, and whether it is adjusted to CPI and/or has a return of premium rider.
6. Existing life insurance: For each spouse, the starting date, term, face amount, and yearly premium of any existing policies.
7. Assumptions: Expected values for inflation, nominal return on portfolio assets, and nominal return on cash.

Now, of course, there is other data that such a calculation would need, including:
1. Life insurance premiums for all relevant ages, terms, face amounts, and ratings for both males and females.
2. Mortality rates, to be used to calculate conservative (e.g., 90th percentile) life expectancies so that the client can avoid running out of money prematurely.
3. Tax rates, brackets, deductions, exemptions, and the like.

And one of the most complex parts of the whole process is calculating the tax effects of taking money out of various types of accounts (i.e., pretax savings, taxable accounts, or Roth accounts), along with the special tax treatment of Social Security payments.

Now that we have the general idea of what input data and algorithms are needed, how would such a program actually solve for optimal sustainable after-tax spending?

Calculating Sustainable After-Tax Spending

One step in this process is to make an initial estimate of spending for the entire conservative lifetime of the longer-lived spouse, simulate withdrawals, taxes, and spending for all the years over which the money will be needed, and see whether there is money left over or not enough to sustain that level of spending. If there is money left over, increase spending, and if there isn't enough, decrease spending.

However, this is just the beginning of the calculations, because we don't know when each spouse is going to die. So, to be able to compute maximum sustainable spending in the worst case, we have to see what happens to that number if one of the spouses dies early or late, and the same for the other spouse. Obviously, this can generate a lot of possible combinations, but fortunately the worst case is generally when one spouse lives a long time and the second spouse dies either immediately or immediately after the termination of a life insurance policy covering that second spouse, so we can reduce the number of simulations and still get good results.

So now we have the base case, with the existing financial and personal picture of the couple. Next, we simulate the results of adding life insurance policies with different face amounts and terms, then running the calculations again to see which, if any, of those additions is effective in increasing sustainable spending.[x]

It would be possible to examine any of these scenarios "by hand," using a spreadsheet for the calculations, looking up the life insurance premiums on the web and running the tax calculations using a commercial tax program. But that is an enormous amount of work that most people either can't or won't undertake, especially if they don't know how much improvement in sustainable spending might result to compensate them for the effort. On the other hand, a program that executes all the calculations searching for the best result would be a lot less work to use, although such a program would require several developer-years to write.

As I have mentioned earlier, there is indeed such a program. To see what it can do to help a married couple figure out how much they can spend, and how they may be able to improve on their current sustainable spending level, let's return to our two sisters from Chapter 1 as they visit their financial planner.

---

[i] The reason that it is not exactly $24,000 a year is that we are assuming that Richard dies at the end of the year, so his Social Security payments have been paid for the year of death. This provides a little extra cash that can be used to boost spending for Mary in the future.

[ii] You may be wondering how I determined the term, face amount, and premium for the life insurance. I promise I'll explain that later.

[iii] To analyze the results of this scenario, we will make some simplifying assumptions, some of which will be relaxed in later iterations of this explanation:

1. They have no other income.
2. They have no financial assets.
3. There is no inflation.
4. The federal tax laws don't change from those in January 2017.
5. They live in a state that doesn't tax Social Security.
6. They are both in excellent health.
7. The first spouse dies at the end of a year.
8. Neither of them lives beyond their 90th percentile of life expectancy.
9. They have no existing life insurance.

[iv] How do we know that they should buy $150K of 15-year term? We'll get to that later in the book.

[v] It would be possible for June to take her survivor's benefit as early as age 60 and her own later, but this introduces even more complexity to the calculations. According to the Social Security Administration: "If a person receives widow's or widower's benefits, ***and*** will qualify for a retirement benefit that's more than their survivors benefit, they can switch to their own retirement benefit as early as age 62 or as late as age 70. The rules are complicated and vary depending on the situation, so talk to a Social Security representative about the options available." (from https://www.ssa.gov/planners/survivors/survivorchartred.html)

[vi] In fact, we do have such a program. More on that in a bit.

[vii] The life insurance rating is needed to estimate the life insurance premium for each spouse, given the other inputs.

[viii] If the Social Security benefit isn't known, it can be estimated from the PIA and starting date.

[ix] Although cost and basis may often be the same in dollar amount, they aren't the same economically. Cost is used in calculating return of premium, whereas basis is used in tax calculations.

[x] There are other possible optimizations I will cover later, including adding annuities and changing the dates when each spouse takes their SS benefit.

Chapter 3
A Visit with the Financial Planner

Back to Our Two Sisters…

June says, “Why don’t we both go see the financial planner together? I could use a refresher on what he was showing me and you need to see it for yourself, too.”

Jane says, “Sure. Let’s make it for tomorrow afternoon. I’ll ask him to come here.”

The next afternoon, Bob, the financial planner, comes to Jane’s house to meet with the sisters. June starts out by asking him to show her the analysis that he had run for her a couple of weeks earlier. He says, “Sure, no problem.” He turns on his computer, double-clicks an icon labeled “Rhino Retirement Analyzer,” and loads a file called “JuneAndJohnSmith.rra.”

Bob says, “This is the main screen that shows the results with your new insurance.” (See Figure 3.1.)

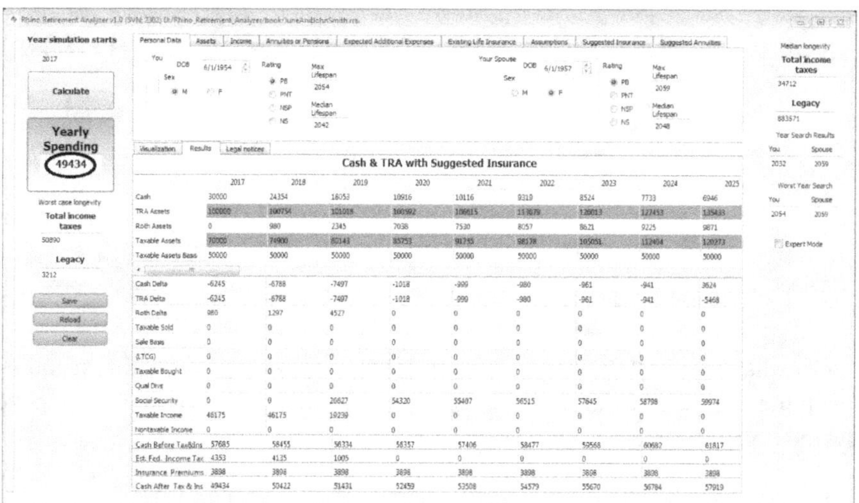

Figure 3.1: The Rhino Retirement Analyzer result screen

Bob continues, “The ‘49434’ in the ‘Yearly Spending’ box is the amount that you would be able to spend every year for the rest of your life even if Jim died at the

DOI 10.1515/9781501506185-003

worst possible time. And that is a 'real,' that is, inflation-adjusted, amount, so it is adjusted for the amount of inflation that we entered as an assumption."

The Comparison between Results with and without Insurance

June continues, "OK, but where is the comparison between the 'with insurance' and 'without insurance' results?"

Bob clicks the "Suggested Insurance" tab, pushes the F4 key, and shows them the comparison screen. (See Figure 3.2)

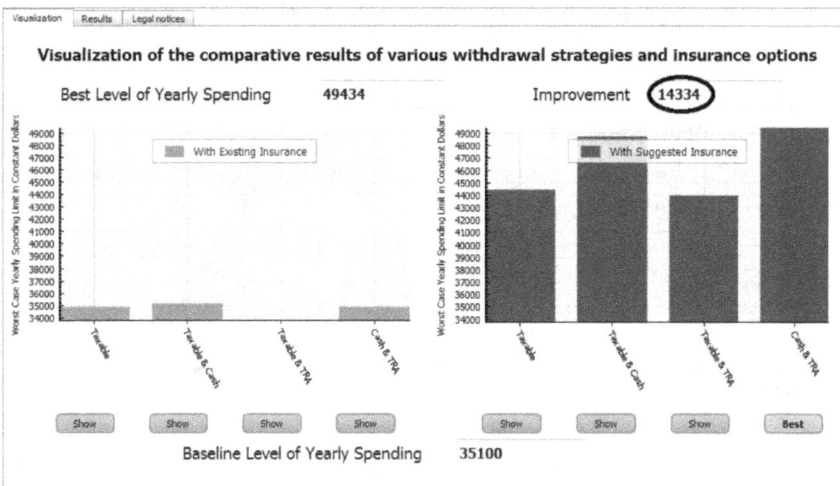

Figure 3.2: The Rhino Retirement Analyzer comparative results screen

Bob explains, "The '14334' is the amount of improvement in sustainable spending with the suggested insurance, compared to the amount you could safely spend without that insurance."

How is the Amount of Life Insurance Calculated?

Jane then asks, "I see that both June and John have $550K in insurance. How was that calculated?"

"Yes," Bob explains, "both June and John needed $550,000 worth of 15-year term, for an estimated yearly premium of about $3,900 for both policies. Now as to how the amount and term were calculated, that's a bit more complicated. The basic idea is that the program tries all the available amounts and terms that the insurance company would write, with a maximum premium of 10% of your yearly cashflow. After it has done that, it picks the one that produces the best improvement in sustainable spending compared with the existing situation."

Including Existing Life Insurance

Jane then asks, "What if we already had some life insurance?"

Bob answers, "Then you would enter that information in the 'Existing Life Insurance' tab, and the program would see if it could improve sustainable spending by adding some more insurance. If not, it wouldn't recommend any additional insurance."

Optimizing the Timing of Social Security

Jane says, "I'm not sure we are planning to take Social Security at the best time. Can it help with that?"

Bob replies, "Yes, it has a Social Security optimization feature too."

Entering Client Personal Data

"But before we calculate anything for you, we need to enter the data for you and Jim."

Jane says, "OK, let's do that." So, Bob clicks the "Clear" button to erase the existing data, then clicks the "Personal Data" tab. (See Figure 3.3.).

Figure 3.3: The Rhino Retirement Analyzer Personal Data tab

Bob says, "What's Jim's birthdate, and yours?"

Jane says, "6/1/1956 and 6/1/1959, respectively."

Bob continues, "Are you both in excellent health? Not taking any medications, no recent serious illnesses, etc.? This is important to estimate your insurance rating and expected lifespan."

Jane says, "Yes, for me. Jim is taking a couple of blood pressure medications and needs to lose 20 pounds or so. Otherwise, he is in good shape."

Bob replies, "OK, I'll put you down as an estimated 'Preferred Best' rating and Jim for 'Preferred Non-Tobacco' (the best and second-best ratings)."

After he enters this data, the resulting tab looks like Figure 3.4.

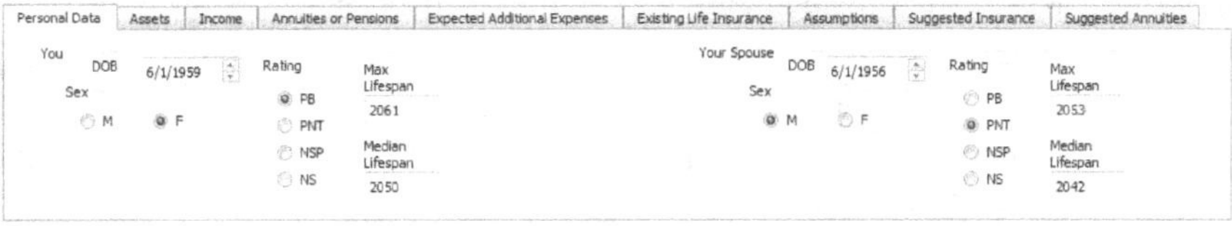

Figure 3.4: The Rhino Retirement Analyzer Personal Data tab with Jane and Jim Smith's data

Entering Client Asset Data

Next, Bob clicks on the "Assets" tab, which looks like Figure 3.5.

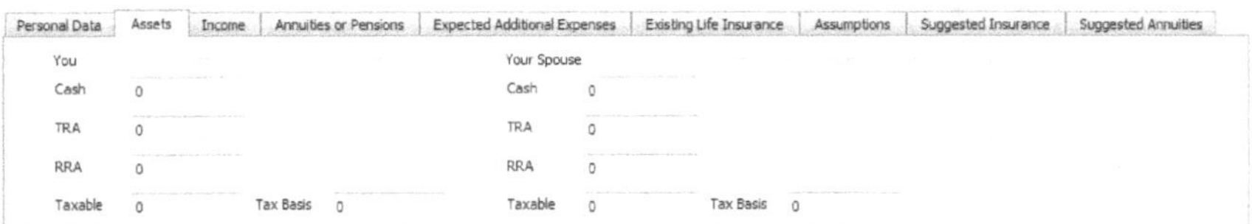

Figure 3.5: The Rhino Retirement Analyzer Assets tab

Bob says, "What do you have in cash, traditional retirement accounts, Roth retirement accounts, and taxable accounts, such as a brokerage account? We can combine the figures for both of you if that's easier."

Jane says, "Yes, let's combine them. The numbers are $30K cash, $100K in traditional retirement accounts, and $70K in taxable. No Roth accounts."

Bob continues, "We also will need the tax basis for the taxable account so the program can calculate capital gains taxes."

Jane responds, “The tax basis for the taxable account is $50K.”

Bob fills in those numbers. (See Figure 3.6.)

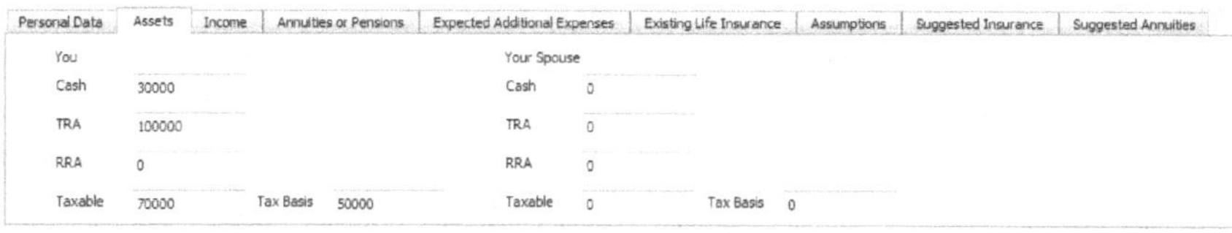

Figure 3.6: The Rhino Retirement Analyzer Assets tab filled in with Jane and Jim Smith’s data

Entering Client Income Information

Bob continues, “Next we have to fill in your income information. Here’s that tab.” (See Figure 3.7.)

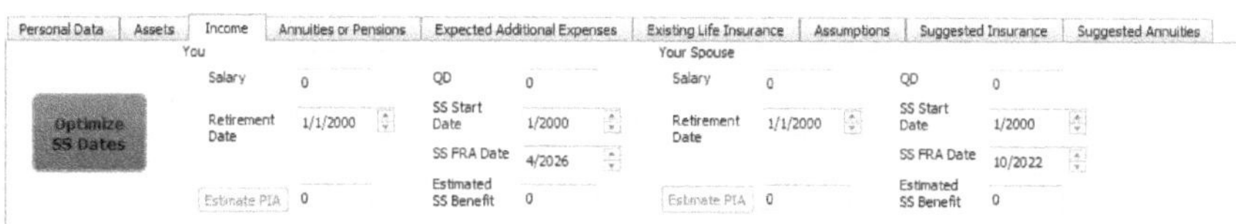

Figure 3.7: The Rhino Retirement Analyzer Income tab

Bob then asks, “What should I put in the Salary and Retirement Date fields?”

Jane says, “$50,000 salary for Jim, retiring in 2021. I’m already retired. What about those other fields, like QD and ‘Estimate PIA’?”

Bob replies, “QD is ‘qualified dividends.’ That is used when you have stocks that pay ‘qualified dividends’ and that you are holding for income only and don’t want to sell. You don’t have any such stocks, right?”

Jane answers, “No, we don’t.”

Full Retirement Age and the Primary Insurance Amount

Bob continues, “FRA stands for Full Retirement Age, which is the age when your Social Security benefit would be your ‘PIA’, which means Primary Insurance Amount. The Primary Insurance Amount is the amount that you would get every month from Social Security if you take your payment at your FRA. Notice that the 'SS FRA Date' fields are already filled in for you and Jim, as that date is based on your birthdates, which we filled in on the 'Personal Data' tab. Are you with me so far?"

She nods, so he continues, "The 'Estimate PIA' buttons, which as you will see are currently dimmed out, are used if you don't know what your PIA is. That is the amount that SS benefits are based on; if you take SS before FRA, then you will get less, and if you take it later than that, you will get more. Have you checked with the Social Security Administration to see what the PIA is for both you and Jim? If you haven't received a recent statement from SSA that projects your PIA, they have a detailed calculator that will calculate it if you have your salary history."

Jane replies, "Actually we do have the PIA figures from SSA. Jim's is $2,509 and mine is $2,526."

Bob continues, "OK, let's put those figures in. We'll set the initial SS starting date for both of you to 7/2021, which is the month after when Jim turns 65. Here's what that Income tab looks like now." (See Figure 3.8.)

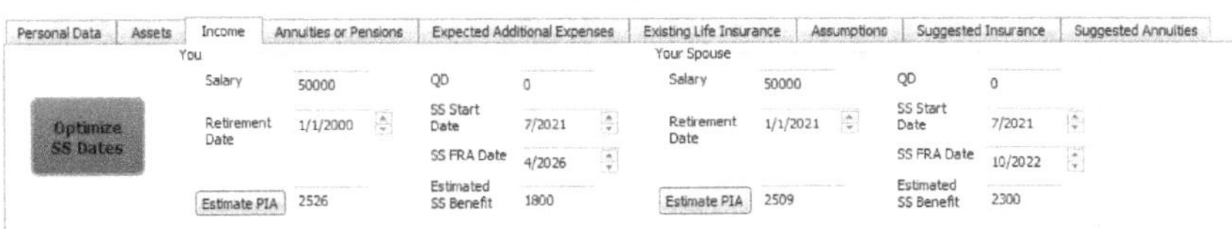

Figure 3.8: The Rhino Retirement Analyzer Income tab with Jane and Jim Smith's data

"I see that the estimated benefits, if you start collecting SS on 7/1/2021, are $1,800 for you and $2,300 for Jim."

Estimating Sustainable Spending before Adding Insurance

"Let's take a look at what your sustainable spending rate would be if you do that, before we start on the insurance calculation. Here's what the current calculation shows." (See Figure 3.9.)

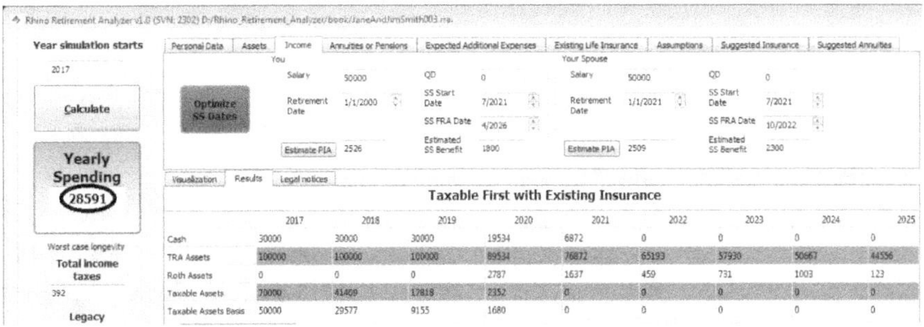

Figure 3.9: The Rhino Retirement Analyzer result screen for Jane and Jim's planned Social Security starting dates

"As you can see, your yearly sustainable spending is only $28,591, but this is very preliminary. We still have to set up the assumptions on rates of return and of inflation, as well as calculating how much life insurance you will need to optimize spending, before we can optimize your SS payment starting dates."

When to Take Social Security

"But even at this point we can run a preliminary SS optimization to see whether you should take it earlier or later than you were planning to do."

He clicks the "Optimize SS Dates" button, which causes the program to try all the possible Social Security starting dates from age 62 to age 72 for Jane, looking for the one that has the best sustainable spending, and then all the possible dates for Jim, looking for the best starting date for him. The SS date optimizer indicates that Jane should start taking SS in June 2021 and Jim in May 2026, which improves the sustainable spending by about $4,000 a year, to $32,576. (See Figure 3.10.)

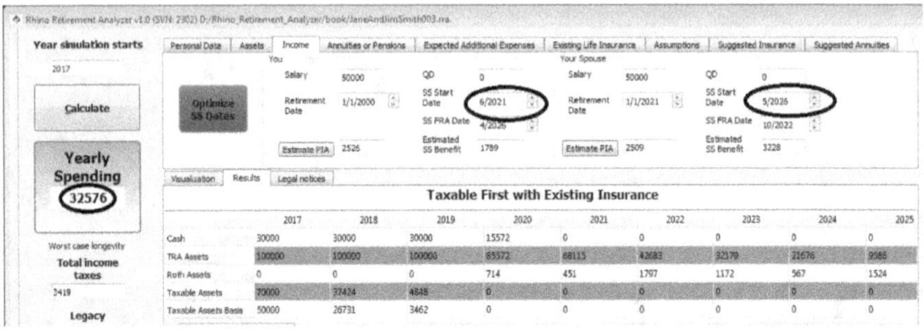

Figure 3.10: The Rhino Retirement Analyzer result screen with Jane and Jim's optimized Social Security starting dates

Annuities or Pensions

Bob continues, "Let's look at the 'Annuities or Pensions' tab next." (See Figure 3.11.)

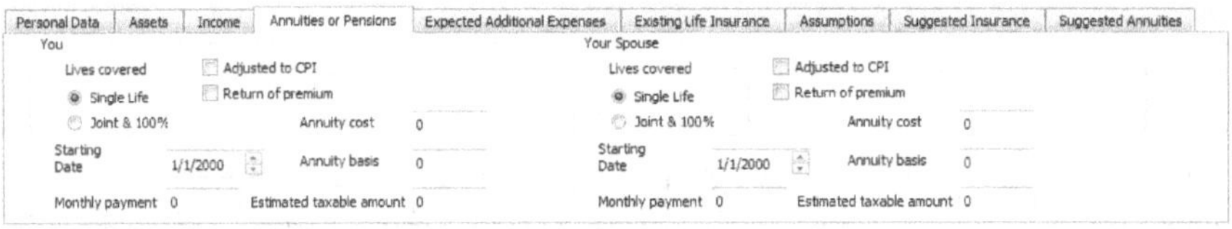

Figure 3.11: The Rhino Retirement Analyzer Income tab

"As you can see, it handles both 'single life' and' joint with 100%-to-survivor' annuities or pensions for either you or your husband, starting any time in the past or the future. The reason for the 'cost' and 'basis' fields is so that the program can estimate the tax effects of getting payments. It also allows inflation adjustment and/or return of premium. You don't have any annuities or pensions, do you?"

Jane replies, "No, we don't."

Expected Additional Expenses

Bob continues, "OK, then let's move on to the next tab, 'Expected Additional Expenses.' This is where you can enter any known specific amounts of money you are planning to spend in the future, like for a new car or an expensive vacation." (See Figure 3.12.)

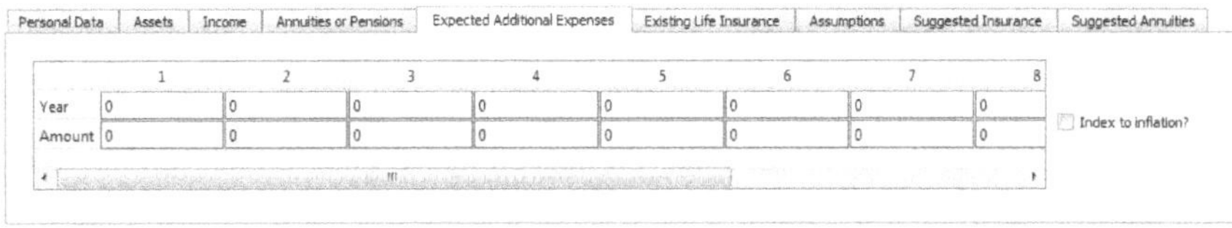

Figure 3.12: The Rhino Retirement Analyzer Expected Additional Expenses tab

Bob says, "Do you have any plans like that?"

Jane replies, "Yes, actually we have a couple of expenses like that. We are planning to take a vacation that will cost about $10,000 in 2018 and a new car in 2020 for $30,000."

Bob says, "OK, then I'll enter those." He does so, resulting in that tab looking like Figure 3.13.

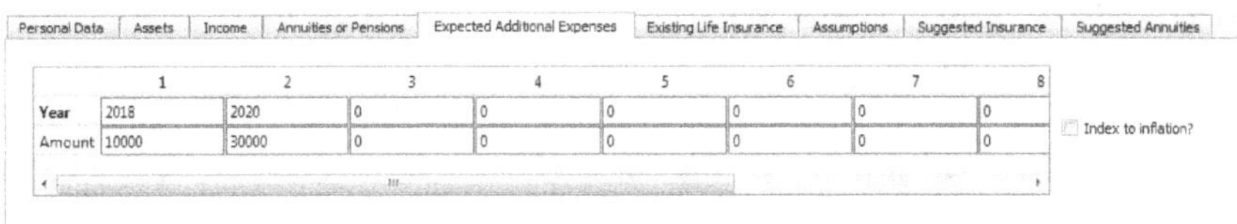

Figure 3.13: The Rhino Retirement Analyzer Expected Additional Expenses tab with Jane and Jim's data

Sustainable Spending Including Additional Expenses

"Now let's see how that affects your overall sustainable spending." (See Figure 3.14.)

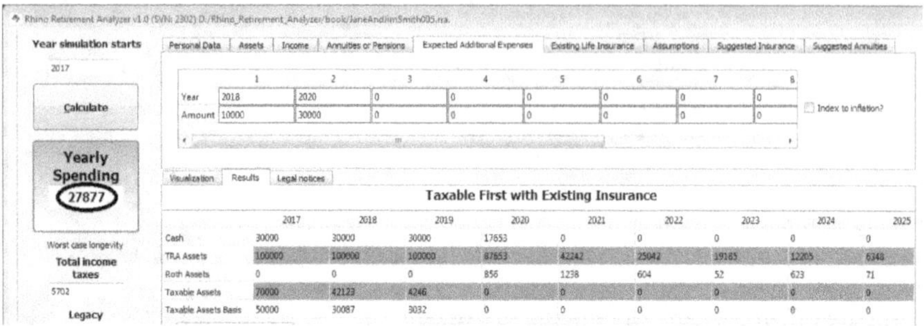

Figure 3. 14: The Rhino Retirement Analyzer result screen after entering Jane and Jim's expected additional expenses

"As you can see, that reduced the projection of your sustainable spending by over $4,000 a year, to $27,877. That's because that extra $40,000 over the next few years won't be available later on. Isn't it helpful to see how that extra spending affects you later?"

Jane says, "Actually that is quite sobering. We may have to rethink the car...."

Bob continues, "One of the advantages of having a program like this is that it makes the effects of those decisions much more visible. Maybe you will want to use it yourself after we get done with our analysis? It's available free on the web."

Indexing for Inflation

Jane adds, "What does that 'Index to inflation' checkbox do?"

Bob says, "We check that if the expense amounts should be adjusted according to the assumed inflation rate. If you have already locked in these amounts, such as by prepaying, then we leave that unchecked. You haven't paid for the vacation or the car, have you?"

Jane says, "No."

Bob adds, "Actually at this point it wouldn't matter because we haven't put in our assumptions for inflation and rates of return on your cash and other assets. The default for all of those is 0%, so checking that box and rerunning produces the same result. But I'm glad you asked about that option. I'll check that box so that the results will be properly adjusted once we put in the assumptions, which we will do shortly. Here's what the screen looks like now." (See Figure 3.15.)

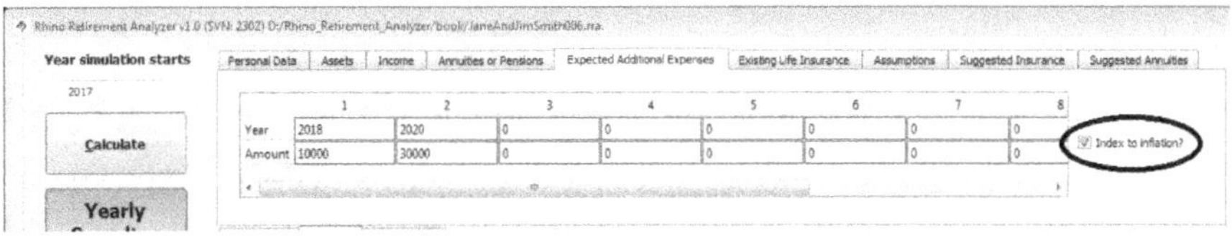

Figure 3.15: The Rhino Retirement Analyzer Expected Additional Expenses tab with "Index to inflation?" checked

Existing Life Insurance

Bob continues, "Now let's look at the 'Existing Life Insurance' tab." (See Figure 3.16.)

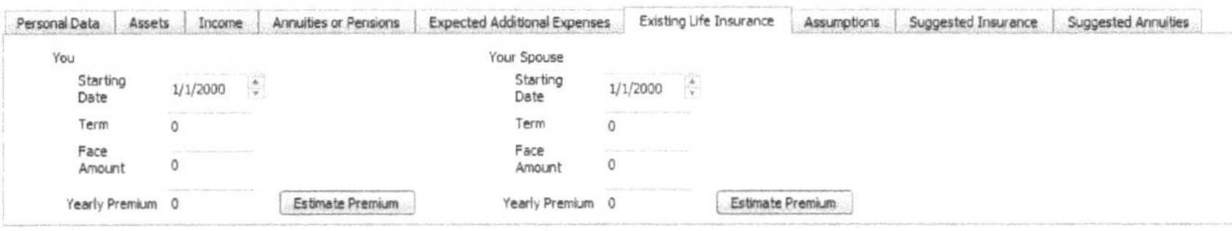

Figure 3.16: The Rhino Retirement Analyzer Existing Life Insurance tab

"From a question you asked before, I don't think you have any current life insurance. Is that right?"

Jane answers, "Yes, that's right."

Assumptions on Inflation and Return on Investments

Bob continues, "OK, then we'll move on to the 'Assumptions' tab and fill that in so we can get some reasonably realistic answers. Here's what that tab looks like now before we fill it in." (See Figure 3.17.)

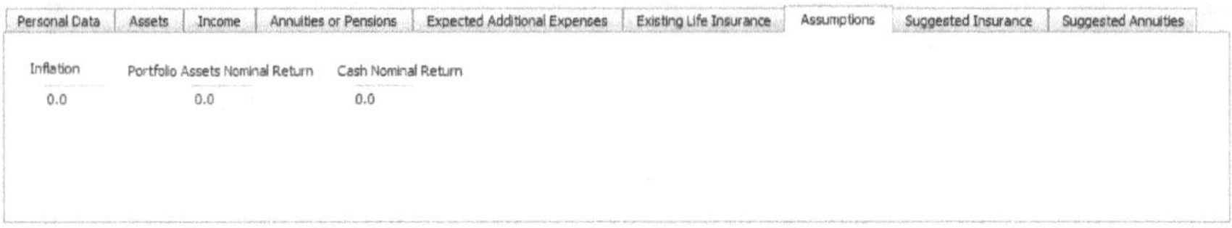

Figure 3.17: The Rhino Retirement Analyzer Assumptions tab

"Let's use the same assumptions as we did with June: 7% return on your portfolio assets (stocks and bonds), 2% return on cash, and 2% inflation. Here's what that tab looks like now." (See Figure 3.18.)

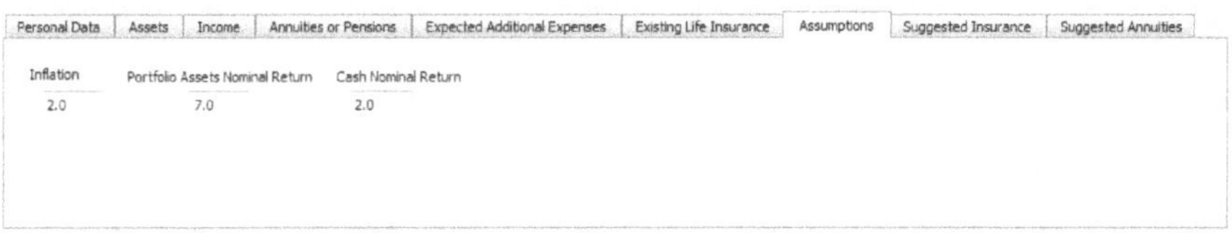

Figure 3.18: Figure 3.18. The Rhino Retirement Analyzer Assumptions tab, filled in

"Of course, now that we have set those assumptions, the results will be different. Let's recalculate and see what sustainable yearly spending you can achieve now." (See Figure 3.19.)

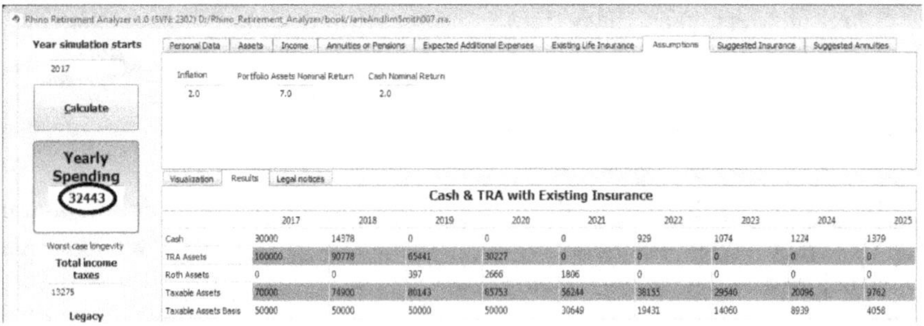

Figure 3.19: The Rhino Retirement Analyzer result screen after entering assumptions

"As you can see, the sustainable spending is back up to about $32,500 even with the expected additional expenses. This is because we now expect some return (7% before inflation) on portfolio assets rather than 0% return (and 0% inflation)

as our previous calculations were using. Of course, no one knows what the actual return will be, but we have to make some assumptions whenever we make projections into the future, and it's nice to see that the differences between the 0% assumption and the positive return assumption aren't gigantic. This suggests that what actually happens might not be too far from these numbers."

The Social Security Optimization after Setting the Assumptions

"Now that we have our assumptions set, let's go back and redo the SS optimization. Here's what we get now." (See Figure 3.20.)

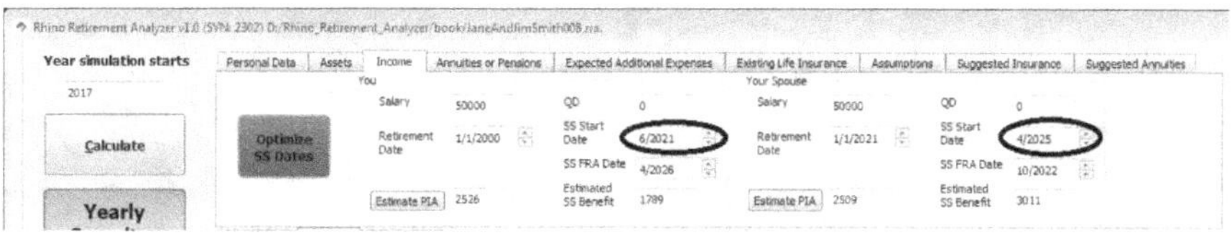

Figure 3.20: The Rhino Retirement Analyzer result screen after redoing SS optimization

"As you can see, that didn't change your SS starting date, although it did change Jim's preferred date by a little over a year. Any questions about this?"

June replies, "Why didn't the sustainable spending change if Jim's SS start date is different?"

Bob answers, "Good question. The answer is that the worst-case scenario is for Jim to die this year, so his theoretical SS starting date doesn't affect the answer... so far. OK?"

How Much Life Insurance Would Optimize Sustainable Spending?

June nods, so Bob continues, "Now let's get to the fun stuff. Namely, would buying term life insurance help you and, if so, what face amount and for how long a term? To find out, let's go to the 'Suggested Insurance' tab, which looks like this right now." (See Figure 3.21.)

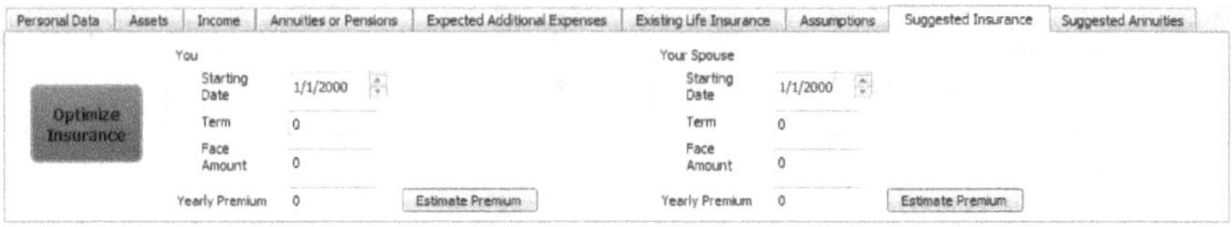

Figure 3.21: The Rhino Retirement Analyzer Suggested Insurance tab

Bob clicks on the "Optimize Insurance" button. (See Figure 3.22.)

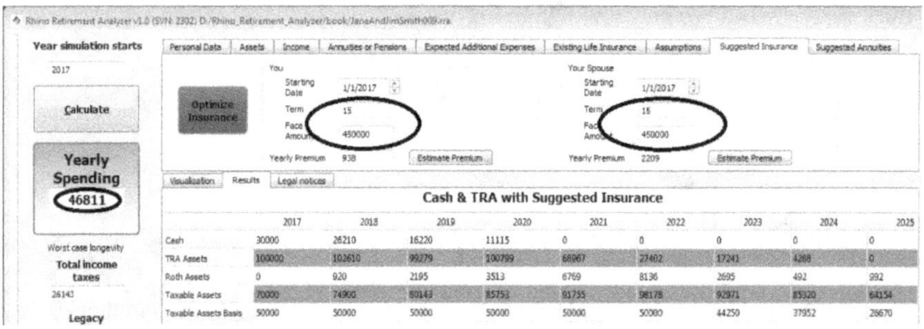

Figure 3.22: The Rhino Retirement Analyzer result screen after calculating suggested insurance

Bob continues, "You can see that it has selected a term of 15 years and a face amount of $450,000 for both you and Jim. The premiums are a lot higher for his policy, because he is older, male, and doesn't have quite as high a rating. The total yearly premium is about $3,150. But look at the improvement in spending; almost $14,500 a year, *after* paying the premiums! How is this possible?"

What is Sustainable Spending?

Before we can answer that question, we need to revisit the notion of "sustainable spending."

First let me make it clear that there is no free lunch here. Buying life insurance doesn't increase the amount one can spend in the best case; that is, when both spouses live a long time (which means past the end of the insurance term, in the case of term life insurance). In fact, in that case they will have paid insurance premiums for a long time with no return, which will obviously reduce the amount they can spend on other things below what it would be otherwise. This means that the expected return on the "investment" of life insurance will be negative. Why spend money on life insurance when the expected return is negative?

For the same reason that it makes sense to buy life insurance in any circumstance: to mitigate the risk of dying "young." The only difference here is the definition of "young." The usual meaning is "while many potential years of paid work lie ahead," whereas here it means "while many potential years of retirement income lie ahead."

Life Insurance is a Perfect Match for the Risk of Dying Early in Retirement

Actually, life insurance mitigates this retirement income risk *better* than it does loss of potential working income, because a young worker is far more likely to become disabled before retirement age than to die before retirement age, and, of course, life insurance will not mitigate that risk. However, since all that is needed to collect retirement income is to continue breathing, life insurance is a *perfect* match for this particular risk: if one stays alive, the retirement income continues, and if one dies during the term of insurance, the surviving spouse collects the face amount, which mitigates the lost retirement income.

Even so, term insurance is fairly expensive at or near retirement age, generally in the thousands of dollars a year for a reasonable amount of coverage for a couple. Why should they spend so much money, when the premiums will obviously reduce the amount of money they can spend if they live a long time?

The answer is that "sustainable spending" means spending in the *worst* case, not in the best case. In most situations, including our example of Jane and Jim Smith, the worst case is that one of the spouses (usually the one with the shorter life expectancy) dies very early in retirement, or even before retirement, whereas the other spouse lives a long time. This case requires their assets to be stretched over the longest time, and thus reduces the amount that can be *safely* taken out each year.

Now, of course, if the couple knew when each of them would die, they could make the calculation on safe spending with certainty. But if it were possible to know that, then life insurance could not exist, so perhaps it is a good thing that it isn't possible! In the real world, the only prudent approach is to estimate spending based on the worst-case scenario. This is where buying life insurance pays off: by cutting off the "left tail" of results where one spouse dies early and the other lives a long time.

How Spending Money on Life Insurance Premiums Can Increase Sustainable Spending

Now we can get back to our specific example and see why it is that spending $4,650 a year on life insurance premiums can increase sustainable spending by over $13,000 a year *after* paying the premiums.

The reason this is possible is that the worst-case scenario without life insurance is that Jim dies in 2017 whereas Jane lives until 2061. (See Figure 3.23.)

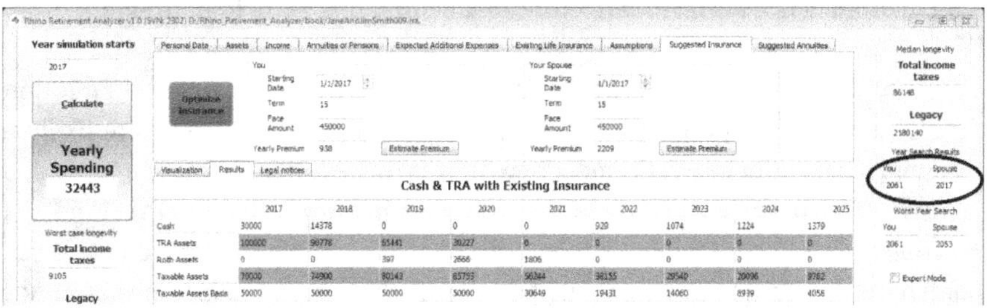

Figure 3.23: The Rhino Retirement Analyzer result screen with no insurance

In this case, their assets must last Jane until 2061. She doesn't take her widow's Social Security benefit until 2021, to avoid the permanent reduction in benefits from taking it early. This means that she can spend only $32,443 a year for the rest of her life if she doesn't want to risk running out of money while still alive.[i]

Now let's look at the results with the suggested insurance. (See Figure 3.24.)

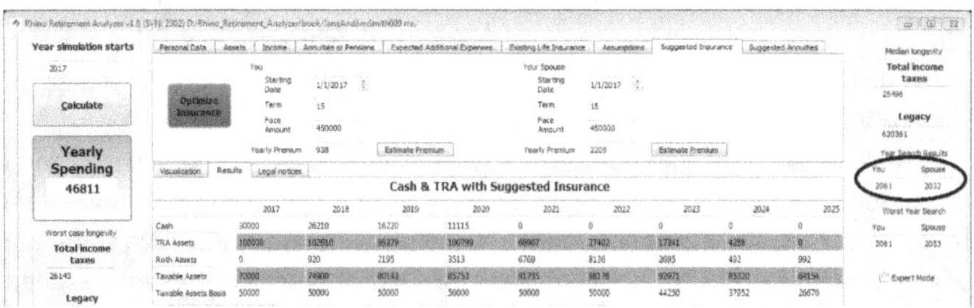

Figure 3.24: The Rhino Retirement Analyzer result screen with suggested insurance

As you can see, in this case the worst case is for Jim to die in 2032, right after his insurance policy expires, while Jane still lives until 2061. The difference of more than $14,000 in sustainable expenses, after paying insurance premiums, comes because in this scenario they get two Social Security payments from 2026 until 2032.

Of course, buying life insurance doesn't guarantee that you will live a long time! But what it *does* guarantee is that if you die before it expires, you will get a payment that can be used to offset the loss of future income. That's exactly why the financial worst-case scenario for this couple *with* life insurance is far better than it is *without* life insurance: if they both live past the end of the insurance, then they collect two Social Security payments for that entire time, whereas if one of them dies while the insurance is still in force, the surviving spouse gets that payment to replace a number of years of lost income.

If you still don't find this absolutely clear, you aren't alone. Let's rejoin Bob and Jane as he goes through it with her again.

Another Look at the Comparative Results with and without Life Insurance

Jane is puzzled by the comparison between her existing situation and what would happen if she bought the recommended life insurance. She says, "But Bob, obviously buying life insurance doesn't affect when one of us dies. How can we have a fair comparison of what happens if we have insurance with what happens if we don't, when the year of death is different? I mean, what would happen if we had insurance and Jim died immediately? Does the program illustrate that?"

Bob replies, "Yes, of course you are right that buying life insurance doesn't affect when you are going to die. The 'Year Search Results' result shows the *worst* years of death for the specified scenario, and those years are different if you have insurance than if you don't, because having the insurance means that the loss of the second Social Security payment isn't as disastrous."

Illustrating Comparative Results with the "Manual Death Years" Feature

"But you're also right that it's hard to follow the comparison with different death rates, so let's use an advanced 'Expert Mode' feature to illustrate the difference between the two scenarios with the same death year. To see the difference, we'll start with the worst-case scenario in the situation where you don't have any life insurance." (See Figure 3.25.)

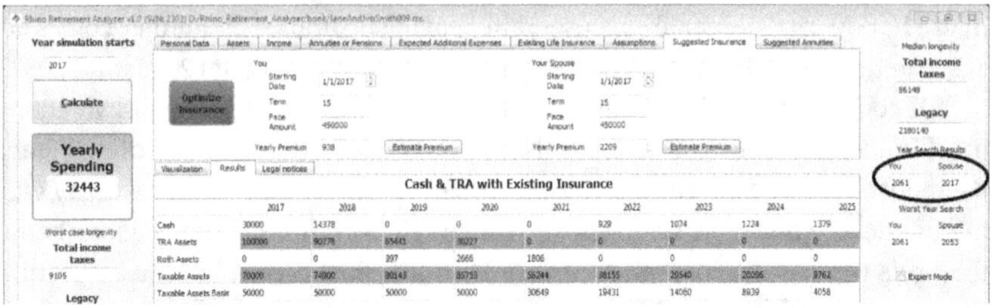

Figure 3.25: The Rhino Retirement Analyzer result screen without insurance

Bob continues, “Now let’s look back at the results with suggested insurance.” (See Figure 3.26.)

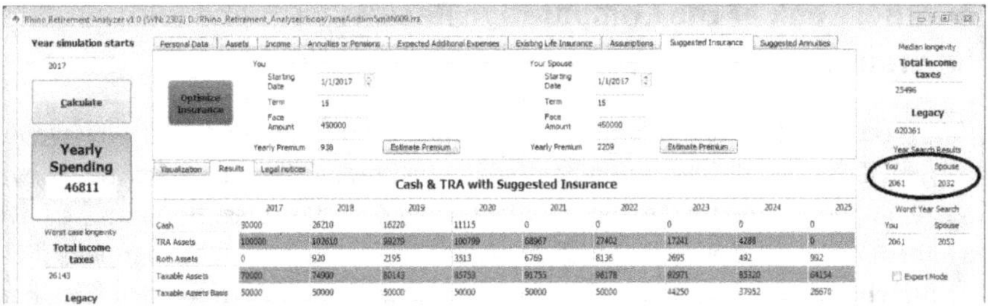

Figure 3.26: The Rhino Retirement Analyzer result screen with suggested insurance

Bob goes on, “As you can see, the worst death date for Jim if you buy the suggested insurance is 2032 rather than 2017 without the insurance. Now let’s look at what happens if we change his death year to 2017 *with* the suggested insurance, then look at the results with the best withdrawal method.” (See Figure 3.27.)

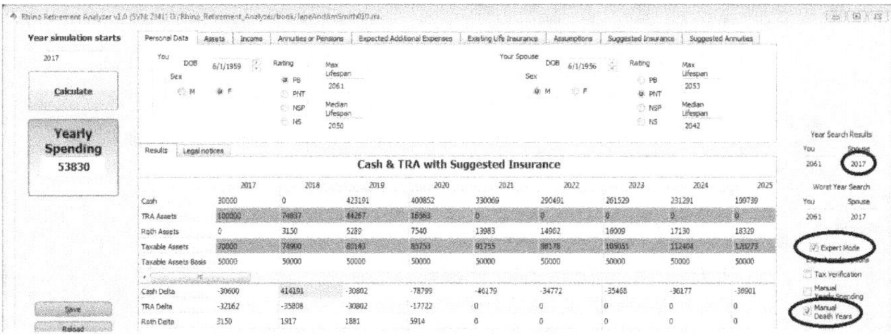

Figure 3.27: The Rhino Retirement Analyzer result screen with suggested insurance and a manually specified death year for Jim

Bob continues, "You can see that we have turned on 'Expert Mode,' set 'Manual Death Years,' then set Jim's death year to 2017. Then I hit the 'Calculate' button to figure out the results."

How the Insurance Payout Fits In

"As you can see when I hover the mouse over the entry for the year 2018 in the row labeled 'Cash Delta' (the blue cell), there is an insurance payout of $450,000. By the way, the reason the payout is in 2018 is that we assume that the person who dies does so near the end of the year (2017 in this case); obviously, this is an arbitrary assumption, but we have to make some assumptions to do the calculations." (See Figure 3.28.)

	2017	2018	2019	2020	2021	2022	2023	2024	2025
Cash	30000	0	423191	400852	330069	290491	261529	231291	199739
TRA Assets	100000	74837	44267	16563	0	0	0	0	0
Roth Assets	0	3150	5289	7540	13983	14962	16009	17130	18329
Taxable Assets	70000	[illegible]	80143	85753	91755	98178	105051	112404	120273
Taxable Assets Basis	50000	50000	50000	50000	50000	50000	50000	50000	50000
Cash Delta	-3060	414191	-30802	-78799	-46179	-34772	-35468	-36177	-36901
TRA Delta	-32162	-35808			0	0	0	0	0
Roth Delta	3150	1917	1881	5914	0	0	0	0	0
Taxable Sold	0	0	0	0	0	0	0	0	0
Sale Basis	0	0	0	0	0	0	0	0	0
(LTCG)	0	0	0	0	0	0	0	0	0
Taxable Bought	0	0	0	0	0	0	0	0	0
Qual Divs	0	0	0	0	0	0	0	0	0
Social Security	0	0	0	0	12088	24659	25153	25656	26169
Taxable Income	0	0	0	0	0	0	0	0	0
Nontaxable Income	0	0	0	0	0	0	0	0	0
Cash Before Tax&Ins	59612	69699	59723	90608	58267	59432	60621	61833	63070
Est. Fed. Income Tax	1134	4593	3719	1647	0	0	0	0	0
Insurance Premiums	4648	0	0	0	0	0	0	0	0
Cash After Tax & Ins	53830	65106	56004	88961	58267	59432	60621	61833	63070

Insurance death benefit of $450000 paid

Figure 3.28: The Rhino Retirement Analyzer result screen with an insurance payout in 2018

How Sustainable Spending Can be Affected by the Year of Death of One of the Clients

Jane says, "Is this right? If Jim dies in 2017, my sustainable yearly spending is about $7,000 more than if he lives until 2032? How does that work?"

Bob replies, "That is because if he lives until 2032, the insurance expires, so you don't get the $450,000 death benefit to make up for the loss in Social Security. Of course, you don't want him to die early, but if he does, you lose much less financially than you would without the insurance."

Jane says, "What if he were to die in an intermediate year, like 2030? How would that affect the result?"

Bob says, "Let's take a look and see. You can see that I've changed the death year to 2030, then I hit the 'Calculate' button to regenerate the results, then I pick the best result and slide the year slider over so we can see years around 2030." (See Figure 3.29.)

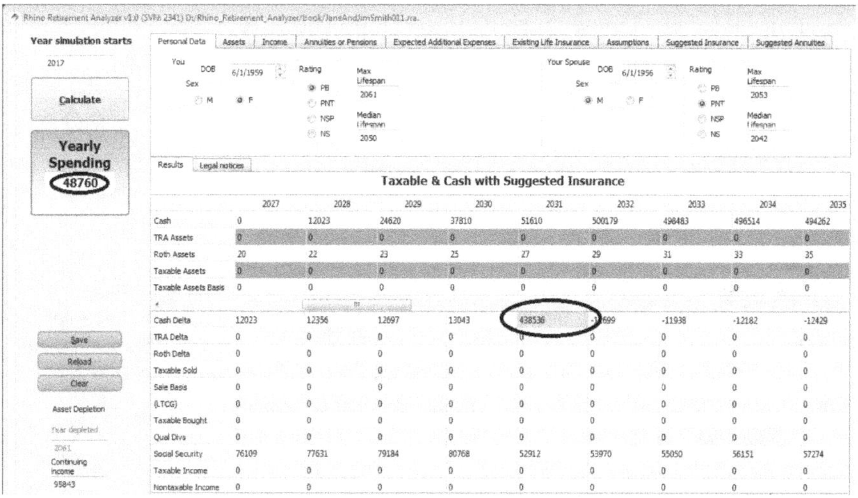

Figure 3.29: he Rhino Retirement Analyzer result screen with an insurance payout in 2031

Bob continues, "The sustainable spending isn't quite as high as the previous one, because the taxable account gets used up right away for spending money. In the previous simulation, the insurance payout in 2018 allowed the taxable account to be preserved as it grew at (the assumed) 7% a year until peaking in 2041 at almost $300K, so it could support another 20 years of spending at a somewhat higher rate than this most recent simulation."

Changing Assumptions May have Nonintuitive Effects

"It isn't always obvious how changing the assumptions, including assumed dates of death, will change the results. That's why it's important to have a tool like this to explore the various possibilities."

"Of course, as with all such tools, it has its own limitations. For example, it never uses an insurance payout to buy more assets in the taxable account, even when that might produce better results, on the basis that a widow (or widower) doesn't want to take on more market risk. Still, some way of estimating what you can safely spend, even though such an effort is inherently imprecise, is a valuable tool."

Jane responds, "OK, that makes sense. I think I have a general idea of what the program does. But can we go over the rows in the spreadsheet? I think I understand the top part with the assets, better than the lower part that shows the money flowing in and out, but I would like to go through the whole thing."

Bob says, “Sure. How much good will it do you if you don’t know what the results mean? This could take a while, though, and I have other clients to see today. How about if we knock off for the rest of the day and start up again tomorrow?”

Jane and June agree, so Bob saves the information and shuts down the program.

---

[i] You may have noticed that the cash after taxes and insurance is noticeably higher in 2018 and 2020 than in the other years. That is because Jane told Bob that they were planning for extra expenses in those years. Obviously, that could be changed if she was worried about spending that much money as a widow, but it is necessary to take account of these extra expenses to make the comparison with the optimized version (with insurance) meaningful.

Chapter 4 Another Visit with the Financial Planner

Bob has been thinking about the best way to explain the result spreadsheet to Jane and June after their questions the previous day. He has decided to go through it line by line starting at the top, because the assets in the top part are where the withdrawals in the bottom part actually come from. So, he starts up the program and reloads the results with the automatic death date calculation.

Year Numbers

Bob begins, “Let’s start at the top, with the year numbers. As you can see, there isn’t room for all the years on the display at once, so the program shows the number of years that will fit. You can use the slider to look at different years.” (See Figure 4.1.)

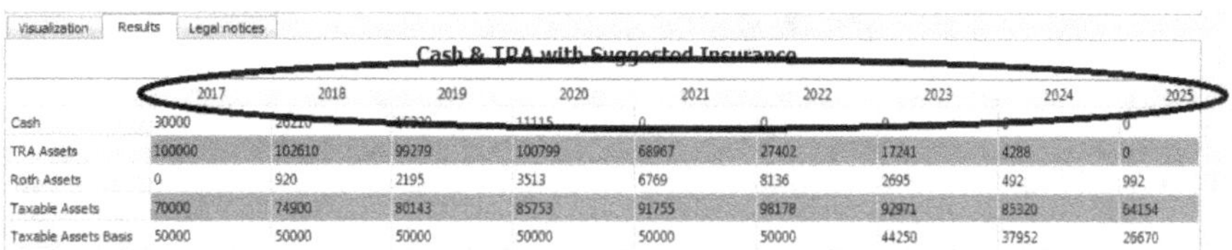

	2017	2018	2019	2020	2021	2022	2023	2024	2025
Cash	30000	[illegible]	[illegible]	11115	0	0	[illegible]	[illegible]	0
TRA Assets	100000	102610	99279	100799	68967	27402	17241	4288	0
Roth Assets	0	920	2195	3513	6769	8136	2695	492	992
Taxable Assets	70000	74900	80143	85753	91755	98178	92971	85320	64154
Taxable Assets Basis	50000	50000	50000	50000	50000	50000	44250	37952	26670

Figure 4.1: The Rhino Retirement Analyzer result screen spreadsheet with the year numbers highlighted

“Of course, the rest of the rows on the spreadsheet follow along with the slider, too, so that you are always looking at the data for the years listed on the top. Here’s what it looks like when we move the slider so that the first year displayed is 2033.” (See Figure 4.2.)

DOI 10.1515/9781501506185-004

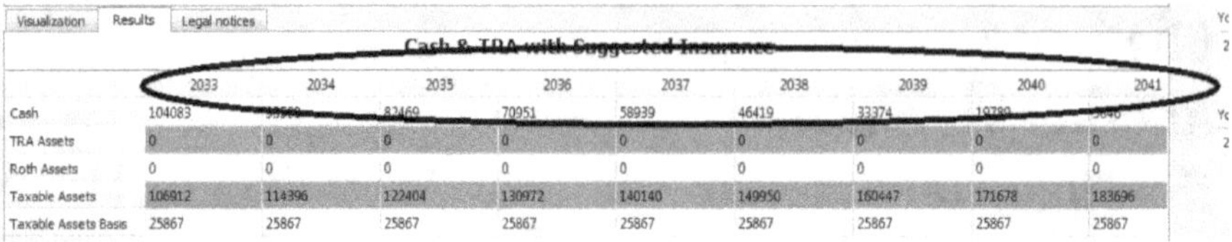

Figure 4.2: The Rhino Retirement Analyzer result screen spreadsheet with the slider moved to show years starting with 2033

June chips in, "That's pretty cool. By the way, this program looks like it was a lot of work to write. Did you write it yourself?"

Bob answers, "No, I didn't write it; the programmer put a free version up on his website."

June replies, "It looks complicated to learn to use."

Bob answers, "It has a pretty good instruction manual and the author responds to questions."

June says, "Well, I had no idea we could get this kind of detail and so many options. Anyway, sorry for the interruption. Let's get back to what all the rows mean on the spreadsheet."

Cash

Bob says, "Sure. The next line, 'Cash,' is the simplest one. It represents the total amount of cash held by both spouses at the beginning of each year. In your case, we have just lumped all the cash into your account rather than dividing it up between your account and Jim's, which is simpler and doesn't make any difference in the results." (See Figure 4.3.)

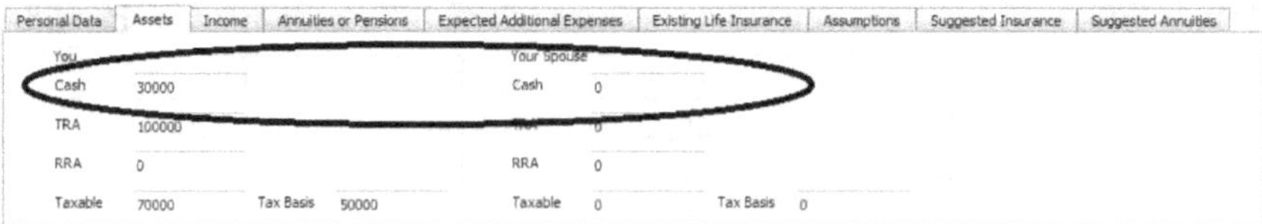

Figure 4.3: The Rhino Retirement Analyzer result screen showing the "Assets" tab

He continues, "The main reason cash is split out from the other assets is because cash tends to have different (usually lower) rates of return than assets like stocks and bonds. So the 'Assumptions' tab has a separate entry for the assumed rate of return of cash." Bob moves the slider back to start at the beginning, 2017, and clicks on the "Assumptions" tab. (See Figure 4.4.)

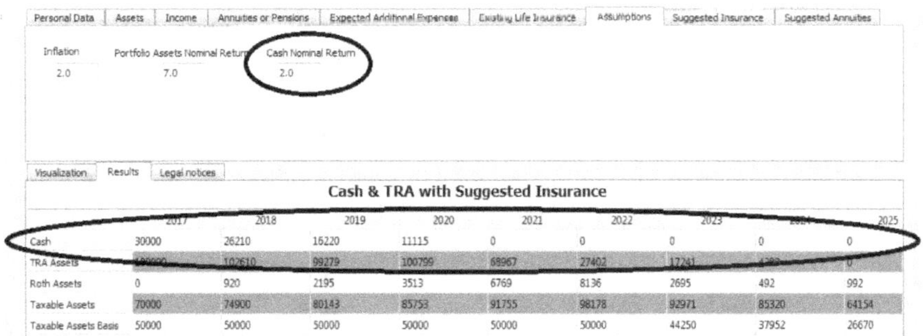

Figure 4.4: The Rhino Retirement Analyzer result screen spreadsheet with the "Cash Nominal Return" assumption and the "Cash" row highlighted

Nominal vs. Real Return

Jane says, "Why does it say 'Nominal' return?"

Bob replies, "Nominal return is the return before inflation. Over a long period of time, inflation causes the dollar to lose a lot of its value, so we have to adjust the amount of spending according to our estimate of inflation, which right now is set to 2.0%. So, if you are making any projections of income and spending for long periods of time, as this program needs to do, it has to account for inflation. There are two main ways to do that: either you can show all the results in 'constant dollars,' that is, with inflation removed, or you can show all the results in 'current dollars,' that is, with inflation included. What you don't want to do is to mix current dollars and constant dollars, because that doesn't make sense."

"This tool shows everything in 'current dollars,' which lose value over time. That's why the 'Cash After Tax & Ins' line at the bottom increases over time to compensate for inflation, rather than being constant. We'll get back to that later in more detail, by the way, but it's relevant here because we are discussing the inflation adjustment." (See Figure 4.5.)

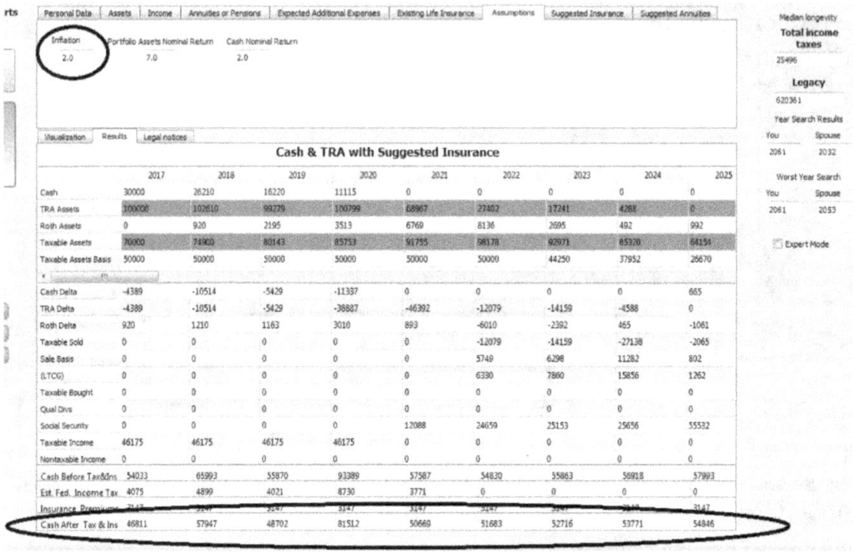

Figure 4.5: The Rhino Retirement Analyzer result screen spreadsheet with the "Inflation" assumption and the "Cash After Tax & Ins" row highlighted

Bob continues, "Does that make sense now?"

Jane answers, "Yes. I seem to recall that you also explained why the entries for 2018 and 2020 have much higher numbers in that 'Cash After Tax & Ins' row. That's because I told you that we were going to be spending extra money in those years, right?"

Bob replies, "Yes, that's why. That information is in the 'Expected Additional Expenses' tab. Here is that tab again." (See Figure 4.6.)

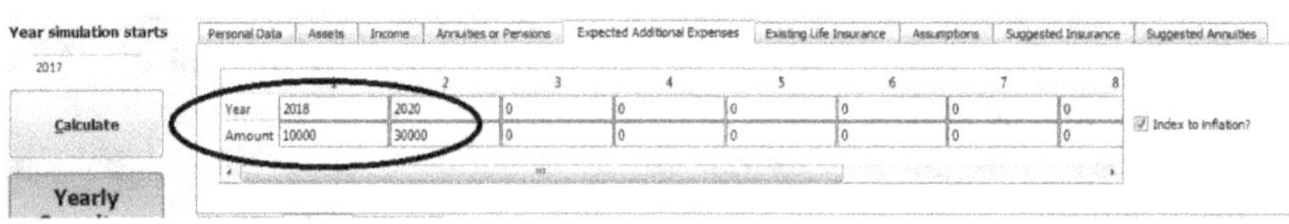

Figure 4.6: The Rhino Retirement Analyzer result screen with the "Expected Additional Expenses" entries highlighted

Jane says, "Yes, I remember that. I assume that if we change our minds about those extra expenses, you can run the program again to see how that affects the results. Is that right?"

Bob answers, "Yes, of course."

The Need for an Annual Review

"In fact, it's one of several reasons that this program should be run *at least* once a year."

"First, of course, the tax calculations change, even if just because of inflation, which increases tax brackets, standard deductions, and a number of other parts of the calculation almost every year. And, of course, once in a while there are changes in the tax laws themselves. But either way, the projections will be more realistic if we run the latest version of the program, which is updated according to the latest tax information available."

"Another reason to rerun the simulations at least once a year is that the results will be different because both of you have survived another year. For example, suppose we run it next year (2018). Obviously, the 'worst-case scenario' can no longer be that one of you dies in 2017, because that didn't happen. That means that the calculations don't have to consider that possibility."

"As you just suggested, you may also make changes in your spending plans, like not taking that vacation or buying the new car, which will affect the sustainable spending level."

"And of course, I don't have to explain that if one of you *does* die, then the results will be much different, if only because there will be only one Social Security payment and possibly an insurance payout."

June contributes her thoughts: "Yes, that makes sense. Can you put it on your calendar to call both of us early next year so we can update the results?"

Bob says, "Sure. I'll do that right now." He enters a note in his reminder program to call them, then continues, "Does either of you have any more questions about the 'Cash' row, or the assumptions?"

Jane and June both shake their heads "no."

Traditional Retirement Account Assets

Bob says, "The next row is the one labeled 'TRA Assets.' This is the total amount that both spouses have in their traditional (pretax) retirement accounts at the beginning of each year." (See Figure 4.7.)

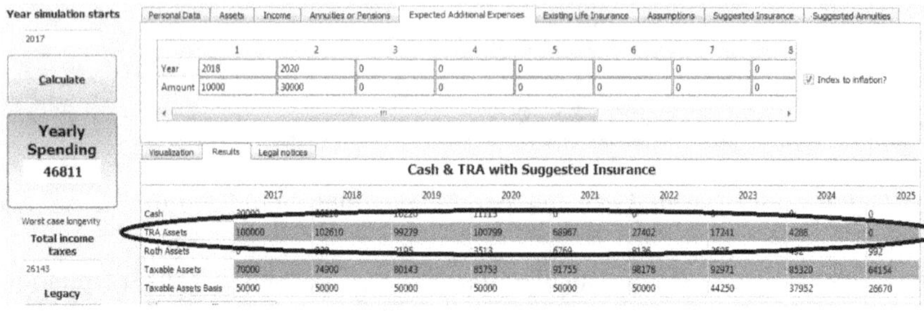

Figure 4.7: The Rhino Retirement Analyzer Visualization screen with the "TRA Assets" row highlighted

Bob continues, "These have to be kept track of separately from other types of accounts because taking money out of them incurs income taxes. Withdrawals of certain amounts, called 'Required Minimum Distributions,' or RMDs, also must start by age 70.5. The program includes the necessity of taking RMDs when calculating how much money you can spend every year."

Withdrawal Strategies to Optimize Taxes

"However, there's a feature of the program that I've blown right past so far: the determination of which accounts to take money out of in which order.

"These methods are what the labels on the 'various withdrawal strategy' bars on the 'Visualization' page refer to." (See Figure 4.8.)

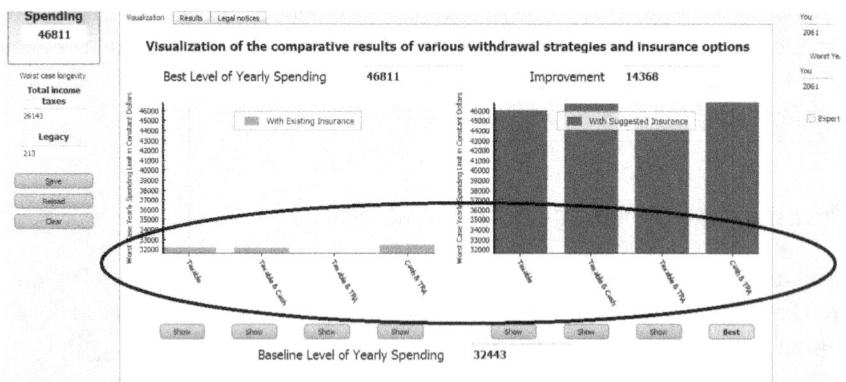

Figure 4.8: Figure 4.8. The Rhino Retirement Analyzer Visualization screen with labels for the different withdrawal strategies highlighted

Bob continues, "As you can see, this screen shows the results of four withdrawal strategies for the situation where you don't have any life insurance (on the left) and the results of the same four withdrawal strategies for the situation where you buy the suggested life insurance (on the right). In your case, as the position of the 'Best' button indicates, the 'Cash & TRA' strategy with 'Suggested Insurance' is the best strategy overall. This means that your best sustainable spending rate would be achieved if you were to buy the suggested life insurance and use your cash and your traditional retirement accounts first, before spending down your other assets (which in your case is just your taxable account balance). Of course, this assumes that the assumptions we have made are accurate."

Four Different Withdrawal Strategies

"I should also explain what the four different strategies mean. 'Taxable and Cash' means that withdrawals will be made from both the taxable account and the cash account until they are exhausted, then the other accounts will be used. 'Taxable' means that withdrawals will be made from the taxable account alone until it is exhausted, then the other accounts will be used. 'Taxable and TRA' and 'Cash and TRA' are similar to 'Taxable and Cash' except for which two accounts will be used first."

"The program tries to maximize sustainable spending using all four of these strategies with both existing and suggested insurance, and displays the 'Best' button below the result that has the highest sustainable spending."

"This was actually the original idea for the program: looking for the best way to take money out of various types of accounts during retirement. Have you ever noticed that although just about every retirement-advice article tells you to take distributions from your accounts in a 'tax-efficient manner,' they never tell you how to figure that out? So, the programmer decided to write a program to try a number of different methods of taking money out, to see which way led to the highest sustainable spending rate."[i]

"Does that make sense?"

June replies, "I recall your briefly mentioning that to me when we went over my results, but I didn't know exactly how the calculation was done. Thanks for the extra explanation."

Other Ways to Improve Sustainable Spending

Jane says, "I think I understand it, but if that was the original idea for the program, why does it have all the other features like Social Security optimization and adding term insurance? Wasn't the original idea good enough? Assuming you know the answer, of course."

Bob replies, "Yes, that is covered in the training for the program. What happened was that the programmer found that the difference in after-tax sustainable spending results, just from taking the money out of the various accounts in the correct order, was noticeable but not enormous. In your case, for example, it's about $1,000 a year, as you can see by comparing the lowest and highest numbers in the 'With Existing Insurance' area."

Assuming the same return on all the different accounts[ii], the reason for the difference in after-tax sustainable spending between one withdrawal method and another is the difference in the tax treatment of money taken out of different accounts. This effect will be different based on your exact situation. For example, if your taxable account has a cost basis *higher* than its current value, you will have losses when you liquidate that account, offsetting some taxable income. On the other hand, if your taxable account has a cost basis *lower* than its current value, you will have to pay some capital gains taxes as you liquidate it. The program takes these effects into account when calculating the results of the different withdrawal strategies. For example, let's look at the 'Taxable & TRA' and 'Cash & TRA' results for your existing insurance. (See Figure 4.9.)

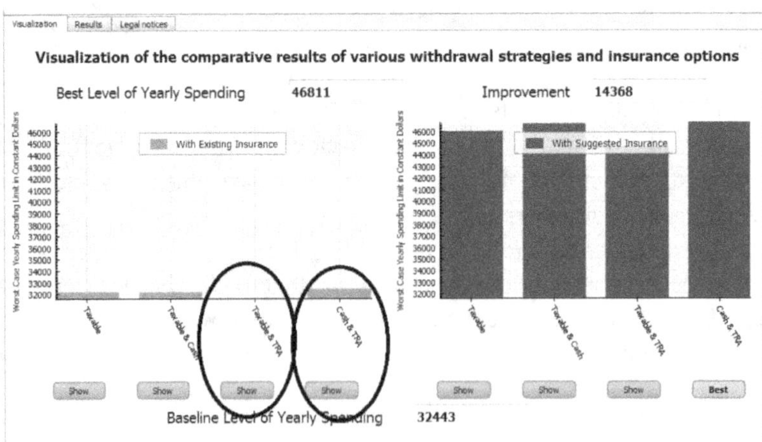

Figure 4.9: The Rhino Retirement Analyzer Visualization screen with the best and worst "With Existing Insurance" results highlighted

Significant Improvements in Sustainable Spending by Adding Insurance

Bob continues, "I know the exact numbers are a bit hard to see on this graph, but that's because it has to represent the much bigger difference between the 'With Existing Insurance' and 'With Suggested Insurance' results, so the display of the much smaller difference among the results within those two groups gets compressed. But we can see the exact difference by clicking the button for the 'Taxable & TRA,' then for the 'Cash & TRA' results and noting how much the 'Yearly Spending' value changes. First, here's the 'Taxable & TRA with Existing Insurance' result, which shows the 'Yearly Spending' as $31,599." (See Figure 4.10.)

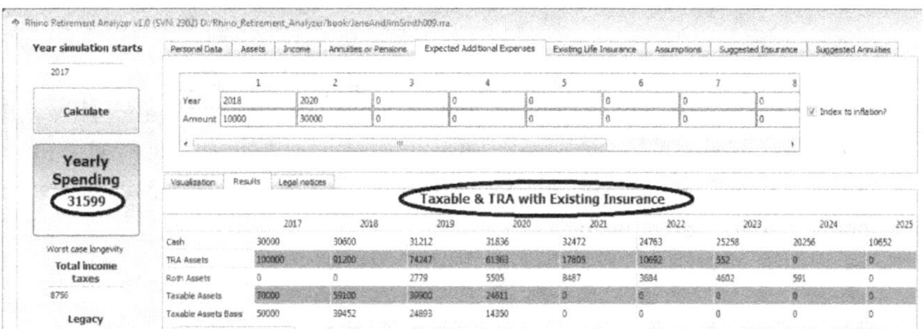

Figure 4.10: The Rhino Retirement Analyzer Visualization screen showing the results for "Taxable & TRA with Existing Insurance"

Bob continues, "And now here's the result for 'Cash & TRA with Existing Insurance,' which shows the 'Yearly Spending' as $32,443." (See Figure 4.11.)

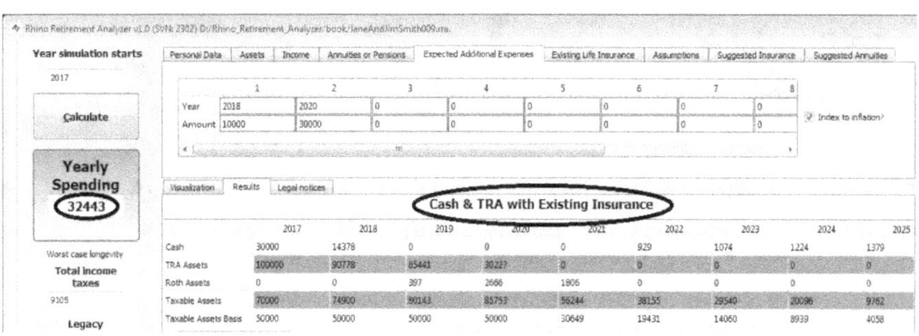

Figure 4.11: The Rhino Retirement Analyzer Visualization screen showing the results for "Cash & TRA with Existing Insurance"

Bob continues, "The difference is a little more than $800 a year, which is nice but not exactly life-changing. So the programmer decided to add some more financial data to see what happened. He was amazed to find that adding term life insurance could make a far larger difference in sustainable spending than just trying to optimize the withdrawals to reduce taxes. It's also much less time-consuming to calculate than searching for the maximum possible improvement in withdrawal methods, so he decided to concentrate on that and the other more powerful optimizations like Social Security timing and annuities (which we'll get to later)."

"Does that answer your question? If so, we can continue with the next row on the spreadsheet."

Jane replies, "Yes, that makes sense now. Go ahead."

Roth Assets

Bob continues, "First, let's switch back to the best result, 'Cash and TRA with Suggested Insurance.' Then, the next row is 'Roth Assets.' This is the total amount that both spouses have in their Roth (post-tax) retirement accounts at the beginning of each year." (See Figure 4.12.)

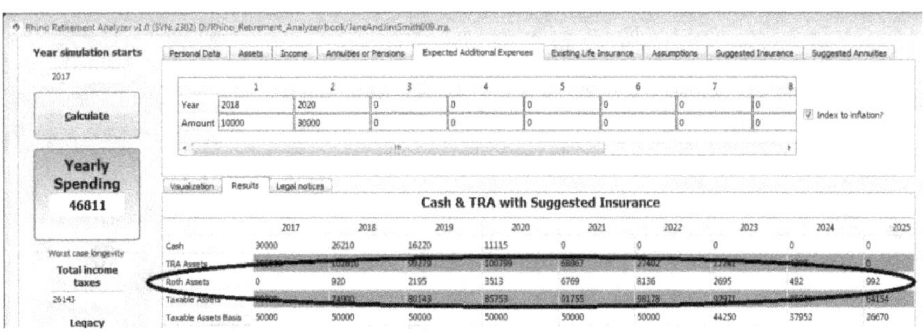

Figure 4.12: The Rhino Retirement Analyzer Visualization screen with the "Roth Assets" row highlighted

Jane says, "We don't have any Roth assets at present, so I see why it starts out as 0. But why does it show them starting in 2018?" (See Figure 4.13.)

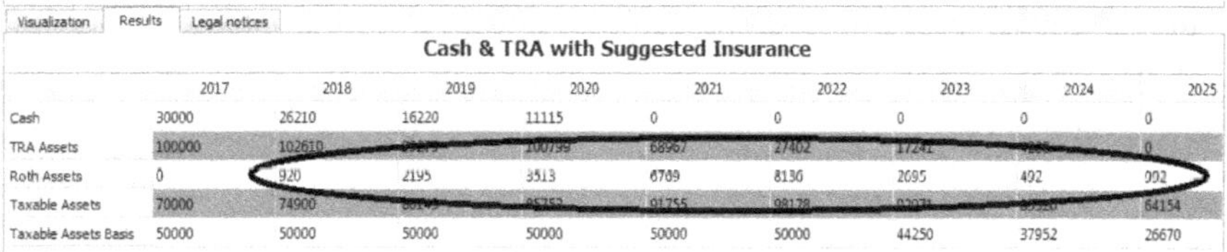

Figure 4.13: The Rhino Retirement Analyzer Visualization screen with nonzero entries in the "Roth Assets" row highlighted

Bob replies, "That's because what the program is trying to do is to make the 'Cash After Tax & Ins' as level as possible in 'real dollars' after accounting for the 'Expected Additional Expenses'. This means that sometimes it has to cash in more of your assets than it needs in one year. When this happens, it puts the extra back into a Roth account, because that has the most favorable tax treatment when you take the money out."[iii]

Jane says, "OK, I guess so, but I don't see the 'Cash After Tax & Ins' row being very level. All the numbers are different."

Bob replies, "That's because of inflation. A dollar now is worth less than a dollar some years from now, so the program increases spending later to make that come out even. But I know it's hard to see the leveling out of spending this way."

"Let's change the inflation rate to 0 and rerun the program, and you'll see that the 'Cash After Tax & Ins' row shows level spending, other than the bumps in 2018 and 2020 for your 'Expected Additional Expenses.'" (See Figure 4.14.)

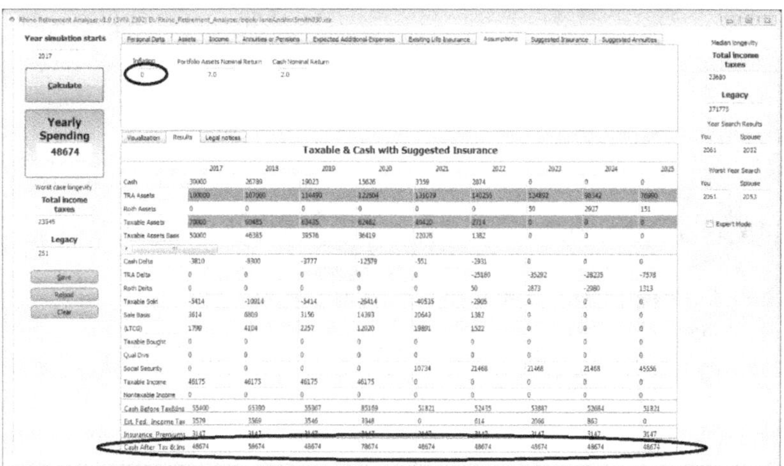

Figure 4.14: The Rhino Retirement Analyzer Visualization screen with the inflation rate set to 0

Jane says, “Yes, now I see it is level. Go ahead with the other rows.”

Bob continues, “OK, first I’ll set the inflation back to 2% and hit the ‘Calculate’ button again.”

Taxable Assets

“The next row is ‘Taxable Assets,’ which is what it sounds like: the total amount that both spouses have in their taxable account or accounts.” (See Figure 4.15.)

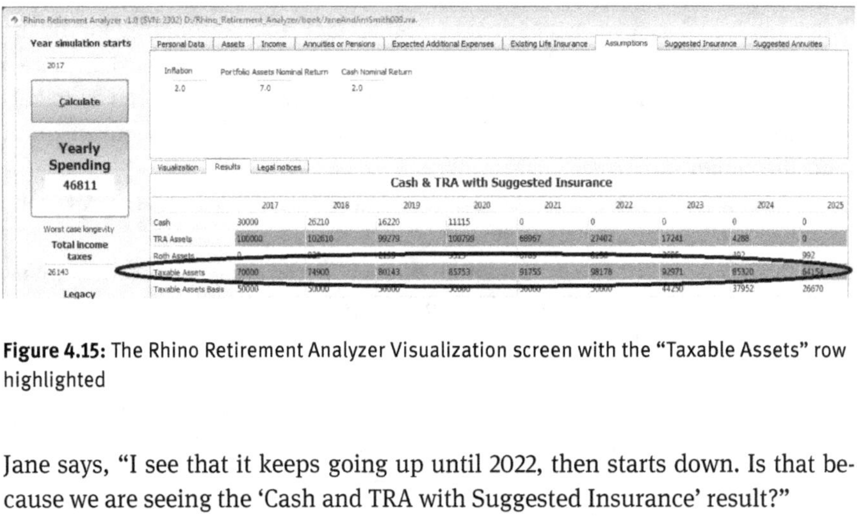

Figure 4.15: The Rhino Retirement Analyzer Visualization screen with the “Taxable Assets” row highlighted

Jane says, “I see that it keeps going up until 2022, then starts down. Is that because we are seeing the ‘Cash and TRA with Suggested Insurance’ result?”

Bob answers, “Yes, exactly. The program has calculated that taking money from cash and your traditional retirement accounts produces the highest ‘Yearly Spending,’ so it exhausts those accounts first.”

Jane says, “OK, got it.”

Taxable Assets Basis

“What about the next row, ‘Taxable Assets Basis’? What is that for?”

Bob replies, “That shows your ‘cost basis’ (how much you paid) for the assets you have in your taxable account at the beginning of each year, which is deducted from the sale price when calculating capital-gains taxes. I’ve also switched back to the ‘Assets’ tab so you can see where the original figure comes from.” (See Figure 4.16.)

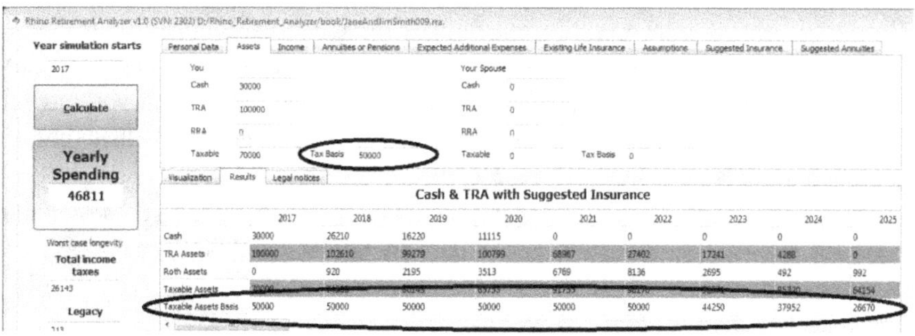

Figure 4.16: The Rhino Retirement Analyzer Visualization screen with the 'Tax Basis' and 'Taxable Assets Basis' entries highlighted

Bob continues, "You can see that your original 'Tax Basis' is $50,000, meaning that you paid that much for the assets in your taxable account. As you can see in the 'Taxable Assets Basis' row, this goes down whenever you sell assets, because you have less left in the taxable account."

"The reason we need to keep track of this is because it affects how much you have to pay in capital-gains taxes. Basically, whenever you sell a taxable asset, you subtract the basis from the sale price to figure your gain; then the capital-gain tax is assessed on that gain. For example, in 2022, the program shows 'Taxable Sold' of $12,079 worth of taxable assets, with a 'Sale Basis' of $5,749, producing a 'LTCG' (long-term capital gain) of (approximately) $6,330." (See Figure 4.17.)

Cash Delta	-4389	-10514	-5429	-11337	0	0	0	0	665
TRA Delta	-4389	-10514	-5429	-38887	-46392	-12079	-14159	-4588	0
Roth Delta	920	1210	1163	3010	893	-6010	-2392	465	-1061
Taxable Sold	0	0	0	0	0	-12079	-14159	-27138	-2065
Sale Basis	0	0	0	0	0	5749	6298	11282	802
(LTCG)	0	0	0	0	0	6330	7860	15856	1262
Taxable Bought	0	0	0	0	0	0	0	0	0
Qual Divs	0	0	0	0	0	0	0	0	0
Social Security	0	0	0	0	12088	24659	25153	25656	55532
Taxable Income	46175	46175	46175	46175	0	0	0	0	0
Nontaxable Income	0	0	0	0	0	0	0	0	0
Cash Before Tax&Ins	54033	65993	55870	93389	57587	54830	55863	56918	57993
Est. Fed. Income Tax	4075	4899	4021	8730	3771	0	0	0	0
Insurance Premiums	3147	3147	3147	3147	3147	3147	3147	3147	3147
Cash After Tax & Ins	46811	57947	48702	81512	50669	51683	52716	53771	54846

Figure 4.17: The Rhino Retirement Analyzer Visualization screen with the 'Taxable Sold', 'Sale Basis' and 'LTCG' entries for 2022 highlighted

Bob continues, “By the way, the reason that ‘Taxable Sold’ is negative is because it is a sale, which reduces the amount you have in your ‘Taxable Assets.’ ‘Sale Basis’ and ‘LTCG’ (long-term capital gains) don’t affect how much you have in assets, just your tax liability, so they aren’t displayed as negative. Does that explain what the taxable basis means?”

Jane says, “I get the general idea, but my tax program does all these calculations for me, so I don’t have to understand the details when it does my taxes. Is that OK here, too?”

Estimating Taxes vs. Precise Tax Calculations

Bob answers, “Yes, absolutely. Remember that this is a retirement estimating program, so you can’t count on its calculating the taxes precisely. That’s what your tax preparation program (or your tax preparer) is for. The tax calculations in this program are used just to estimate how much you will have to take out of savings each year; there is no way to know exactly what tax brackets are going to be even next year, much less 30 years in the future, even if we assume that tax laws aren’t going to change in all that time.

“Of course, no one else knows that either, so that’s not a weakness of this program compared to any other program that tries to estimate future taxes; they are all in the same position.”

“I’ll bet you are ready to knock off for the day, right? This is a lot of information to absorb in one session.”

Jane and June both nod, so Bob says “OK, how about if we get together tomorrow and go over the middle rows in the spreadsheet, the income sources?”

Jane looks at June, who says, “I’m in. We are going to be retired for a long time, and you don’t get two chances at planning retirement.”

Jane adds, “Yes, I agree. Most people spend more time deciding which car to buy than they do on one of the biggest decisions in their lives. I don’t want to make that mistake.”

Bob says, “OK, how about 1 PM tomorrow, back here?”

They nod, so he shuts down the program and closes up his laptop.

---

[i] See Appendix E for more on this topic.

[ii] Most users will probably assume that cash earns less return on average than portfolio assets, but that assumption is separate from the tax effects.

[iii] The program assumes that the Roth account has been set up already for a long enough time (five years, as of this writing) that any earnings taken out are tax-free.

Chapter 5
The Withdrawal Source Section of the Spreadsheet

Bob spent some time overnight thinking about Jane and June's questions and comments on the previous day's session. Since Jane had said she was less comfortable with the lower part of the result page than the top part, Bob took some more pains with this part.

So, he opens up his computer and reloads the data from the previous day, switches to the "Assumptions" tab, and points to the withdrawal source section of the spreadsheet. (See Figure 5.1.)

Cash Delta	-4389	-10514	-5429	-11337	0	0	0	0	665
TRA Delta	-4389	-10514	-5429	-38887	-46392	-12079	-14159	-4588	0
Roth Delta	920	1210	1163	3010	893	-6010	-2392	465	-1061
Taxable Sold	0	0	0	0	0	-12079	-14159	-27138	-2065
Sale Basis	0	0	0	0	0	5749	6298	11282	802
(LTCG)	0	0	0	0	0	6330	7860	15856	1262
Taxable Bought	0	0	0	0	0	0	0	0	0
Qual Divs	0	0	0	0	0	0	0	0	0
Social Security	0	0	0	0	12088	24659	25153	25656	55532
Taxable Income	46175	46175	46175	46175	0	0	0	0	0
Nontaxable Income	0	0	0	0	0	0	0	0	0

Figure 5.1: The Rhino Retirement Analyzer result screen with the "withdrawal source section" of the spreadsheet row highlighted

Cash Delta

"Let's start with the first row in that area, 'Cash Delta.'" (See Figure 5.2.)

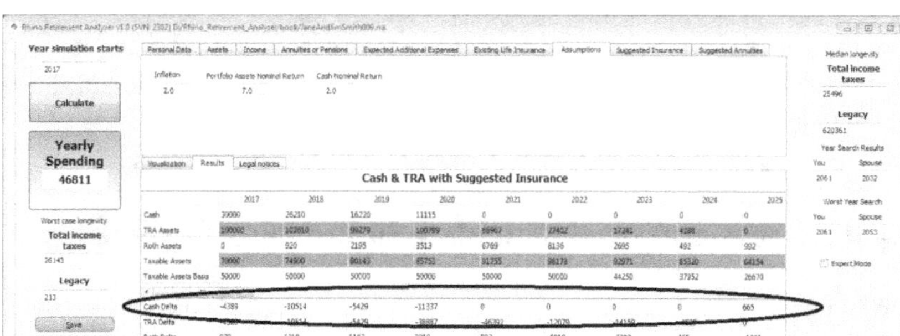

Figure 5.2: The Rhino Retirement Analyzer result screen with the "Cash Delta" row highlighted

DOI 10.1515/9781501506185-005

Bob continues, "'Delta' is a math term meaning 'change in something.' In this case, 'Cash Delta' means 'change in your cash holdings.' So, if we look at the entry for 'Cash' at the beginning of a year, then add the 'Cash Delta' entry for that year, we should get *almost* the 'Cash' entry for the beginning of the next year. For instance, if we add the 'Cash' entry for 2017, which is $30,000, to the 'Cash Delta' for that same year, which is -$4,389, we get $25,611. The 'Cash' entry for 2018 is $26,210, which is $599 more. Where did that $599 come from? June?" (See Figure 5.3.)

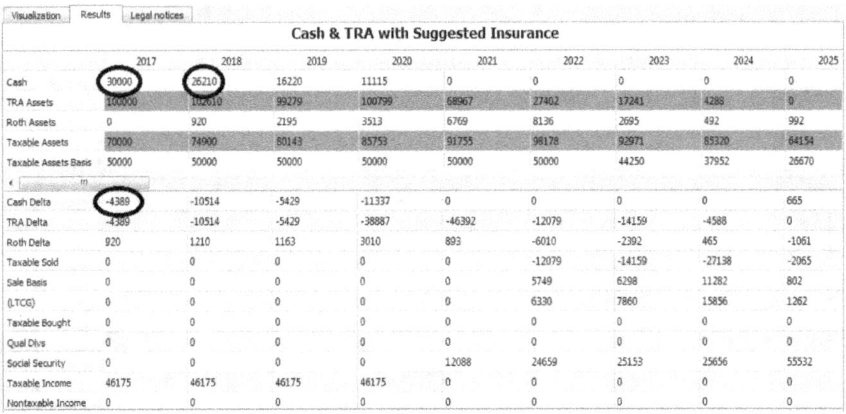

Cash & TRA with Suggested Insurance

	2017	2018	2019	2020	2021	2022	2023	2024	2025
Cash	30000	26210	16220	11115	0	0	0	0	0
TRA Assets	100000	102610	99279	100799	68967	27402	17241	4288	0
Roth Assets	0	920	2195	3513	6769	8136	2695	492	992
Taxable Assets	70000	74900	80143	85753	91755	98178	92971	85320	64154
Taxable Assets Basis	50000	50000	50000	50000	50000	50000	44250	37952	26670
Cash Delta	-4389	-10514	-5429	-11337	0	0	0	0	665
TRA Delta	-4389	-10514	-5429	-38887	-46392	-12079	-14159	-4588	0
Roth Delta	920	1210	1163	3010	893	-6010	-2392	465	-1061
Taxable Sold	0	0	0	0	0	-12079	-14159	-27138	-2065
Sale Basis	0	0	0	0	0	5749	6298	11282	802
(LTCG)	0	0	0	0	0	6330	7860	15856	1262
Taxable Bought	0	0	0	0	0	0	0	0	0
Qual Divs	0	0	0	0	0	0	0	0	0
Social Security	0	0	0	0	12088	24659	25153	25656	55532
Taxable Income	46175	46175	46175	46175	0	0	0	0	0
Nontaxable Income	0	0	0	0	0	0	0	0	0

Figure 5.3: The Rhino Retirement Analyzer result screen showing the entries needed to estimate the Cash for 2018

June says, "Well, that's almost $600, which is 2% of the starting amount in 2017. I see that the 'Assumptions' tab shows 2.0% as the 'Cash Nominal Return.' Is that how it is calculated? And if so, why isn't it exactly $600?"

Bob replies, "Go to the head of the class! Yes, the difference is the interest. As to why it isn't exactly $600, that's because the program is optimized for speed rather than accounting exactness. If it were a tax-preparation program, it would have to do all the arithmetic precisely, but that is much more complex and slower even on today's very fast machines."

Why it's Not Important to Calculate Future Results Precisely

"Now of course it seems as though it would be better to get perfectly correct answers than taking shortcuts like this. But in fact, there *are no* perfectly correct answers anyway. Even if we can assume that we are getting exactly 2% on cash, we don’t know exactly what the return on our other assets is going to be, nor do we know what the tax brackets will be for any year that isn’t over yet. In fact, it would be a miracle if the first two digits of the ‘Yearly Spending’ number were correct, so a few dollars here or there make no difference in the accuracy of a projection of this type. Does that make sense?”

June replies, “I think so. Whatever projection the program makes isn’t going to come out exactly right anyway, because it depends on data that we won’t have until after the fact. So, the fact that the arithmetic isn’t exact doesn’t matter. Is that right?”

Traditional Retirement Account Delta

Bob answers, “Yes, that’s exactly it. OK, now let’s move on to the next row, ‘TRA Delta.’ Jane, what should that represent?” (See Figure 5.4.)

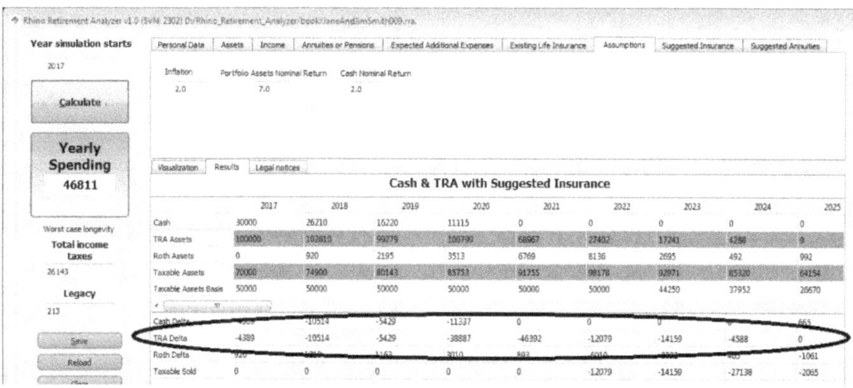

Figure 5.4: The Rhino Retirement Analyzer result screen with the “TRA Delta” row highlighted

June replies, “That should be how much we should take out of the ‘Traditional Retirement Accounts,’ right?”

Bob says, “Right.”

Jane continues, “I see that in this case we start taking money out of that account right away. Is that because we get a higher ‘Yearly Spending’ level by using that money first and preserving the taxable account balance?” (See Figure 5.5.)

Cash Delta	-4389	-10514	-5429	-11337	0	0	0	0	665
TRA Delta	-4389	-10514	-5429	-38887	-46392	-12079	-14159	-4588	0
Roth Delta	920	1210	1163	3010	893	-6010	-2392	465	-1061
Taxable Sold	0	0	0	0	0	-12079	-14159	-27138	-2065
Sale Basis	0	0	0	0	0	5749	6298	11282	802
(LTCG)	0	0	0	0	0	6330	7860	15856	1262
Taxable Bought	0	0	0	0	0	0	0	0	0
Qual Divs	0	0	0	0	0	0	0	0	0
Social Security	0	0	0	0	12088	24659	25153	25656	55532
Taxable Income	46175	46175	46175	46175	0	0	0	0	0
Nontaxable Income	0	0	0	0	0	0	0	0	0

Figure 5.5: The Rhino Retirement Analyzer result screen with the first TRA withdrawal highlighted

Bob replies, "Yes, the program has projected that 'Cash & TRA' looks like the best withdrawal method in your particular case, given our assumptions. So, in this case, you would hang on to the taxable account until you have used up most of the cash and traditional retirement accounts."

Roth Delta

"Let's continue with the 'Roth Delta' row." (See Figure 5.6.)

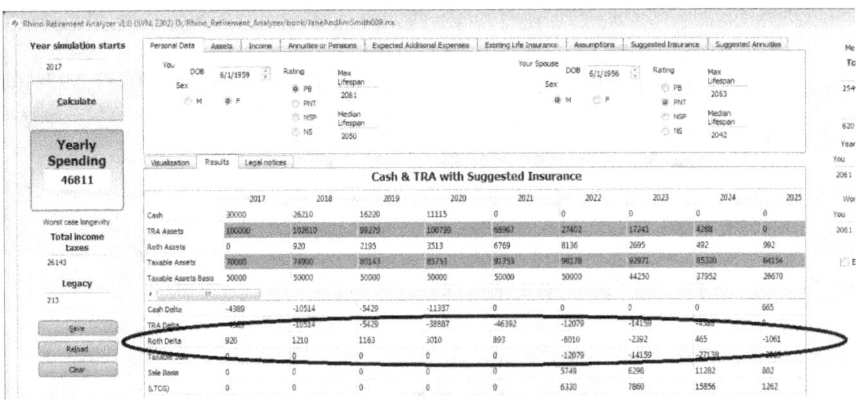

Figure 5.6: The Rhino Retirement Analyzer result screen with the "Roth Delta" row highlighted

Jane says, "We discussed this a bit yesterday. I know it starts out as 0 because we don't have a Roth account set up yet. The deposits starting in 2017 are from 'extra money' that we get from Jim's salary, right? It doesn't seem like we ever have any 'extra money' that isn't accounted for, but I guess that's fairly normal."

Bob answers, "Yes, I'm afraid that is normal. However, if you want to have about the same 'real' spending level (that is, after tax and inflation) for the rest of your life, you must save money while you have more income, so that you will have it to spend later. This is just a special case of that general rule."

June interjects, "Is that how the program works? It tries to level spending out for the rest of the couple's life?"

Bob replies, "Yes, that is the idea, aside from the 'Expected Additional Expenses,' it looks for the maximum level after-tax, inflation-adjusted cash flow if one spouse dies at the worst possible time. Wow, that's a mouthful!"

June says, "Can you give us an idea of how it does that? We don't need every step, but just the general approach? Assuming you know, of course."

Bob answers, "Yes, the 'theory of operation' is covered in the documentation that I studied to be able to use the program effectively, so I should be able to explain that. But I'd rather finish the explanation of the withdrawal source section of the spreadsheet first, if you don't mind."

They nod in agreement, so he continues with the next row, "Taxable Sold." (See Figure 5.7.)

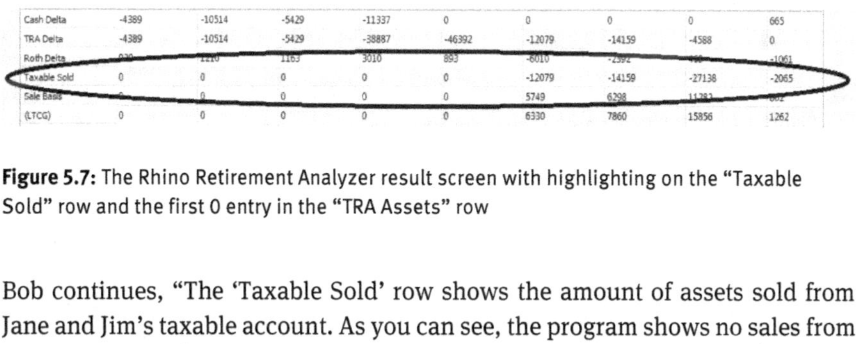

Cash Delta	-4389	-10514	-5429	-11337	0	0	0	0	665
TRA Delta	-4389	-10514	-5429	-38887	-46392	-12079	-14159	-4588	0
Roth Delta	[illegible]	1210	1163	3010	893	-6010	-2392	[illegible]	-1061
Taxable Sold	0	0	0	0	0	-12079	-14159	-27138	-2065
Sale Basis	0	0	0	0	0	5749	6298	11282	[illegible]
(LTCG)	0	0	0	0	0	6330	7860	15856	1262

Figure 5.7: The Rhino Retirement Analyzer result screen with highlighting on the "Taxable Sold" row and the first 0 entry in the "TRA Assets" row

Bob continues, "The 'Taxable Sold' row shows the amount of assets sold from Jane and Jim's taxable account. As you can see, the program shows no sales from that account until 2022, as it has you selling off your TRA assets to preserve your taxable account balance as long as possible. In your particular case, selling TRA assets and drawing down your cash turns out to be the approach that gets the highest after-tax cash flow (as always, if the assumptions turn out to be correct). Any questions on this row?"

They both shake their heads.

Sale Basis

Bob continues, "The next row, 'Sale Basis,' usually inspires some questions. Let me explain it first, though." (See Figure 5.8.)

Cash Delta	-4389	-10514	-5429	-11337	0	0	0	0	665
TRA Delta	-4389	-10514	-5429	-38887	-46392	-12079	-14159	-4588	0
Roth Delta	920	1210	1163	3010	893	-6010	-2392	465	-1061
Taxable Sold	0	0	0	0	0	-12079	[illegible]	-27138	-2065
Sale Basis	0	0	0	0	0	5749	6298	11282	802
(LTCG)	0	0	0	0	0	6330	7860	[illegible]	1262
Taxable Bought	0	0	0	0	0	0	0	0	0

Figure 5.8: The Rhino Retirement Analyzer result screen with the "Sale Basis" row highlighted

Bob goes on, "What that row shows is how much you paid for the assets in your taxable account that were sold in the 'Taxable Sold' entry for the same year. Let's look at the entries for the 'Taxable Sold' and the 'Sale basis' rows in 2022." (See Figure 5.9.)

Cash Delta	-4389	-10514	-5429	-11337	0	0	0	0	665
TRA Delta	-4389	-10514	-5429	-38887	-46392	-12079	-14159	-4588	0
Roth Delta	920	1210	1163	3010	893	-6010	-2392	465	-1061
Taxable Sold	0	0	0	0	0	-12079	-14159	-27138	-2065
Sale Basis	0	0	0	0	0	5749	6298	11282	802
(LTCG)	0	0	0	0	0	6330	7860	15856	1262
Taxable Bought	0	0	0	0	0	0	0	0	0
Qual Divs	0	0	0	0	0	0	0	0	0
Social Security	0	0	0	0	12088	24659	25153	25656	55532
Taxable Income	46175	46175	46175	46175	0	0	0	0	0
Nontaxable Income	0	0	0	0	0	0	0	0	0

Figure 5.9: The Rhino Retirement Analyzer result screen with the "Taxable Sold" and "Sale Basis" entries for 2022 highlighted

"In 2022 you would be selling $12,079 worth of assets from your taxable account, as shown in the 'Taxable Sold' cell for that year. What you paid for that $12,079 worth of assets is $5,749. Any questions so far?"

Jane says, "Yes, two. First, where did that $5,749 amount come from? Second, why does it matter how much we paid for the assets we are selling?"

Bob replies, "The $5,749 is calculated from the 'Taxable' and 'Tax Basis' entries in the 'Assets' tab, the $12,079 sale amount, and the 7% 'Portfolio Assets Nominal Return' assumption." (See Figures 5.10 and 5.11.)

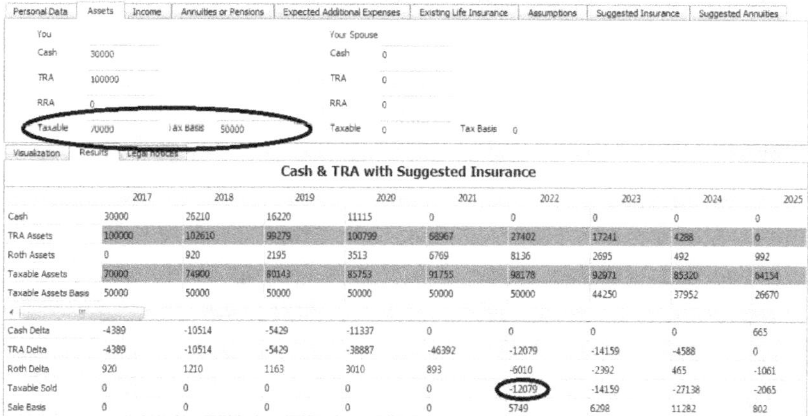

Figure 5.10: The Rhino Retirement Analyzer result screen with highlighted "Taxable" and "Tax Basis" entries on the "Assets" tab and the Taxable Sold cell for 2022

Figure 5.11: The Rhino Retirement Analyzer result screen with "Portfolio Assets Nominal Return" highlighted

Bob continues, "First we multiply the year 2022 starting taxable account value of \$98,178 by 1.07 (adding 7% return), so at the end of 2017, that taxable account should be worth \$105,050. Then if you are selling \$12,079 out of \$105,050, that is (let me get out my calculator) ... a bit less than 11.5% of your taxable assets. So, we take 11.5% of your 'Tax Basis' of \$50,000, which is \$5,750. The actual number on the spreadsheet is \$5,749, which is a bit less than \$5,750, so it looks as though our calculation is right. Does that answer your first question?"

Jane replies, "Yes."

Bob then continues, "Now, as for why this matters, it affects your taxes."

Long Term Capital Gains

"See the next row, labeled '(LTCG)'?" (See Figure 5.12.)

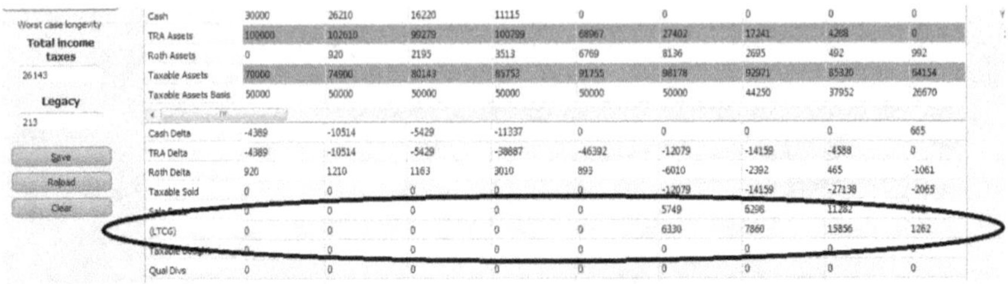

Figure 5.12: The Rhino Retirement Analyzer result screen with the "LTCG" row highlighted

Jane nods her head.

Bob continues, "LTCG stands for 'long term capital gains.'[i] This is a special type of income that has better tax treatment than many other types of income. The maximum tax rate for such gains is 20% unless you have a *lot* of taxable income, much more than you and Jim have. In fact, you can pay as little as 0% tax on capital gains if your other income is low enough. It is calculated on the amount you get for selling assets ('proceeds') minus the amount you paid for those same assets ('cost basis'). So we need to know the cost basis of the assets being sold. That's what the 'Sale Basis' row represents."

"Of course, these rules are subject to change at any time by Congress, but since no one knows what the tax laws will be in the future, all we (or anyone else) can do is use current law for our projections.

"Do you have any questions on this row?"

Jane answers, "I understand that capital gains taxes apply only when we sell. If so, we can time the sales to reduce taxes, right?"

Bob replies, "Yes, that is possible. The problem if you have mutual funds is that you can't control when *they* sell, which can also cause you to incur a tax liability. If you have individual stocks or other assets that aren't part of a mutual fund, you can generally decide when to sell. There are exceptions to that rule too, but they don't apply in most cases."[ii]

"Any other questions on this row?"

Both sisters shake their heads.

Taxable Bought

Bob continues, "The next row, 'Taxable Bought,' is basically reserved for future use, since the current version of the program doesn't ever buy assets in the taxable account." (See Figure 5.13.)

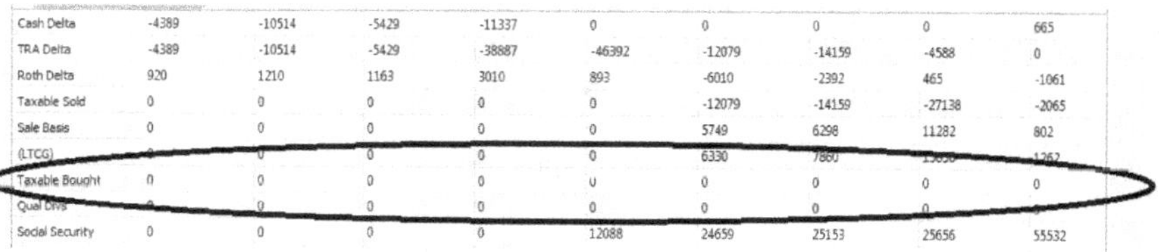

Figure 5.13: The Rhino Retirement Analyzer result screen with the "Taxable Bought" row highlighted

Bob continues, "Instead, as we've already seen, if there is extra income, it buys Roth assets to the extent that is feasible based on tax law. Any questions on this?"

Both sisters indicate that they are satisfied.

Qualified Dividends

Bob continues, "The next row is used if you have reported any 'qualified dividends' on the 'Income' tab." (See Figure 5.14.)

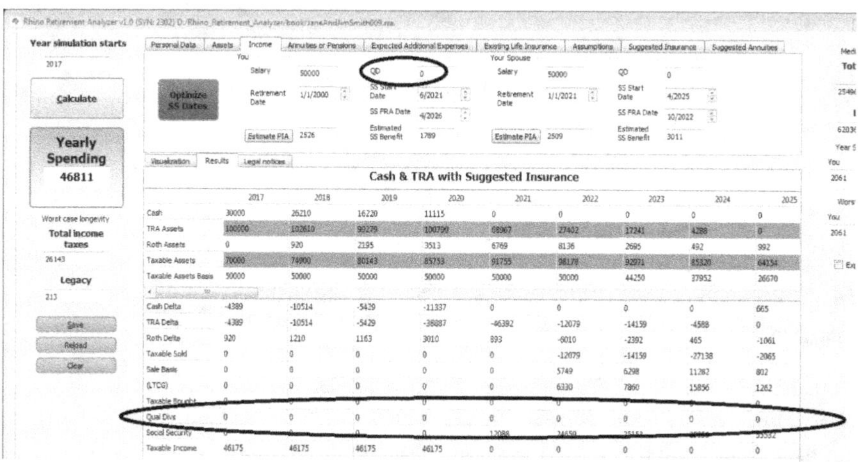

Figure 5.14: The Rhino Retirement Analyzer result screen highlighting the "Qualified Divs" row and the "QD" entry on the "Income" tab

"However, since you don't have any such dividends, this row will be filled with zeroes. Any questions on this?"

Jane says, "What makes a dividend 'qualified,' and why is that important?"

Bob replies, "It depends on the company meeting certain qualifications in the tax law. If you get a dividend reporting tax form from the company, it should say on the form whether the dividend is qualified. It's important because qualified dividends get capital gains tax treatment (very favorable) rather than ordinary income tax treatment (unfavorable). Any other questions?"

The sisters shake their heads.

Social Security

Bob continues with the explanation of the next row, "Social Security." (See Figure 5.15.)

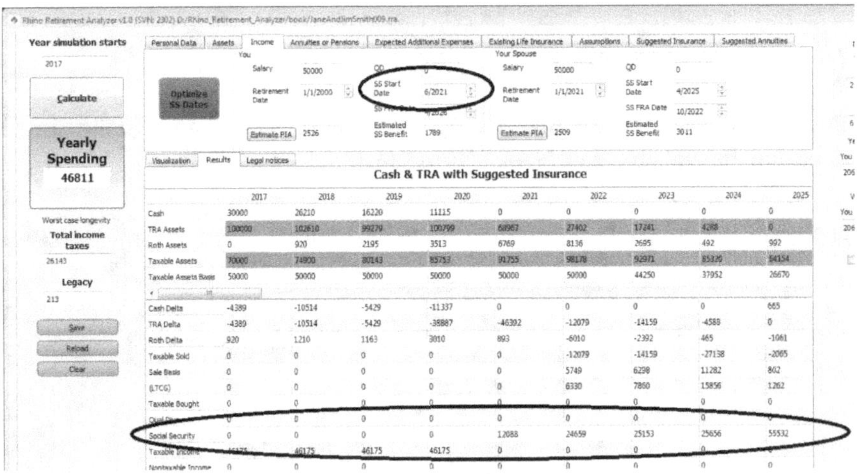

Figure 5.15: The Rhino Retirement Analyzer result screen highlighting the "Social Security" row and Jane's Social Security start date

Bob continues, "As you can see, this assumes that you start taking Social Security in June 2021, which is why the amount for that year is only $12,088. Do you remember how that date was chosen?"

Jane replies, "I recall that you clicked the 'Optimize SS Dates' button after we put in the return assumptions. Is that right?"

Bob says, "Yes, that's right."

Taxable Income

"The next row is 'Taxable Income'." (See Figure 5.16.)

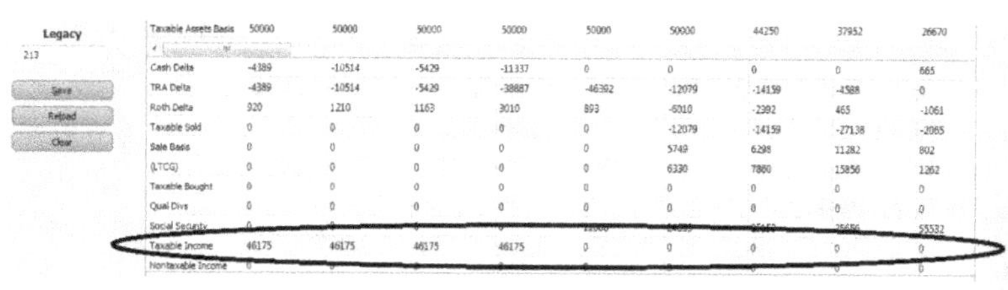

Figure 5.16: The Rhino Retirement Analyzer result screen with the "Taxable Income" row highlighted

Bob continues, "In your case the entries on this row are just Jim's salary until his planned retirement in 2021, after deducting the FICA tax but before income taxes, amounting to $46,175 a year. Do you have any questions on that?" (See Figure 5.17.)

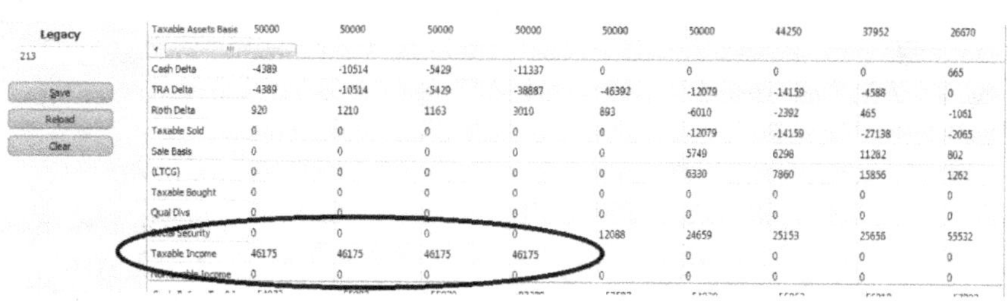

Figure 5.17: The Rhino Retirement Analyzer result screen with the "Taxable Income" row for years 2017 through 2020 highlighted

Jane answers, "Yes, I do have a couple of questions. Why is FICA deducted but not income taxes? And what else could go on that Taxable Income row, even if it doesn't apply to us right now?"

Bob replies, "Well, for your first question, that's because FICA taxes are a flat percentage that can be calculated just from your salary income, so the program can just display 'salary after FICA' as a fixed number that can be used toward your spending allotment. On the other hand, income taxes on your salary depend on your other income, which depends in turn on how much we are selling from your taxable accounts or withdrawing from your retirement accounts. Thus, the program has to estimate income taxes after figuring out both of those numbers. Does that make sense now?"

Jane nods her head, so Bob continues, "Now for your second question, if you had an annuity, then some of the money that you get from it is considered taxable income and some is considered nontaxable, because it represents the return of part of the premium you paid for the annuity."

Nontaxable Income

Jane says, "Is that what the next row, 'Nontaxable Income,' is for?" (See Figure 5.18.)

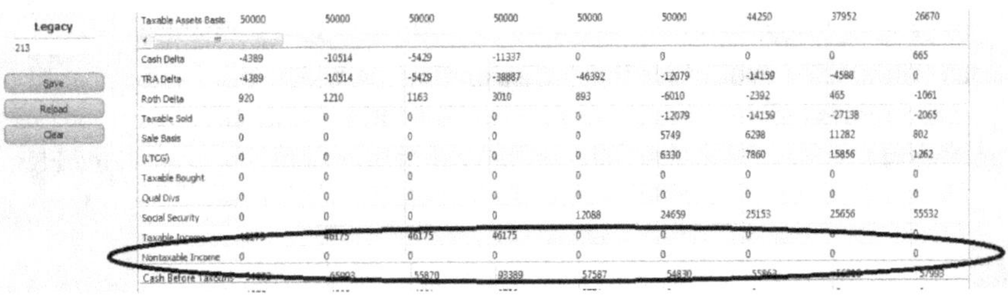

Figure 5.18: The Rhino Retirement Analyzer result screen with the "Nontaxable Income" row highlighted

Bob says, "Yes, that's right. The nontaxable part of any annuity payments goes there, but so far, anyway, you don't have any annuities, so all of the numbers are 0."

"That finishes off the 'withdrawal source section' of the spreadsheet. I'm sure you will also want to go over the last section, the 'cash, taxes, and insurance premiums' section, since that's where the 'rubber meets the road.' But I think we've done enough for today. How about if we continue tomorrow at 1 PM?"

Jane and June both nod, so Bob shuts down the program and closes up his laptop.

---

[i] The program assumes that you have owned the assets in your taxable account for at least a year, so that any gains on assets you sell from that account will have the more favorable tax treatment given to long-term capital gains.

[ii] One of the situations that can force a holder to sell is a hostile takeover of a company, especially one that takes the company private.

Chapter 6
Cash, Taxes, and Insurance Premiums
The Next Day...

Bob opens up his computer and loads the data from the previous day. Then he switches to the "Income" tab and says, "Here's the cash, taxes, and insurance premiums section of the spreadsheet. Let's go over them today." (See Figure 6.1.)

Cash Before Tax&Ins	54033	65993	55870	93389	57587	54830	55863	56918	57993
Est. Fed. Income Tax	4075	4899	4021	8730	3771	0	0	0	0
Insurance Premiums	3147	3147	3147	3147	3147	3147	3147	3147	3147
Cash After Tax & Ins	46811	57947	48702	81512	50669	51683	52716	53771	54846

Figure 6.1: The Rhino Retirement Analyzer result screen with the "cash, taxes, and insurance premiums" section highlighted

Cash before Taxes and Insurance

Bob continues, "The first line of this section, labeled 'Cash Before Tax&Ins,' is pretty simple. It represents the total amount of cash that would be available for spending if there were no income taxes or insurance premiums." (See Figure 6.2.)

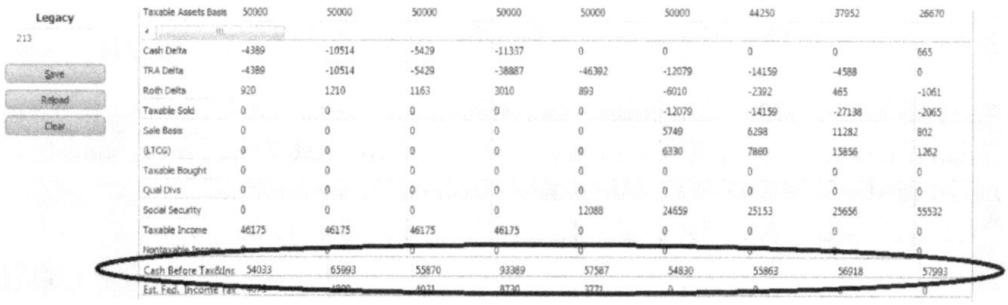

Taxable Assets Basis	50000	50000	50000	50000	50000	50000	44250	37952	26670
Cash Delta	-4389	-10514	-5429	-11337	0	0	0	0	665
TRA Delta	-4389	-10514	-5429	-38887	-46392	-12079	-14159	-4588	0
Roth Delta	920	1210	1163	3010	893	-6010	-2392	465	-1061
Taxable Sold	0	0	0	0	0	-12079	-14159	-27138	-2065
Sale Basis	0	0	0	0	0	5749	6298	11282	802
(LTCG)	0	0	0	0	0	6330	7860	15856	1262
Taxable Bought	0	0	0	0	0	0	0	0	0
Qual Divs	0	0	0	0	0	0	0	0	0
Social Security	0	0	0	0	12088	24659	25153	25656	55532
Taxable Income	46175	46175	46175	46175	0	0	0	0	0
Nontaxable Income	0	0	0	0	0	0	0	0	0
Cash Before Tax&Ins	54033	65993	55870	93389	57587	54830	55863	56918	57993
Est. Fed. Income Tax	[illegible]	4899	4021	8730	3771	0	0	0	0

Figure 6.2: The Rhino Retirement Analyzer result screen with the "Cash Before Tax&Ins" row highlighted

"This is computed by adding the entry for that year in 'Taxable Income,' 'Nontaxable Income,' 'Qual Divs,' and 'Social Security,' then adding that sum to the amount taken from the various accounts: 'Cash,' 'TRA Assets,' 'Roth Assets,' and

DOI 10.1515/9781501506185-006

'Taxable Assets.' So, for your case, in 2017 that can be calculated as $46,175 (Taxable Income) + $4,389 (the sum taken from cash) + $4,389 (the sum taken from your traditional retirement account) - $920 (the amount put into your Roth account), which comes out to ... (enters numbers into calculator) $54,033, which is the entry in the 'Cash Before Tax&Ins' for 2017."

"Does either of you have any questions about this entry?"

Jane and June both shake their heads no.

Estimated Federal Income Tax

Bob continues, "OK, let's take a look at the next row, 'Est. Fed. Income Tax.'" (See Figure 6.3.)

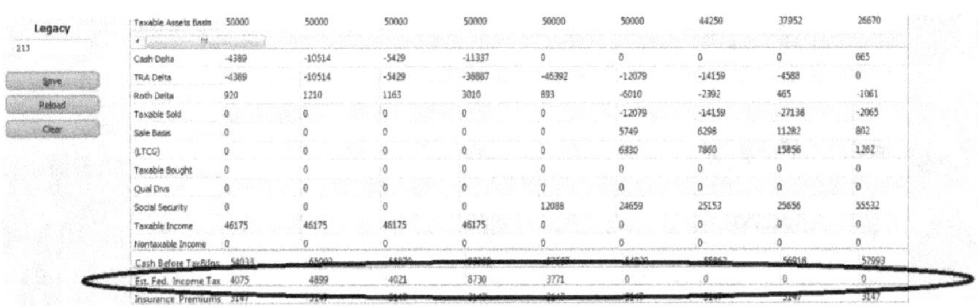

Taxable Assets Basis	50000	50000	50000	50000	50000	50000	44250	37952	26670
Cash Delta	-4389	-10514	-5429	-11337	0	0	0	0	665
TRA Delta	-4389	-10514	-5429	-38887	-46392	-12079	-14159	-4588	0
Roth Delta	920	1210	1163	3010	893	-6010	-2392	465	-1061
Taxable Sold	0	0	0	0	0	-12079	-14159	-27138	-2065
Sale Basis	0	0	0	0	0	5749	6298	11282	802
(LTCG)	0	0	0	0	0	6330	7860	15856	1262
Taxable Bought	0	0	0	0	0	0	0	0	0
Qual Divs	0	0	0	0	0	0	0	0	0
Social Security	0	0	0	0	12088	24659	25153	25656	55532
Taxable Income	46175	46175	46175	46175	0	0	0	0	0
Nontaxable Income	0	0	0	0	0	0	0	0	0
Cash Before Tax&Ins	54033	[illegible]	[illegible]	[illegible]	[illegible]	[illegible]	[illegible]	56918	57993
Est. Fed. Income Tax	4075	4899	4021	8730	3771	0	0	0	0
Insurance Premiums	3147	[illegible]	[illegible]	[illegible]	[illegible]	[illegible]	[illegible]	3147	3147

Figure 6.3: The Rhino Retirement Analyzer result screen with the "Est. Fed. Income Tax" row highlighted

Bob continues, addressing Jane, "As I hope the name makes clear, this is the estimated federal income tax that you and Jim would pay under this scenario for the next nine years. Do you have any questions about this?"

Jane replies, "Yes, I do have a couple of questions about the federal tax row. First, I assume this means that the program doesn't estimate any state taxes. Is that right?"

Bob replies, "Yes, that's right. Of course, it would be possible to estimate those, too, but since every state that has an income tax has different rules for how to compute that tax, that would increase the complexity substantially. So, it is the one significant area that is omitted in the software. Fortunately, since we live in a state with no income taxes, we don't have to worry about that complication at this point. What's your other question?"

Jane says, "What happens to the taxes after 2025?"

Bob replies, "As I think I've shown you before, information for other years is visible if you slide the slider above the withdrawal source section of the spreadsheet, so here's the estimation for years 2025 to 2033. Does this answer your question?" (See Figure 6.4.)

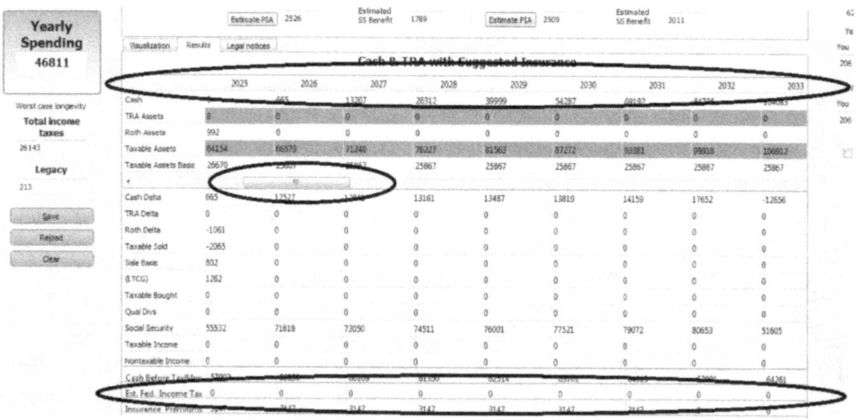

Figure 6.4: The Rhino Retirement Analyzer result screen with the slider, the year number row, and the "Est. Fed. Income Tax" row highlighted

Jane answers, "Wow, that is interesting. No income taxes after 2025? I see that our income keeps going up with inflation, so why don't we have to pay income taxes?"

Bob replies, "That is largely the result of the favorable tax treatment of Social Security, which makes up your entire income at that point in time. Of course, tax laws can and do change, but that particular benefit of Social Security payments has been around for a long time."

Jane says, "Sounds good to me. What's next?"

Insurance Premiums

Bob replies, "The next row is 'Insurance Premiums,' which shows how much total premium you and Jim would pay for life insurance every year until one of you dies. Let's move the slider back to the present so we can see the next few years." (See Figure 6.5.)

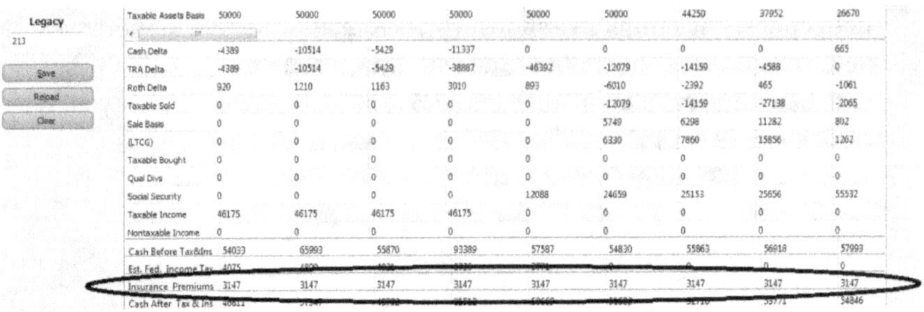

Legacy

213

Save

Reload

Clear

Taxable Assets Basis	50000	50000	50000	50000	50000	50000	44250	37952	26670
Cash Delta	-4389	-10514	-5429	-11337	0	0	0	0	665
TRA Delta	-4389	-10514	-5429	-38887	-46392	-12079	-14159	-4588	0
Roth Delta	920	1210	1163	3010	893	-6010	-2392	465	-1061
Taxable Sold	0	0	0	0	0	-12079	-14159	-27138	-2065
Sale Basis	0	0	0	0	0	5749	6298	11282	802
(LTCG)	0	0	0	0	0	6330	7860	15856	1262
Taxable Bought	0	0	0	0	0	0	0	0	0
Qual Divs	0	0	0	0	0	0	0	0	0
Social Security	0	0	0	0	12088	24659	25153	25656	55532
Taxable Income	46175	46175	46175	46175	0	0	0	0	0
Nontaxable Income	0	0	0	0	0	0	0	0	0
Cash Before Tax&Ins	54033	65993	55870	93389	57587	54830	55863	56918	57993
Est. Fed. Income Tax	4075	[illegible]	[illegible]	[illegible]	[illegible]	0	0	0	0
Insurance Premiums	3147	3147	3147	3147	3147	3147	3147	3147	3147
Cash After Tax & Ins	[illegible]	[illegible]	[illegible]	[illegible]	[illegible]	[illegible]	[illegible]	53771	54846

Figure 6.5: The Rhino Retirement Analyzer result screen with the "Insurance Premiums" row highlighted

Jane asks, "Why just until one of us dies? Does a surviving spouse have to stop paying his or her life insurance premium?"

Bob replies, "The program assumes that the life insurance has served its purpose after the first spouse dies. Of course, you could keep paying the premium until the end of the term,[i] but it isn't needed any more to protect the income of the surviving spouse, which is the reason that the program suggested the insurance in the first place. Thus, it no longer shows that premium in its projections after the death of the first spouse, as you can see happens in this scenario in 2032. Does that make sense?" (See Figure 6.6.)

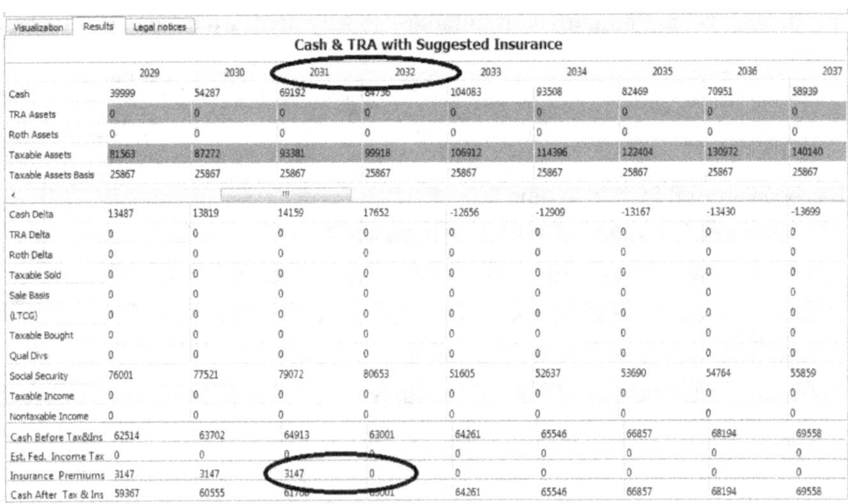

Visualization | Results | Legal notices

Cash & TRA with Suggested Insurance

	2029	2030	2031	2032	2033	2034	2035	2036	2037
Cash	39999	54287	69192	[illegible]	104083	93508	82469	70951	58939
TRA Assets	0	0	0	0	0	0	0	0	0
Roth Assets	0	0	0	0	0	0	0	0	0
Taxable Assets	81563	87272	93381	99918	106912	114396	122404	130972	140140
Taxable Assets Basis	25867	25867	25867	25867	25867	25867	25867	25867	25867
Cash Delta	13487	13819	14159	17652	-12656	-12909	-13167	-13430	-13699
TRA Delta	0	0	0	0	0	0	0	0	0
Roth Delta	0	0	0	0	0	0	0	0	0
Taxable Sold	0	0	0	0	0	0	0	0	0
Sale Basis	0	0	0	0	0	0	0	0	0
(LTCG)	0	0	0	0	0	0	0	0	0
Taxable Bought	0	0	0	0	0	0	0	0	0
Qual Divs	0	0	0	0	0	0	0	0	0
Social Security	76001	77521	79072	80653	51605	52637	53690	54764	55859
Taxable Income	0	0	0	0	0	0	0	0	0
Nontaxable Income	0	0	0	0	0	0	0	0	0
Cash Before Tax&Ins	62514	63702	64913	63001	64261	65546	66857	68194	69558
Est. Fed. Income Tax	0	0	0	0	0	0	0	0	0
Insurance Premiums	3147	3147	3147	0	0	0	0	0	0
Cash After Tax & Ins	59367	60555	[illegible]	[illegible]	64261	65546	66857	68194	69558

Figure 6.6: The Rhino Retirement Analyzer result screen with the insurance premium cutoff entries highlighted

Jane says, "But if this projection shows Jim dying in 2032, why isn't there an insurance payout? Shouldn't there be one?"

Bob says, "The program is designed to be as conservative as possible, so if a spouse dies during the last year of an insurance term, it assumes that he or she dies after the policy has expired, which of course means that there wouldn't be a payout."

Jane says, "OK, I get it. It says premiums. Is there anything else that can go on that row other than the term life insurance that the program recommends?"

Bob says, "Yes, there is. First, if you already have some life insurance, the premiums for that policy (or those policies) will be included on that line until the projected date of death as well as premiums for the suggested new policies. Second, the program also can suggest the purchase of a single-premium annuity, in which case the premium for that annuity will be shown on that row in the first year. That applies mostly to people who have quite a bit in assets, but I can show you what (if anything) it would do for you after we get through the long-awaited explanation of how the program works, if you're interested."

Jane says, "Actually, my mother has been hinting at giving us some cash while she's still alive rather than making us wait for an inheritance. So maybe it would be a good idea to see how that might affect our sustainable spending in our retirement."

Bob replies, "Yes, buying an annuity can make a sizable difference in sustainable spending, depending on your age, assets, and the assumptions we make about how much the market will return. Before we discuss that, I'll need to do some research on annuity prices so I'll have something to show you."

Jane answers, "Sure, then let's finish the spreadsheet explanation and get through how the program works, if you are okay with that."

Bob replies, "I am fine with that."

Cash after Taxes and Insurance

"The last row on the spreadsheet is 'Cash After Tax & Ins.' That is really the bottom line, both physically and logically. It tells you how much you can spend every year, in inflated dollars according to our inflation estimate. Let's move the year slider back to the present so we can see the first few years." (See Figure 6.7.)

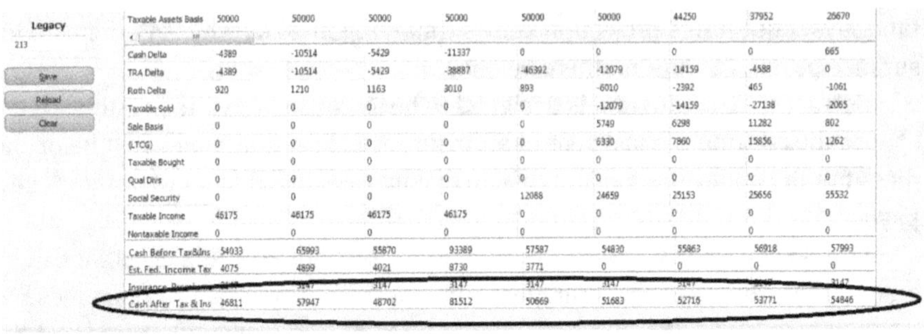

Figure 6.7: The Rhino Retirement Analyzer result screen with the "Cash After Tax & Ins" row highlighted

Jane says, "I see most of the entries in that row go up a bit every year from the previous year, but the entries for 2018 and 2020 are considerably higher than the numbers on either side. Is that because of the 'Expected Additional Expenses'?"

Bob replies, "Yes, that's why. Here's the 'Expected Additional Expenses' tab that shows those numbers, and you can see that they occur in 2018 and 2020." (See Figure 6.8.)

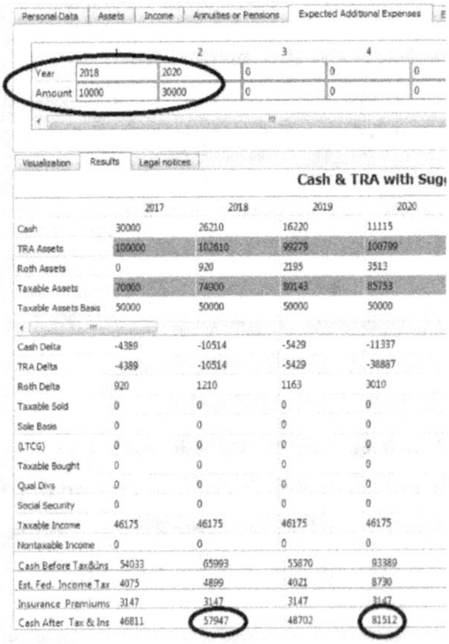

Figure 6.8: The Rhino Retirement Analyzer result screen with the Cash After Tax & Ins entries for 2018 and 2020 and the additional expenses for years 2018 and 2020 highlighted

Bob continues, "Any other questions for today, or should we just call it a day and get back together tomorrow at 1 PM to discuss how the program actually does its job?"

Both sisters agree to continue the next day, so Bob shuts down the program and closes his laptop.

---

[i] Actually, in most cases you can even keep a term policy in force beyond the end of the level term period, but the premiums rapidly escalate to unaffordable levels, so that is only done in very rare circumstances beyond the scope of this discussion.

Chapter 7
Calculating Sustainable Retirement Spending

Bob begins by saying, "The basic idea is that the Rhino Retirement Analyzer creates what we refer to as a 'simulation' of what would happen given the starting assets and income, if each spouse dies in a specific year. The simulation starts with the existing assets and income information and the assumed year of death for each spouse. The program then estimates how much money would be left over if the couple spent no money from 'now' (the beginning of the year in the 'Year simulation starts' field) until the second spouse's death."

"It does this calculation by adding their income for each year to the amount of assets they had at the beginning of the year, then applying the return assumptions on the 'Assumptions tab' to increase their total assets.

"It does this for all the years until the second spouse dies. Once it has the amount they would have left over at that point if they hadn't spent any money, it can estimate how much money they *could* spend every year without running out until the second one dies. Does that make sense so far?"

June replies, "I'm not sure. Why does it figure out how much money they would have if they didn't spend any? That doesn't sound very realistic, or even relevant to the problem of how much they could spend."

Bob answers, "Yes, of course, that isn't realistic. But it *is* relevant. Let's see if I can explain it with a very simplified example."

A Very Simplified Example of the Sustainable Income Calculation

"Let's take the case of a single person. We will assume that she has no income, she doesn't earn any money on her assets, she wants to spend the same amount every year, and she doesn't care about leaving any legacy to her heirs. In that case, the amount of money she has right now has to last until she dies, and she can spend all of it. So, if we assume when she is going to die, we can just divide the amount of money she has by how many years she is going to live. For example, if she has $1,000,000 and we assume that she is going to live 10 years, she can spend $100,000 a year. Does *that* make sense?"

June says, "OK, I'm with you so far."

Bob says, "Good. Now let's assume that she gets 5% interest on her assets. In that case, the first year she will earn $50,000 in interest. For the moment, let's ignore taxes on that interest. We might think that the $50,000 can be

DOI 10.1515/9781501506185-007

added to the $100,000, so she can spend $150,000 the first year. But that leaves her with $900,000 after the first year, which means the second year her interest is only $45,000. That means if she spends all the interest in addition to the $100,000 from principal, she can spend only $145,000 the second year. Obviously the same will happen the third year, reducing her spending to $140,000. Following me so far?"

June says, "Yes, I see that this approach means a decreasing amount of spending every year. So obviously that won't work if the idea is to keep spending constant."

A Well-Known Solution to the Problem of Level Payments When there is Interest being Paid

Bob replies, "Right. Fortunately, this is a well-known problem in finance. In fact, it is exactly the same problem as paying off a mortgage, where at the beginning most of the money goes to interest and at the end most of the money goes to principal. If you've ever seen a 'mortgage amortization schedule,' you know what I'm referring to. The only difference is which way the money flows; with a mortgage, the borrower starts *owing* a sum of money, say $100,000 and ends up paying off the debt. In this case, the retiree starts by *owning* $100,000 and ends up with no assets. But the mathematical calculations are the same ... as long as we know exactly when the retiree dies. Of course, we don't actually know that, but we can analyze the results for any individual year of death. Does that make sense?"

June says, "Yes, actually I have looked at the amortization schedule for our mortgage. We have only about five years left on our mortgage, and most of the payment goes to principal now. So, if I'm understanding this, most of the spending money for a retiree comes out of principal at the end of life. Is that right?"

Bob answers, "Yes, that's how it works."

Conservative Estimates of Lifespan

Jane interjects, "But how do you know how long the widow is going to live? With a mortgage, the term is fixed in advance, but not with retirement. What if she lives too long and runs out of money?"

Bob replies, "Yes, that would be a bad result. That's why the program uses a conservative approach when figuring possible years of death. It assumes that each person could live long enough to outlive 90% of their contemporaries, so there is only a 10% chance of outliving their assets. This is called the '90th percentile of lifespan,' which is how we will refer to it in the future. Since we don't know exactly how long the widow is going to live, we have to do the calculations for each possible date of death up to that point."

Jane answers, "OK, but what about that 10% chance? Won't they be in really bad financial shape if that happens?"

Bob responds, "Then they will still have whatever retirement income continues until death. Social Security is the big one for most people, but some people also have pensions. And if someone is *really* worried about living too long, there's a solution to that problem as well, which I've already mentioned briefly: 'life annuities.' We'll get into those later."

Jane replies, "As long as I know there is a solution, I can wait to hear about it. Let's go on with the explanation of how the program does the calculations."

Bob continues, "OK, so now we have accounted for interest. The adjustment for inflation is almost the same as the one for interest, because we have to increase the spending in inflated dollars every year by the same percentage to keep 'real spending' constant. Can we skip the details on this part?"

June and Jane nod "yes," so he continues.

"Now let's consider the effect of income on the results. The amount of money you can spend is equal to your income (after taxes) added to the amount you withdraw from savings. So, if the income is the same every year, we can just add it to the amount that is withdrawn from savings every year. Is that obvious?"

June and Jane nod again, so he moves on.

Adding the Other Spouse Back into the Lifespan Calculation

Bob continues, "The next complication is that there are two spouses, not just one. So instead of just accounting for all the feasible years of death of one spouse, we have to consider what happens if one spouse dies early and the other lives a very long time. With the information we're dealing with so far, the only effect is that we have to make the money last until the 90th percentile of longevity of the spouse who has a longer possible lifespan, but there are other effects that I'll explain shortly. Any questions about this so far?"

Longevity Calculations

Jane says, "I have a question: How does it estimate the longevity of the spouses?"

Bob replies, "Remember the 'Personal Data' tab, where we selected an estimated insurance rating?" (See Figure 7.1.)

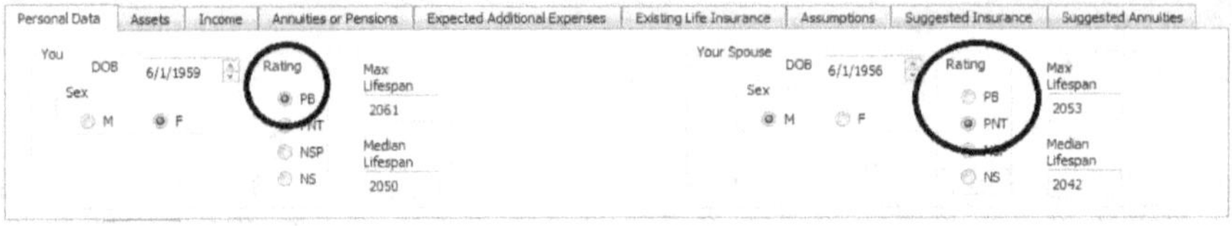

Figure 7.1: The Rhino Retirement Analyzer result screen with insurance ratings highlighted

"The program uses those estimated ratings, along with the life insurance premium rates that it has stored, to estimate mortality rates for each spouse. The calculation starts with the standard mortality rates published by the Social Security Administration, which keeps track of when each Social Security recipient dies. Then it adjusts those mortality rates based on the insurance ratings; the higher the rating, the lower the mortality rate. Then it adds up the mortality rates from the beginning of the simulation until the cumulative probability of death reaches 90%, which means we have reached the 90th percentile of life expectancy for this spouse. Does that make sense?"

Jane says, "I'm not sure. Can you give a simplified example?"

Bob says, "Sure. Let's assume we have an 80-year-old female, and a mortality table that says that the average person of that age and sex has a 10% chance of dying in the next year. In that case, out of 1,000 80-year-old females, 900 of them will survive to their 81st birthday. Then let's say that an average 81-year-old female has a 20% chance of dying in the next year, so we have 900*0.8, or 720 remaining at age 82. Continuing in this same vein, we will assume 30% mortality from age 82 to 83, so that there are 576 remaining females at age 83; 40% mortality from age 83 to 84 leaves 345 females; 50% mortality from age 84 to 85 leaves 173 remaining. Then assuming 60% mortality from age 85 to age 86, we get 69 remaining."

"So this means, with these artificial numbers, we have passed the 90th percentile of longevity for an average 80-year-old female at age 86. In the program, 'average' corresponds to the 'NS' rating, which stands for 'Non-smoker.' Are you with me so far?"[i]

Jane says, "Those aren't the real mortality rates, just ones you have made up for this simplified example, right?"

The Effect of Insurance Ratings on Lifespan Estimates

Bob replies, "Yes, that's right. Now let's see what happens if the rating is 'PB,' which stands for 'Preferred Best.' The program assumes that someone with a rating of 'PB' has roughly half the mortality risk of someone in the 'NS' category.[ii] So in that case, the calculations would go like this:"

"We have an 80-year-old female, and the made-up mortality table says that the average person of that age and sex has a 10% chance of dying in the next year. But in this case, rather than an average 80-year-old female, we are assuming a PB (Preferred Best) 80-year-old female. So we have to cut the mortality in half for each year. In that case, out of 1000 PB 80-year-old females, only 5% will die in the next year, so 950 of them will survive to their 81st birthday. Then the PB 81-year-old female has a 10% chance of dying in the next year, so we have 950*0.9, or 855 remaining at age 82. Continuing in this same vein, we will assume 15% mortality from age 82 to 83, so that there are 727 remaining females at age 83; 20% mortality from age 83 to 84 leaves 581 females; 25% mortality from age 84 to 85 leaves 436 remaining. Then assuming 30% mortality from age 85 to age 86, we get 305 remaining. At a 35% mortality rate from age 86 to 87, we still have 198 remaining women. At 40% mortality from age 87 to 88, we end up with 119, and with 45% mortality from age 88 to 89, we have 65 remaining women.

"So this means, with *these* artificial numbers, we have passed the 90th percentile of longevity for a Preferred Best 80-year-old female at age 89, three years later than for a 'standard' 80-year-old female. Of course, the real numbers are different, but the method of calculation is the same. Does that clarify how the longevity calculations work?"

Jane says, "So the better the rating, the lower the mortality, and the longer the potential lifespan. Is that right?"

Bob replies, "Yes, I think you have it."

Median and Maximum Lifespan Estimates

Jane continues, "Can we see the lifespan estimates somewhere? I'd like to see what the program calculates. I've seen some of those 'how long will you live?' quizzes on the Web and wonder how the program's numbers compare."

Bob replies, "Sure. The program displays 'Median Lifespan,' which is its estimate of what is usually called 'life expectancy,' and 'Max Lifespan,' which is its estimate of your 90th percentile lifespan, on the 'Personal Data' tab." (See Figure 7.2.)

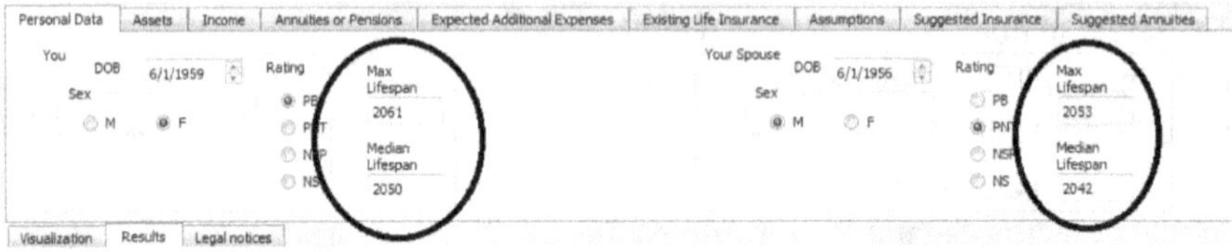

Figure 7.2: The Rhino Retirement Analyzer Personal Data tab with the lifespan estimates highlighted

Jane answers, "Hmm, that's interesting, and a bit scary, looking at the median lifespan dates of 2050 for me and 2042 for Jim. Does that mean that I'm likely to be a widow for eight years starting in 2042?"

Bob replies, "Yes, according to the actuarial tables that the program uses, and assuming that the insurance ratings that I've entered for you and Jim are right. But remember that it isn't *very* likely that both you and Jim will live to exactly your life expectancy. These are only estimates, not promises."

Jane says, "OK, I'll keep that in mind."

June interjects, "So is it bad to have a very good insurance rating because your long life expectancy means your money has to last longer?"

Bob replies, "Yes, it is true that your money has to last longer. But, on the other hand, you can insure yourself against the early death of one of the spouses much more inexpensively, because the term life insurance premiums are so much lower for people with excellent ratings."

June comes back with, "Well, I was mostly kidding, but that is a good point! Go on with the explanation."

Adding in the Income of the Spouses, Including Social Security Benefits

Bob continues, "The next piece of the puzzle that we should consider is income of the two spouses. Of course, it is possible (as in your cases) that at least one spouse is earning money through employment at the beginning of the simulation, and that money from employment is added to the 'pot' of money that can be used for spending. However, most people are going to retire within a few years of doing these calculations, and are likely to be retired for much longer than they will still be working. So most of the income that the program has to take account of is going to be retirement income."

"While some people have pensions and/or annuities, which are entered on the 'Annuities or Pensions' tab, the main source of retirement income for most people is Social Security, so I'll go over that first."

"It is no exaggeration to say that Social Security rules are *complicated*. As a result, the program can't take account of all of them, but it does include the effects of a number of the more common situations, especially the effect of one spouse of a married couple dying."

Financial Effects of One Spouse Dying Early in Retirement

"As I've explained before, exploring this outcome is the main benefit of the program. To vastly oversimplify, when one spouse dies, the other spouse gets just the greater of their two Social Security benefits. This is what causes the big drop in income at widowhood, and is where term life insurance can help out so significantly."

"But at this point in the explanation of the program, what we need to consider is how that possible death at a relatively early point in retirement affects the amount that can safely be spent every year. We can see part of that effect by looking at the Social Security income for the period between 2020 and 2026 in Jane's simulation without any additional insurance." (See Figure 7.3.)

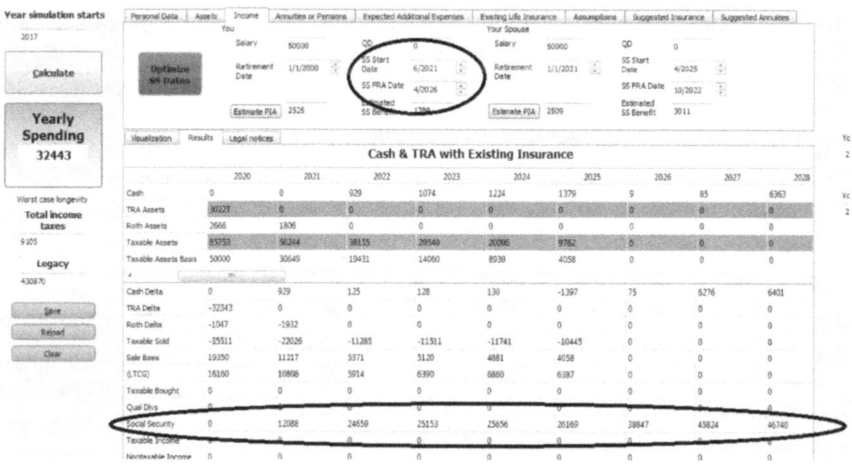

Figure 7.3: The Rhino Retirement Analyzer result screen with the "Social Security" dates and result row highlighted

"This simulation shows Jim dying in 2017, since that is the worst year for him to die if he doesn't have any insurance. You will notice that in 2020, you have no Social Security income, because you are too young to get it on your own record.

So instead, you wait until June of 2021, when you turn 62, and claim your (reduced) benefit at that time. So what happens in 2026, when your Social Security benefit jumps from about $26,000 to almost $39,000, then to almost $46,000 in 2027? Can you guess?"

Jane answers, "2026 is when I start taking Jim's benefit, right?"

Bob says, "Absolutely right! Apparently, you have been doing your research. Why do you take it then?"

Jane replies, "Because that is the year I get to my full retirement age. If I take it before then, I don't get as much."

Bob answers, "Yes, that is correct. Actually, you don't start taking his benefit until April 2026, because that's when you reach 66 and 10 months. That's the full retirement age for someone born in 1959."

Jane then says, "But couldn't I start taking his benefit as a widow when I get to age 60? There's a special rule for that, isn't there?"

Bob replies, "Yes, but that would reduce your Social Security income *permanently* by 28.5% compared to waiting until your full retirement age.[iii] That's why the program doesn't use that approach. Instead, it assumes you will take your own benefit as soon as you can take it (at age 62), then switch to Jim's benefit as soon as you reach full retirement age and can take his benefit without reduction."[iv]

Finding the Sustainable Spending Level without Inflation or Taxes

Bob says, "Now back to how the program figures out how much you can spend. As I mentioned earlier, it starts by assuming that you won't spend any money and figures out how much you would have at the end of your lives. To do this, it takes the income for each year (Social Security, salary, annuities, and pensions) starting from now until the later of the two deaths. Then it adds the assumed returns for your assets to the amount you have saved at the beginning of the simulation.

"So now it knows how much money you would have at the end of both lives if you didn't spend any money. Why is this useful?"

"To see how this helps, let's take a very oversimplified example. Let's say that the total amount of money you would have at the end of your life without spending any money is $1 million, your 90th percentile life expectancy is 40 years, and there is no inflation or taxation. In that case, we could simply divide $1 million by 40 to come up with sustainable spending of $25,000 per year. Does that make sense?"

Jane says, "Yes, I can see if we had a total of $1 million to spend over 40 years, without any inflation or taxes, we could spend $25,000 a year. Go on."

Adding in the Effects of Inflation and Estimated Federal Income Taxes

Bob continues, "So the program can start with that number of $25,000 yearly income and do the following for each year as long as either of you is alive:"

1. Start with the assets at the beginning of the year;
2. Add any income for the year, including Social Security and salary income;
3. Add the assumed return on assets;
4. Subtract the assumed spending rate (starting at $25,000);
5. Subtract estimated federal taxes and any insurance premiums;[v]
6. Increase spending to match the assumed inflation rate.

"Now, since taxes and inflation will cause your assets to shrink faster than the original oversimplified calculation assumed, the simulation will find that instead of your money lasting until your last year, you will be short a certain amount at that time.

"Let's assume that you would be short $100,000 at the end of your life. In that case, the program reduces spending by $100,000/$1,000,000, or 10%, resulting in a starting spending allowance of $22,500 instead of $25,000."

"It then runs the simulation again for all the years, to see whether you would have money left over or still be short at the end. If you would have money left over, it increases spending by a similar calculation (amount left over/number of years), and, of course, if you would still be short, it reduces spending in the same way. Eventually, the amount of sustainable real after-tax spending per year changes by only a few dollars, at which point it stops and records the result. This approach to finding the solution to a math problem is called 'successive approximation.' Does it make sense so far?"[vi]

Jane answers, "Mostly, but why does it have to do this repeated calculation? Why can't it figure the answer out directly?"

Why the Program Uses Successive Approximation to Find the Sustainable Spending Level

Bob replies, "The main reason it has to do the calculations this way is because of taxes. Tax calculations are complex, which makes it difficult to calculate a level after-tax spending amount directly. It's a lot easier (although still not trivial) to compute taxes on a particular level of income to figure out how much you can spend after taxes, so the program tries a number of different spending levels to see what the maximum allowable spending would be. Does that answer your question?"

Jane says, "So if the entire tax code was 'your tax is 10% of your income,' the program could do it directly?"

Bob replies, "Sure, assuming that the definition of 'income' were simple enough. I doubt we will have to 'worry' about that possibility any time soon though."

Jane agreed that situation wasn't very likely.

Running the Calculation for Different Potential Years of Death to Find the Worst-Case Death Year Scenario

Bob continues, "OK, so now we have one simulation that says, 'If you and Jim both die in the selected years of death, you can spend this much money every year without running out of money before you die.' But, of course, we don't know exactly when either of you will die, so the program needs to do the same calculations for all the other years of death that we are going to consider. As it does that, it keeps track of which years of death for each spouse result in the lowest allowable spending. When it gets done with the calculations for the entire lifespan of each spouse, it presents the results for the worst years of death as the 'Yearly Spending' number."

"It does all of the above for all four different 'withdrawal strategies' for both the existing insurance and the proposed insurance, and displays the 'Best' button below the result that has the highest sustainable yearly spending in the worst-case death year scenario."

"I realize that's a lot to absorb. Any questions?"

Jane says, "I certainly have questions. First, what do you mean by 'it keeps track of which years of death for each spouse result in the lowest allowable spending'? Obviously, it doesn't know when we will die, so how does it figure that out? Does it try every year of death for both of us until the end of time, or what?"

Bob says, "Well, to be completely certain to find the worst years of death for both of you, it would have to try every possible year between now and the end of the actuarial tables, which go up to at least age 100.[vii] Since you are 58 and Jim is 61, that would be at least 42*39 possibilities, or over 1,600 combinations of death dates. That would take a noticeable amount of time to calculate even with a fast computer, so the programmer decided to limit the combinations based on the assumption that one spouse living as long as possible would use up the assets to the greatest possible extent. So the program assumes that one of the spouses lives to the 90th percentile of his or her life expectancy and combines that assumption with all possible death years for the other spouse. Obviously, this needs to be done for each spouse as the possibly long-lived one."

"In your particular case, your 90th percentile life expectancy isn't over until 2050, which means 34 possible years of death to consider, and Jim's 90th percentile life expectancy reaches to 2042, which means 26 possible years of death to consider. So the total number of combinations of death years is only 34 + 26, or 60, rather than over 1,600. That's one of the reasons that the program can recalculate the results for all the death year possibilities in a few seconds even on a reasonably old computer like the one I'm using."

"More important, though, is how long it takes to run the optimizations like the insurance optimizer. In that case, the program has to try a lot of different insurance amounts and terms and recalculate the results for all of the different death years for each combination of insurance amounts and terms. That can take 15 seconds or more even with the 60 or so death year combinations that it uses, and might take 8 or 10 minutes if it tried all of the death year combinations. That would make the program a lot less user-friendly!"

Jane answers, "Yes, I can see waiting around for 10 minutes to see how much insurance I should buy would probably not be much fun. Anyway, we already know that the results are just a guide, not a precise answer to something that isn't knowable in advance."

Bob continues, "Agreed. What's your next question?"

Jane answers, "You just touched on it: the insurance optimizer. How does that work?"

The Term Life Insurance Optimizer

Bob replies, "This is the hardest part to explain, but I will give it a shot. The program tries a number of different term life insurance policy face amounts and terms for both spouses. It starts by calculating the maximum face amount that would be needed to replace the lost income from SS (and a single-life annuity if that spouse has one)."

"Then it selects the shortest term it handles (10 years in the free program's case) and the lowest amount that makes sense to issue and then calculates the premiums based on that term and face amount, given the insurance rating of each spouse. Once the program has the total premium, it calculates the sustainable spending and records that result."

"Next it increases the term in steps up to the maximum available for each spouse and reruns the calculation and saves that result. Once it gets to the end of the available terms (20 years in the free program's case), it starts over with the next face amount for the shortest term and does the same steps for that face amount. In each of these calculations, it has to take account of how long a term the insurance company will allow for each age, and limits the premiums to a maximum 10% of the couple's cash flow."

"The rates used in the free version of the program (that is available for download) are samples obtained from web sources, but insurance companies or agents can have the program customized to include their actual rates, which obviously would be more convenient if they are going to sell policies based on those rates."

"Once it has done all of those calculations, it knows which combination of policies (if any) would improve sustainable spending the most, so that's the one it recommends. OK so far?"

Jane says, "Actually I have several questions already. What do you mean by 'lowest amount that makes sense to issue'? Also, why does the term depend on how old you are, and why do they care if you spend more than 10% of your cash flow on insurance?"

Why Buying Small Amounts of Insurance isn't Cost-Effective

Bob replies, "Small amounts of insurance are too expensive to make sense for the protection they provide, because the cost to the company of doing the investigative work to decide whether you are a good risk is too high for them to be thorough. It may cost an insurance company several hundred dollars for the paramedic exam and doing all the paperwork to get your doctors' records collected and examined. They are willing to do that for a large enough premium, but the premiums for small policies won't pay them back. So they issue small policies with 'relaxed' underwriting, which makes the premiums a lot higher per dollar of face amount. That's one of the reasons that the 'affordable' policies that you sometimes get direct mail for aren't really very affordable: they have to assume that anyone who takes them up on such an offer is not in very good health, because if they were, they could buy an underwritten policy instead. The sample rates begin at face amounts of $100,000 because that's the lowest amount of fully underwritten insurance that was available on the websites that the programmer collected them from.[viii] Does that make sense now?"

Jane nods, so Bob continues, "For your next question: each company has rules about which policies it will issue on each person. The rates built into the free version of the program for 20-year-level-premium term go up only to age 64. From 65 to 69, the maximum term is 15 years, and from 70 to 74, the maximum is 10 years. The program takes account of that in trying the different policies; that is, it won't consider a 20-year policy for someone who is 65 or older, since that isn't possible with the rates it has built in."

"Now as to your last question: again, each company has its own rules about how much of a person's income can go to life insurance, and the rates in the free version of the program use 10% as the limit."

"I don't know the exact reasons for these limitations, but we have to work with what the insurance companies are willing to do. Does that answer your questions?"

Jane answers, "Yes, you've answered those questions, but now I have another one. What if the actual company that you use has different rules from the ones in the free version of the program, or different premiums for that matter?"

Bob replies, "Most companies have fairly similar rules for age and income limits, and I don't think any of them that I use limit 20-year or shorter term policies for anyone under 65. Obviously, I will check that before we apply for your policies."

Why the Exact Premiums aren't Critical

"As to the rates, fortunately the exact rates aren't critical in figuring out how much term insurance you need, so using the sample rates will give pretty good results even if they are off by 15% or 20%. And as we have already discussed, no one knows exactly what is going to happen in the future, so any calculations we make are only a guideline anyway, not anything you can take to the bank (so to speak)."

June interjects, "Wait a minute! How can the insurance premiums not be critical? Wouldn't a 15% or 20% difference affect the overall results by 15% or 20%?"

Bob replies, "No, actually they wouldn't affect the results nearly that much, because the insurance premiums are lot smaller than the change in sustainable spending from buying the insurance. Let's look at an example to see how much the difference would be."

"First, take a look at the results with the built-in premiums, where Jane's premium is $938 a year for a 15-year, $450,000 policy, and Jim's premium is $2,209 for the same amount and term. That produces a sustainable yearly spending rate of almost $47,000." (See Figure 7.4.)

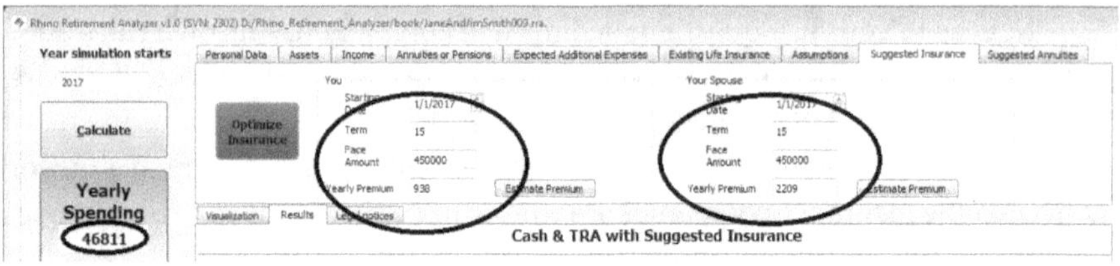

Figure 7.4: The Rhino Retirement Analyzer result screen with the "Suggested Insurance" terms, face amounts, premiums, and sustainable spending highlighted

"Now let's increase both premiums by 20% to $1,126 and $2,651, respectively, and rerun the calculation." (See Figure 7.5.)

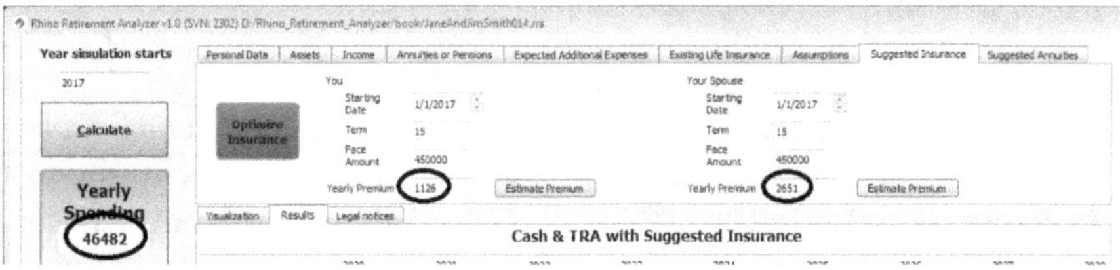

Figure 7.5: The Rhino Retirement Analyzer result screen with the changed premiums and sustainable spending

"As you can see, the sustainable spending result is only different by about $300 a year, which is less than 1% of their total spending. The insurance premium difference is greater than that, at about $600 a year, but the premiums end at Jim's worst-case death year, 2032 (which also happens to be when the level premium term expires). Since those premiums don't continue for Jane's entire life, the effect on her sustainable spending should be less than that $600 a year difference. Does that make sense to both of you?"

June asks, "What do you mean about the level premium term expiring? Doesn't the insurance policy expire at the end of the term?"

Bob replies, "No, term insurance doesn't actually expire at the end of the term. What expires is the term during which the premium is level. You can keep it in force if you want to after that point, but only at enormously higher rates that don't make sense for most people, and certainly aren't appropriate for this use. So the program just assumes that the policy terminates at the end of the level premium term. Does that answer your question?"

June nods, but then Jane says, “OK, but can we rerun the insurance optimizer to make sure this doesn’t affect how much we should buy?”

Bob replies, “No, the insurance optimizer can use only the built-in rates. We can override it by changing the premiums, as I just did, but if we rerun the optimizer, it will go back to its ‘normal’ rates. However, we can see that the effect of changing the rates by as much as 20% isn’t very significant, so we don’t have to worry about that.”

Jane nods.

Bob says, “OK, any other questions so far?”

Jane says, “Yes: Are the four ‘strategies’ for withdrawals the only possible ones?”

Bob replies, “No, those are just four of the more common ways. Actually, there are an almost unlimited number of ways that you could take money out of your accounts. In fact, the original version of the program was designed to search for an optimal way to do that,[ix] but it turned out that the order in which you take money out has much less effect on sustainable spending than adding term insurance does. So the programmer changed the focus of the program to look at insurance (including annuities) rather than the order in which to withdraw from various accounts. Do you have any other questions about this?”

Jane shakes her head, so Bob continues, “OK, let’s change the premiums back to the default ones in the program, and then cover the Social Security optimizer.” He reloads the previous saved file and switches to the “Income Tab.” (See Figure 7.6.)

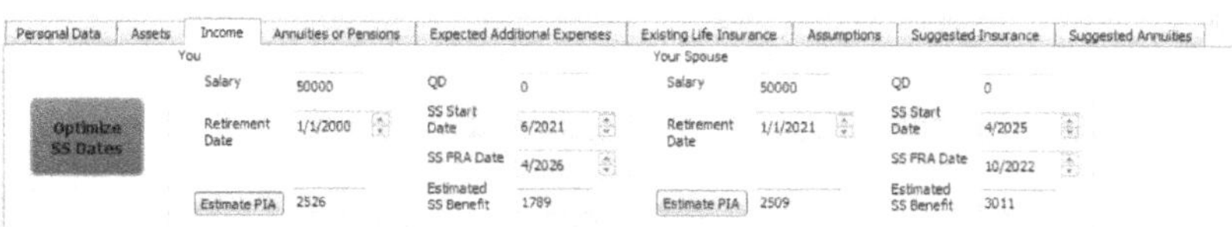

Figure 7.6: The Rhino Retirement Analyzer screen showing the “Income Tab”

Optimizing Social Security Claiming Dates

Bob continues, “As I think you saw before, clicking the ‘Optimize SS Dates’ button tells the program to search for the best dates for each spouse to start SS. Would one of you like to guess how it works? It’s not that much different from the way the insurance optimizer works.”

June says, "I'll give it a shot. Does it try all the different dates that each spouse could start SS to see which date produces the highest sustainable spending? That would be quite a number of different possibilities!"

Bob replies, "Very good! That's how it works. As to how many different possibilities, roughly how many do you think there might be?"

June says, "Well, you can start any month from 62 to 70, so that would be 8 years * 12 months, or 96, right?"

Bob answers, "Close, but not quite. The correct answer is 97, because you can start any time from age 62 and 0 months to 70 and 0 months, so there are 12 possible months for each age from 62 to 69 and one month at 70 and 0 months."

June replies, "Oh yes, I forgot about the last possible starting month!"

Bob says, "Don't worry about it. You got very close. But that is just for one spouse. What happens when we add in the other spouse?"

June replies, "If the program tried all of the possible combinations for each spouse, that would be 97 * 97 possibilities. That must be close to 10,000 altogether!"

Bob says, "Yes, it is quite a few. Let me get the exact number." He punches in 97 *97 on his calculator and gets the answer 9,409, which he shows them. "So do you think that's what the program does?"

June replies, "No, that would take too long compared to what I see happening when you run the SS optimizer. I'll bet it does each spouse separately so there would be 'only' 194 possibilities instead of 9,409. Right?"

Bob says, "Yes, that is exactly right! Again, the programmer thought that it would be better to get a good answer rapidly (in about 40 seconds on this computer) than a 'perfect' one after a long delay (over half an hour), since there is no 'perfect' answer anyway. OK so far?"

They nod, so he continues, "Now as to how it actually calculates the effects of a different starting date: For each starting date, it has to calculate the estimated benefit based on the 'PIA' (Primary Insurance Amount) and the rules for early or late claiming. Then it runs the calculation for all of the different death year combinations just as it does when I hit the 'Calculate' button. As it goes through all the possible starting dates, it keeps track of which date each spouse should start Social Security to obtain the best sustainable income level. When it gets done, it resets the starting date for each spouse according to that result. Does that make sense?"

Both sisters nod, so he continues by saying, "There is more to cover, mostly about annuities, but I think the explanation of that feature of the program will make more sense after we see if you can benefit from an annuity. How about if we look into an annuity tomorrow at 1 PM?"

They agree, so he shuts down the program and closes his laptop.

[i] Smokers have far greater mortality at every age than nonsmokers. As a result, their insurance premiums are generally so high as to make it infeasible to use term life insurance to hedge against early death. That's why the program doesn't handle ratings that are assigned to smokers.

[ii] The relative mortality risk of the different ratings is based on the premiums that the program uses by default, and may vary depending on exactly which insurance company the program is customized for.

[iii] See https://www.ssa.gov/planners/survivors/survivorchartred.html, which uses an example of a full benefit of $1,000: "The $1,000 benefit would be reduced to $715 for anyone who started receiving survivors [sic] benefits at age 60."

[iv] Of course, there are cases where a widow has no other assets and has to take the *permanently* reduced widow's benefit as soon as possible, which is at age 60. But that disastrous situation can't happen if they have even a modest amount of life insurance to bridge the gap, so the program is even more valuable in those cases.

[v] The program also has to adjust tax brackets, deductions, and other tax-related numbers each year, based on the assumed rate of inflation.

[vi] Note that this is not exactly how the program actually operates; it takes returns and inflation into account in making the initial spending estimate, to reduce the number of times it has to re-estimate sustainable spending and speed up the overall process. But this method would work.

[vii] Different actuarial tables have different ending dates, but the youngest age where any of them ends will be at least age 100 in these days of fairly long lifespans.

[viii] The sample rates include a "price break" starting at $250,000 face amount that makes that more affordable in many cases than a $200,000 policy, so the program skips the $200,000 face amount.

[ix] See Appendix E for a brief discussion of this topic.

Chapter 8
Adding an Annuity

Bob has planned to talk Jane and June through the impact annuities can have, and the benefit and the cost alternatives. Shortly after they arrive, he loads data from his previous day's research and says, "I found some annuity quotes for you.. But before we look at them, first let me explain why you might want an annuity."

"Although the program uses conservative estimates for lifespan, there is no way to tell how long you will actually live. This means that no matter how many years' spending we plan for, you could run out of money if you live too long."

"That is, unless you buy an annuity. An annuity is the only source of income that you can't outlive. The way it works is that you give a big chunk of money to the insurance company, and then they pay you every month as long as you are alive.[i] So if you are concerned about outliving your income, an annuity is the solution. Does that sound like something you would like to hear about?"

Jane says, "Sure, I might as well know as much as possible about my options. Go ahead."

Bob continues, "OK, then here's the 'Suggested Annuities' tab showing the first set of figures, for a 'plain' immediate annuity that pays out a fixed amount every month, starting 4/20/2017, and which keeps paying as long as either you or Jim is alive." (See Figure 8.1.)

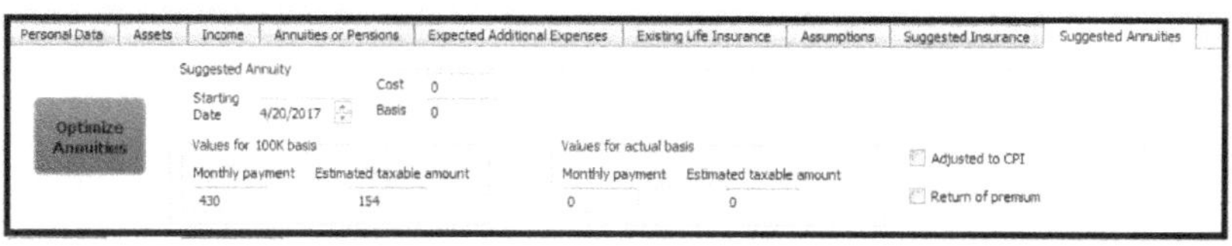

Figure 8.1: The Rhino Retirement Analyzer with the "Suggested Annuities" tab highlighted

Bob continues, "You can see that so far we don't have an actual monthly annuity payment, just the amounts that you could buy for $100,000, which are the numbers for 'Monthly payment' and 'Estimated taxable amount' in the 'Values for 100K basis' box." (See Figure 8.2.)

DOI 10.1515/97815015.6185-008

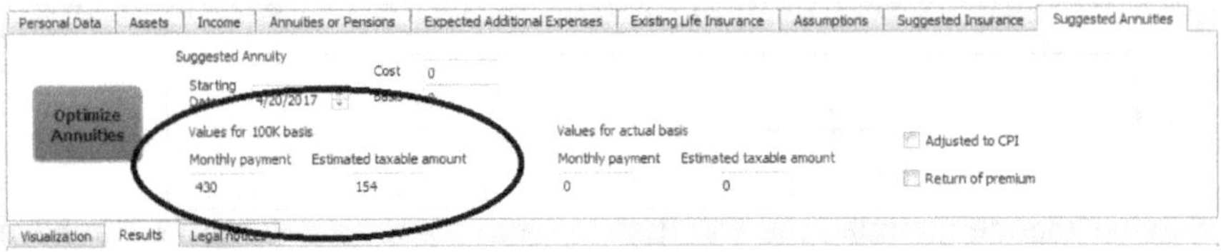

Figure 8.2: The Rhino Retirement Analyzer with the "Values for 100K basis" box on the "Suggested Annuities" tab highlighted

Bob continues, "I found the 'Monthly payment' amount at immediateannuities.com by putting in $100,000 for the amount to be invested. The 'Estimated taxable amount' is calculated by the program, based on your ages and the amount of the payment. Clear so far?"

Jane says, "Not really. What does $100,000 have to do with my situation? That's not how much my mother is thinking of giving me."

Bob replies, "The way the program works is that I give it the amount of payment that $100,000 can buy just to get it started; this causes the program to try a number of different amounts to invest and sees which one provides the most sustainable spending. It's like the way it searches for how much insurance you need to optimize sustainable spending, as we saw when we ran the insurance optimizer the other day. We can go over exactly how the annuity optimizer works tomorrow if you want to."

Jane says, "Yes, let's do that, but first show me what it does."

Bob continues, "OK, the next thing I will need to know is roughly how much your mother is thinking of giving you. You said it would be cash, not stocks, right?"

Jane answers, "Yes, that's what she had in mind. The amount she was thinking of is $500,000."

Bob's eyes light up and he says, "Well, that should improve your sustainable spending noticeably. First, here's what your assets look like now, without that extra $500,000, and of course without any annuity purchase." (See Figure 8.3.)

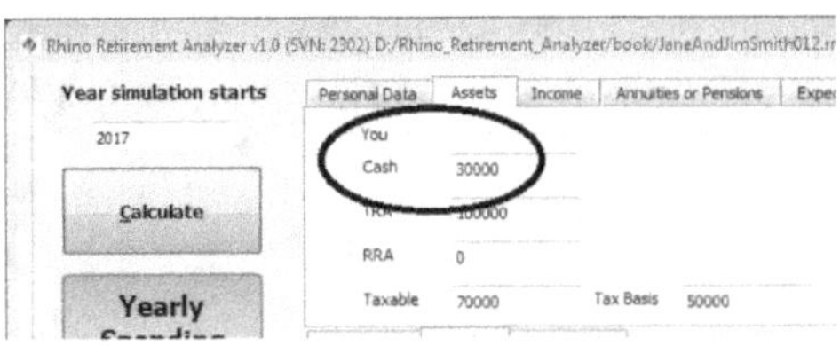

Figure 8.3: The Rhino Retirement Analyzer with the Cash entry on the "Assets" tab highlighted

Bob continues, "Now let's add $500,000 to your cash, which leaves it looking like this." (See Figure 8.4.)

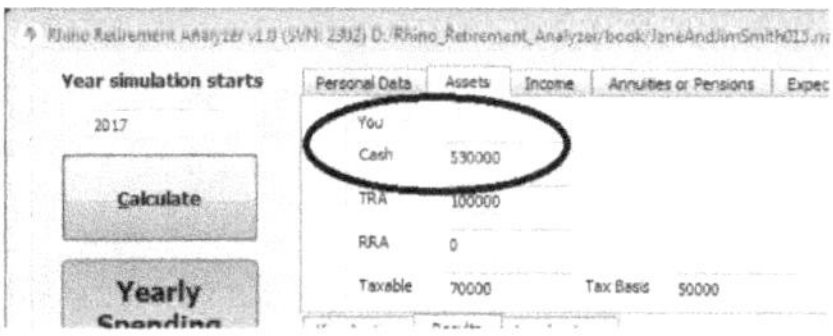

Figure 8.4: The Rhino Retirement Analyzer with the new Cash entry of $530,000 highlighted on the "Assets" tab

Jane says, "I don't see anything different other than the new cash amount. Was something else supposed to happen?"

Bob answers, "No, until we tell the program to recalculate, it won't make changes."

He clicks the "Calculate" button, resulting in Figure 8.5.

Figure 8.5: The Rhino Retirement Analyzer with the new sustainable spending result of $62,620 highlighted

Bob says, "So far, this is nothing new other than that since you have more money, you can spend about $16,000 more per year based on the extra money and the return on investment figures we have in the program now for your cash assets. Now let's see what it suggests for an annuity. By using this Suggested Annuities tab, the program will optimize the amount of sustainable spending, just like always, and we can find out what the amount of the annuity should be." He switches to the "Suggested Annuities" tab and clicks the "Optimize Annuities" button, producing the result in Figure 8.6.[ii]

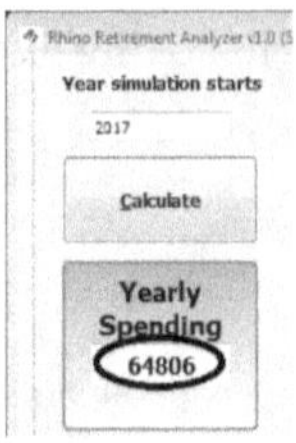

Figure 8.6: The Rhino Retirement Analyzer result after adding an annuity, with the new sustainable spending result of $64,806 highlighted

Bob says, "That didn't make very much difference, only about $2,000 a year, but then we haven't checked what effect changing the return and inflation assumptions might have. That might make a lot more difference, since the amount you get from a straight life annuity isn't dependent on the market but is guaranteed.[iii] Let's compare the results with and without the annuity if we assume that there is no inflation and no return from your portfolio assets." He reloads the previous version of the data with the extra $500,000 in cash but without purchasing an annuity, sets the return and inflation assumptions to 0, then hits the "Calculate" button. (See Figure 8.7.)

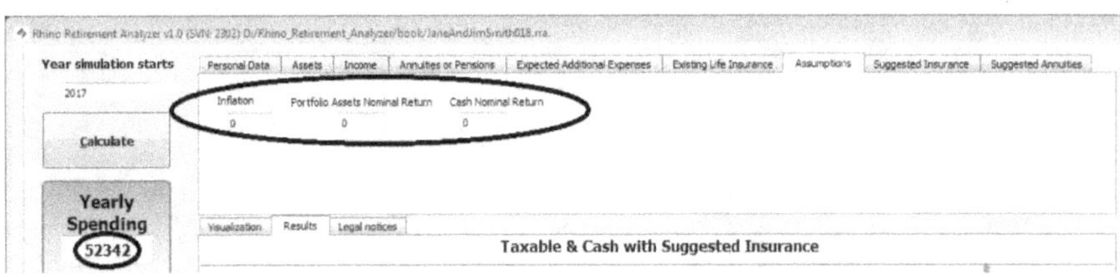

Figure 8.7: The Rhino Retirement Analyzer result with the new $500,000 in cash, without an annuity, and with the assumptions and new sustainable spending result of $52,342 highlighted

Bob continues, "That really hurt the sustainable spending compared to the results with the more optimistic assumptions of 2% inflation and cash returns, and 7% portfolio returns. Now let's see how the annuity version does with the zero assumptions." He switches to the "Suggested Annuities" tab and hits the "Optimize Annuities" button. (See Figure 8.8.)

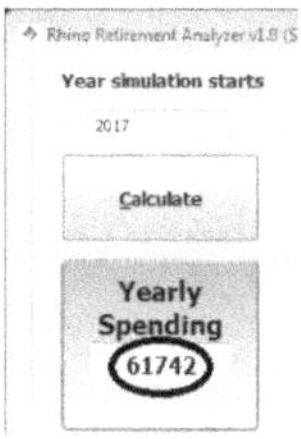

Figure 8.8: The Rhino Retirement Analyzer result with the added $500,000 in cash, with an immediate annuity purchased with $350,000, and with the new sustainable spending result of $61,742 highlighted

Bob says, "That makes a pretty big difference, over $9,000 a year, compared to the situation in which you don't buy the annuity. So even though the annuity doesn't make much difference if we use the optimistic assumptions, if the market isn't cooperative, then you would do a lot better with the annuity than without it, although of course you would have $350,000 less in cash in the event that you needed a lot of cash for some reason."

Jane responds, "OK, but what's the chance that the market will have no return at all for the rest of my life? That doesn't sound very likely."

Bob replies, "I agree that doesn't sound very likely to happen for the rest of your life, but the problem is what the experts call 'sequence of returns risk.' That is, if the market's performance is bad right after you retire, you may use up your assets too fast and not have enough left when it recovers to benefit from that recovery. This program doesn't model that particular situation directly, but what we can do is to set the yearly spending to the amount calculated with the optimistic assumptions, then change the assumptions back to no return and no inflation and see how fast you would run out of money." He reloads the data with the optimistic assumptions and no annuity (as shown in Figure 8.5), then changes the assumptions to no returns and no inflation, turns on "Expert Mode" and checks "Manual Yearly Spending," then hits the "Calculate" button. (See Figure 8.9.)

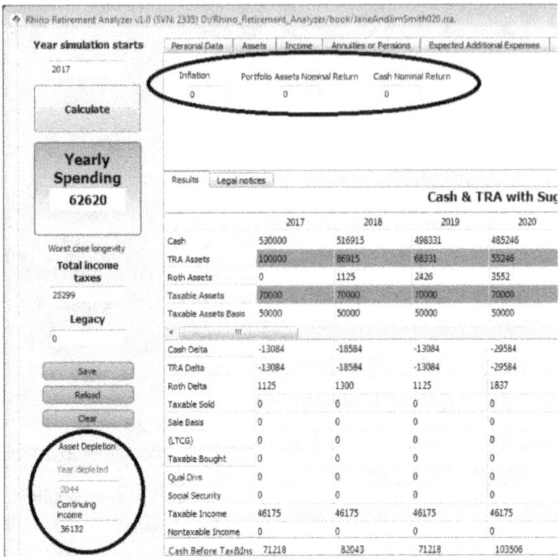

Figure 8.9: The Rhino Retirement Analyzer result with the new $500,000 in cash, without an annuity, and with the assumptions set to no inflation and no return, using the "Manual Yearly Spending" feature

Bob continues, "This shows what would happen if you spent the 'correct' amount according to the prior optimistic assumptions, whereas in reality you got 0% inflation and 0% returns.[iv] If you did that, you would run out of assets in 2044, although you would still have $36,132 a year to spend after that. Now let's see what happens if we buy the annuity using the optimistic assumptions but have adverse market results of 0% for inflation and returns." (See Figure 8.10.)

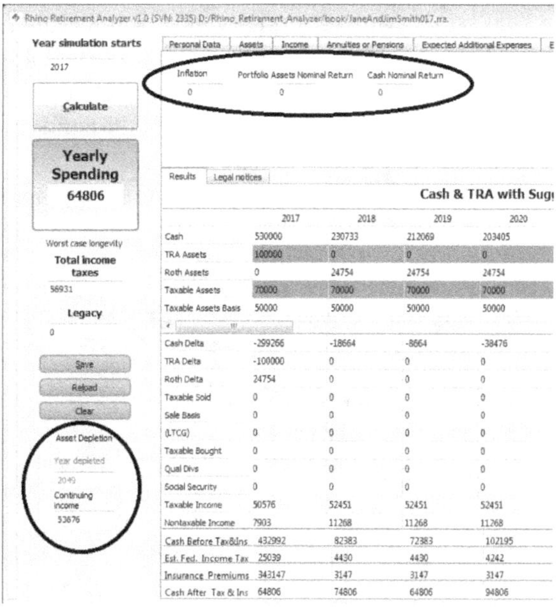

Figure 8.10: The Rhino Retirement Analyzer result with the new $500,000 in cash, with an annuity, and with the assumptions set to no inflation and no return, using the "Manual Yearly Spending" feature

Bob continues, "Note that this gives you an additional five years before you run out of assets (until 2049 rather than 2044), and also increases your continuing income (from Social Security and the annuity) by almost 50%, so you won't have to go back to work at age 85. Of course, if this cost you a significant amount of income under the optimistic assumptions, I can see why you might not want to do it, even though it improves the results significantly with adverse results. But fortunately, the annuity performs slightly better than the nonannuity case even with the optimistic assumptions. So this seems like a pretty good way to reduce your dependence on market returns."

"On the other hand, annuities have their downsides too. Your money is locked up so you can't get at it. Current interest rates are low and might go up. If that happened, you could get more income if you waited to purchase an annuity. And you don't have to worry about not being able to qualify for an annuity if you wait, as you do with life insurance, because the insurance company doesn't ask for health information when selling an annuity as they do with life insurance. So there's no big rush. What do you think?"

Jane answers, "Of course I'll discuss it with Jim and see what he thinks, but I agree that I'd rather be safe than sorry. So, I think the annuity makes a lot of sense."

Bob replies, "In the meantime, how about if we get together at 1 PM tomorrow to go over how the annuity optimizing feature of the program works?"

Jane and June both agree, so Bob closes down the program and his laptop.

---

[i] All references to annuities in this book refer only to fixed life annuities, which pay a pre-determined amount of money every month so long as the annuitant is alive. There are a number of other types of annuities, but none of them is appropriate for this application.

[ii] Chapter 9 will discuss how the annuity optimizer works.

[iii] Of course, all annuity payment guarantees depend on the financial health of the issuer, but the amount to be paid doesn't fluctuate with the stock or bond markets.

[iv] Those optimistic assumptions were that you would get 7% before inflation on your portfolio assets with 2% inflation and 2% return on cash.

Chapter 9
Can an Annuity Improve Sustainable Retirement Spending?

Bob begins by saying, "Adding an annuity that pays you for the rest of your life may be able to improve your sustainable spending. But how can we tell whether an annuity will help, and if it will help, how much should you spend on it? The annuity optimizer is intended to answer those questions."

"The way it works is fairly similar to the way the insurance optimizer works, although of course there are differences because the effect of annuities is different from the effect of life insurance: Annuities pay as long as you are alive, whereas life insurance pays only if you die during the term of the insurance. Let's start by reviewing the 'Suggested Annuities' tab in more detail."

He reloads the version of the data with the extra $500,000 but no annuity, then clicks the "suggested annuities" tab, resulting in the situation seen in Figure 9.1.

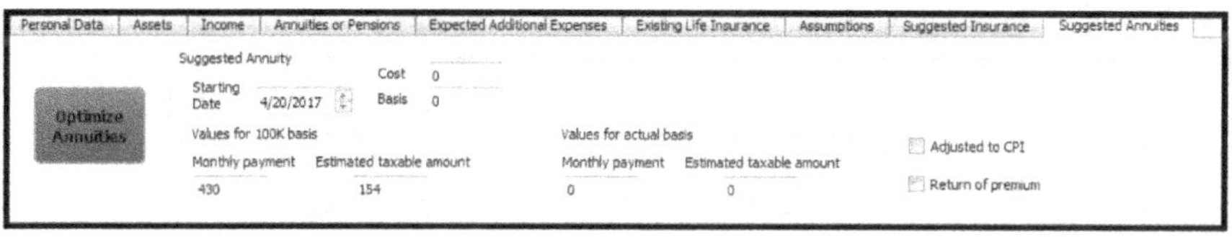

Figure 9.1: The Rhino Retirement Analyzer with the "Suggested Annuities" tab highlighted

Bob continues, "The annuity optimizer calculates the effects of different annuity premiums starting with $50,000 and increasing by $10,000 with every step until it has tried every amount up to ½ of your total assets. Whichever of those results gives the highest sustainable spending is the winner. To do this, it uses the monthly payment and estimated taxable amount for $100K premium as bases for its calculations." (See Figure 9.2)

DOI 10.1515/9781501506185-009

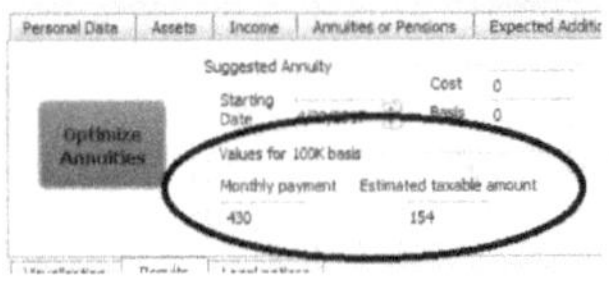

Figure 9.2: The Rhino Retirement Analyzer with the "Value for 100K box" on the "Suggested Annuities" tab highlighted

Where to Find Annuity Payment Information

Bob continues, "I found the 'Monthly payment' amount at immediateannuities.com by putting in your and Jim's ages, saying that you wanted to start payments immediately, and selecting $100,000 for the amount to be invested. The 'Estimated taxable amount' is the result that immediateannuities.com calculated for payments starting 'immediately' (a month after I entered the data), given your ages and an investment of $100,000. Clear so far?"

Jane says, "I know you explained this before, but why did you specify the investment as $100,000 rather than the amount that my mother is thinking of giving me?"

Bob replies, "Well, of course we could have directly put in the amount your mother is thinking of giving you and checked to see how much that would improve your spending. But the idea of the optimizer is to try different investment amounts to see which would improve your spending the most (assuming any of them would cause an improvement in the first place). That's why we always put in the payment amount that you could get for a $100,000 investment. Once the program has that number, it tries a number of different amounts to invest and sees which one provides the most sustainable spending. It's like the way it searches for how much insurance you need to optimize sustainable spending by trying a number of possible terms and face amounts."

Why Knowing the Exact Starting Dates of an Annuity is Important

Jane says, "Ok, I do remember that. But why does it matter exactly what date the payments start? I don't remember that being an issue with the life insurance policies the program recommended."

Bob responds, "Annuity rates fluctuate a lot more than life insurance rates. Most life insurers change their premiums every year or two, whereas annuity rates can change every day. The reason is that annuity rates are very dependent on interest rates, because when the insurance company writes an annuity policy, they are committing to paying you a set amount every month for the rest of your life, based on the amount that you invested with them. Now of course some of that calculation is based on their estimate of how long you will live, just as life insurance rates are, but in the case of life insurance they are promising to make only one payment at a future date, assuming you are still insured when you die. If you outlive the term of insurance, they don't have to pay anything, so in that case, interest rates are almost irrelevant. But let's assume that they do have to pay your survivor when you die. In that case, they have been collecting premiums and investing them, so interest rates do matter somewhat. But at least with the current very low rates, they don't earn very much on those invested premiums, so a small change in interest rates doesn't affect them very much."

Bob continues, "On the other hand, with an annuity policy, they know that they will have to pay you for the rest of your life, based on the amount you invested with them. Let's suppose that they expect to make 5% every year on an investment of $100,000. In that case, vastly oversimplifying by ignoring the fact that you will die one day as well as the insurance company's profit margin, they can pay you $5000 a year. But if interest rates go down to 4%, they can pay you only $4000 a year. So, a 1% reduction in interest rates reduces the amount they can pay by 20%. And remember, as soon as they commit to paying you a set annuity payment, they have to keep doing that *no matter what* happens to interest rates after that point, so they have to be very careful what they promise. Since interest rates fluctuate every day, so do annuity rates."

"For this reason, an annuity quote is good for only a few days; if you wait too long, we'll have to get another quote. Does that make more sense now?"

Jane answers, "Yep. Ok, what's next?"

Deferred Annuities Can Also Improve Sustainable Retirement Spending

Bob replies, "Although the annuity quotes I got for you before were for an 'immediate' annuity that, as the name indicates, starts paying (almost) immediately, the program doesn't require payments to start right away. It can also handle 'deferred' annuities that don't start paying for quite a while, so long as the monthly payment is known in advance. Let's look at an example of such a deferred annuity right now to see if it might be better than the immediate annuity that we looked at yesterday."

Bob goes to the immediateannuities.com web site and puts in Jane's and Jim's birth dates, selects $100,000 as the amount to be invested, and sets the starting income date to '10 years', which results in a quote of $736/month, of which $460 a month is estimated to be taxable, with a starting date of 5/5/2027. Then he hits the "Optimize Annuities" button, resulting in Figure 9.3.

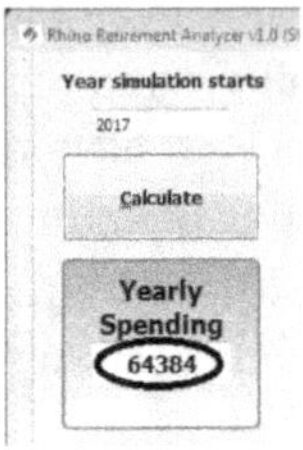

Figure 9.3: The Rhino Retirement Analyzer with a deferred annuity where payments start in 2027

Bob continues, "Let's compare that 'Yearly Spending' number of $64,384 to the immediate annuity result that we got earlier." He reloads that previous result, which is shown in Figure 9.4.

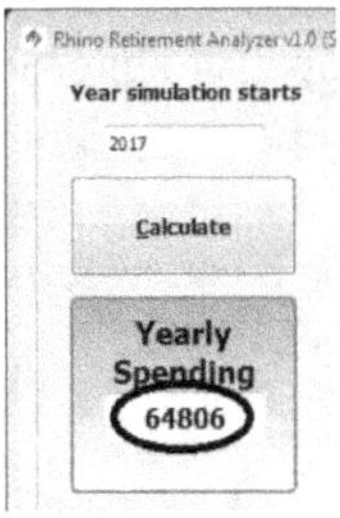

Figure 9.4: The Rhino Retirement Analyzer with an immediate annuity

"Well, it looks like the immediate annuity is producing a better 'Yearly Spending' value, at $64,806, so there's no point in deferring the income. Does either of you have any questions on this?"

What Happens after the Death of One or Both Annuitants?

June says, “Yes, I do. What happens if Jane or Jim dies? Do the payments continue?”

Bob replies, “Yes, all of the annuities that the program suggests are the type called ‘Joint & 100%’, meaning that the payments continue unchanged until the death of the second spouse.”

Jane adds, “Ok, but what happens when both of us die? Do our heirs get anything?”

Bob answers, “That depends on the rules of the annuity that you purchase. Some annuities will pay the remainder of the original investment to the estate of the second spouse to die. For an annuity like that, we check the ‘Return of Premium’ checkbox, on the ‘Suggested Annuities’ tab. If that is checked, then the remainder of the premium will go into your estate.”

“Actually, the quotes from immediateannuities.com include annuities with and without the return of premium feature. What do you think happens to the payment if you want to add that feature?”

Jane says, “I imagine the payment would go down because in that case they would need to pay out money if we both died before we got the whole premium back, which they wouldn’t have to do otherwise.”

Bob replies, “Absolutely correct. Want to guess how much it would go down?”

Jane answers, “Hmm, maybe 10%?”

Bob says, “Well, the monthly payment per $100K is only about 3% lower, at $418 per hundred thousand, but let’s take a look and see whether it affects the suggested purchase amount.” He enters the new monthly payment of $418 and the new estimated taxable amount of $151, checks the “Return of premium” checkbox, then clicks the “Optimize Annuities” button. The resulting screen looks like Figure 9.5.

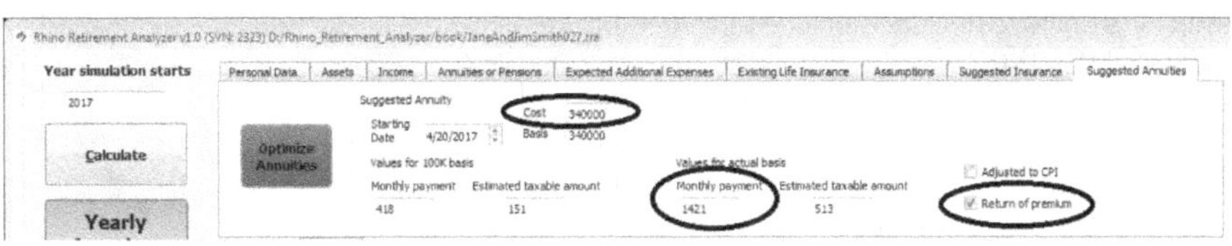

Figure 9.5: The Rhino Retirement Analyzer with an immediate annuity that has the return of premium feature, showing the new payment of $1421, the new estimated taxable amount of $513, and the new yearly spending of $64,507

Bob continues, "Hmm, interesting. Apparently, the recommended annuity purchase amount is still $340,000, so the payment went down about 3%, just as the payment per $100K did. The yearly sustainable spending accordingly went down about $300/year. So, the return of premium feature wouldn't cost much in your case. What does that mean?"

Jane says, "It must mean that they expect that we will probably live long enough to get the whole premium back without the refund. Right?"

Bob replies, "Right. If both of you were older, then that feature would be more expensive, because then they would have a bigger chance of having to pay your heirs some money after you both died. This is also true of single-life annuities with the premium refund feature, because it is more likely that one person will die in a relatively short period time than that two people will both die during that time."

"So would you like to keep the annuity with return of premium, considering that it doesn't cost you very much? Obviously it would improve your legacy if both of you did happen to die early."

Jane answers, "Yes, since it doesn't cost that much I think we should pick that option."

Bob nods, and is going to continue, but then June chips in with, "I have another question."

Adjusting Annuity Payments to CPI

"What about that other option, 'Adjusted to CPI'? What does that do?"

Bob replies, "CPI is short for 'Consumer Price Index'. You can also buy annuities with inflation adjustments that increase the payments according to the increase in the CPI. Of course, those annuities are more expensive than those that just pay the same amount every month so long as you (or your joint annuitant if it is a joint annuity) are alive. For example, the quotes I got for Jane and Jim include that option too. Here's what the results look like for that option." (See Figure 9.6)

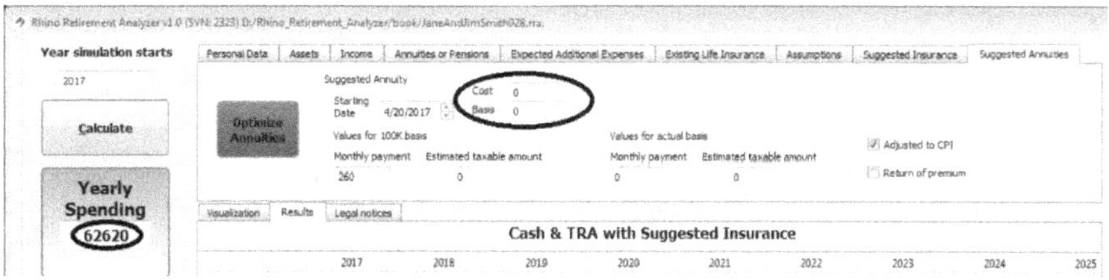

Figure 9.6: The Rhino Retirement Analyzer with an attempt to use an immediate annuity that has the "Adjusted to CPI" feature, showing that this particular annuity does not improve spending compared to the situation without the annuity

Bob continues, "Notice that in this case the program is not recommending the purchase of an inflation-adjusted annuity because it would reduce 'Yearly Spending' assuming that our inflation projection is accurate. So if we want to investigate the possibility of adding the CPI adjusted annuity, we will have to adjust our inflation expectations to a point where such an annuity would improve spending. This is again a way to reduce risks, in this case the risk of higher than anticipated inflation, at the cost of a slightly lower sustainable spending if our assumptions are correct. Do you want to try that?"

June answers, "No, I don't think that will be necessary. I'm happy with the existing assumptions."

Bob continues, "Also notice that the 'estimated taxable amount' is 0. That number comes from the annuity quotation from immediateannuities.com. Your tax person should be able to calculate the actual taxable amount. Any other questions on the topic CPI adjustments?"[i]

June shakes her head.

Bob continues, "Okay, let's go back to the previous annuity calculation with the return of premium feature, and go over the rest of the features that we haven't discussed yet, starting with the left-hand side of the main screen." (See Figure 9.7)

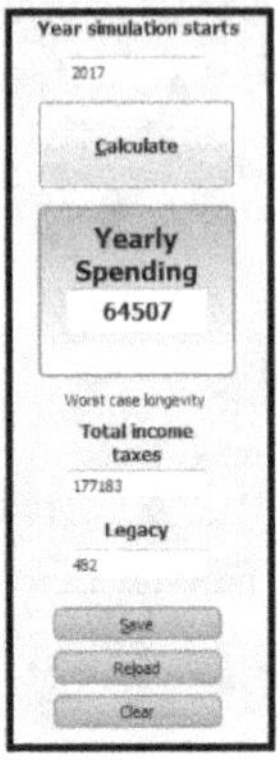

Figure 9.7: The Rhino Retirement Analyzer with the left side of the main screen highlighted

Bob continues, "The first field on that left-hand side is 'Year simulation starts'. That defaults to the current year, but we can change that if we want to start in a different year. Of course most of the time we will want to begin the calculations this year, but there are a couple of reasons that we wouldn't want to do that:"

1. If we are near the end of the year, we might want to start with the next year, partly because we won't be able to buy the insurance or annuity and have it start this year anyway.
2. If we want to compare results that we calculated last year with those from this year, then we need to be able to change the starting date of the calculations so that they begin last year rather than this year.

"The next field is 'Yearly Spending', which we've already discussed in detail. But to summarize, that is how much money you can spend every year from now until your conservatively estimated life expectancy, without running out of money while you are still alive. That is the current amount of spending, and is adjusted every year according to our estimate of inflation, which is why the 'level spending' doesn't look level but seems to increase every year; it's actually level in 'real dollars', with the exception of any 'Expected Additional Expenses', which are added in the years that they are expected to occur. Any questions so far?"

Why we Might Want to Compare Last Year's Projections with this Year

Jane says, "Why would we need to compare to last year's results?"

Bob replies, "When we get together again next year, then we will need to rerun the results because (I assume) both you and Jim have survived until next year, so that's one less year that we have to worry about either of you dying in. And, of course, your term insurance will have one less year to go, and there will be different inflation numbers, tax brackets, and other variables. So, this should be done at least once a year, and more frequently if anything changes significantly so that the previous results wouldn't be meaningful anymore."

Jane asks, "What sort of changes would do that?"

Bob replies, "If there is a major change in taxes, that would require the program to be updated and we'd need to rerun it with the new information. Or if you win the lottery, get an inheritance, or anything else that affects your assets significantly. Any more questions on that?"

Worst Case Longevity Results

Both sisters shake their heads, so he continues, "Next we have the 'Worst case longevity' box, which shows the estimates for two very important amounts: the total income taxes that you and your spouse will pay during your remaining lifetimes ('Total income taxes'), and the amount of money that you will leave to your heirs after both of you die ('Legacy'), assuming that the years of death for both spouses are the ones that the program computes as causing the lowest sustainable spending."

June asks, "I understand the total taxes, but why is the legacy such a low number in all of the cases you have shown us so far? It's not usually 0 as it is in this case, but it's always pretty small compared to the yearly spending."

Bob explains, "Ideally it would always be 0 because the program is trying to figure out how the maximum amount you can spend without running out of money before the second spouse dies. Any amount left over is money you could theoretically have spent while you were alive. However, it usually can't get it down to 0, for a couple of reasons: First, because spending even a little more in an earlier year can cause an increase in taxes which could make you run out too early, and second, because the calculations aren't done to the dollar for reasons we've discussed before. Does that make sense now?"

They nod, so Bob clicks on the "Personal Data" tab, then says, "Okay, now let's move to the right side of the screen." (See Figure 9.8)

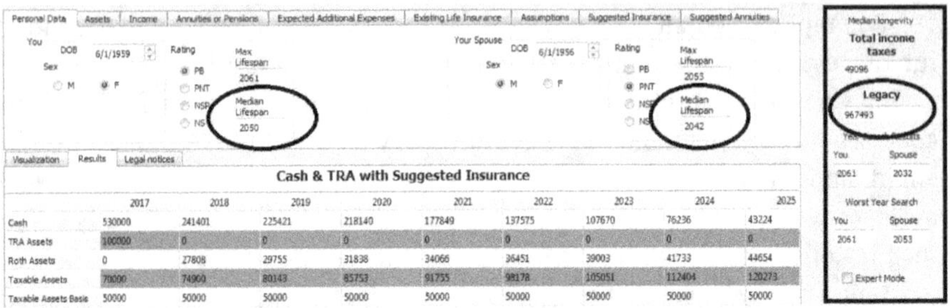

Figure 9.8: The Rhino Retirement Analyzer with the right side of the main screen, the median longevity years, and the median longevity legacy highlighted

Median Longevity Results

"The top box, labeled 'Median longevity', has information corresponding to the information in the 'Worst case longevity' box on the left, except in this case the numbers for income taxes and legacy are based on both of you surviving to your median longevity ('life expectancy'), which in this case is 2050 for Jane and 2042 for Jim. Since this is considerably better financially than the worst case in which you live until 2061 and Jim dies in 2032, you end up leaving a significant legacy, estimated at almost a million dollars. Any questions about this?"

The Worst Case Years of Death

Neither of the sisters has any questions, so he continues, "Next, we have the 'Year Search Results' box, which shows the years of death for both you and Jim that the program has determined would produce the lowest sustainable spending." (See Figure 9.9.)

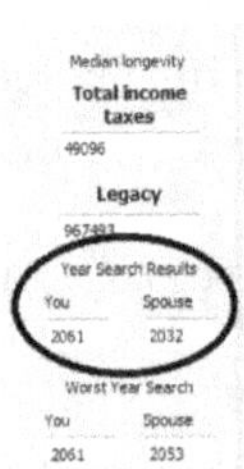

Figure 9.9: The Rhino Retirement Analyzer with the "Year Search Results" box highlighted

"As is normally the case, the worst death years for sustainable spending are that you live until your 'Max Lifespan', which is your 90th percentile life expectancy, whereas Jim dies immediately after your suggested insurance expires in 2032." He clicks on the "Suggested Insurance" tab, then slides the year slider over to show years 2031 and 2032, resulting in a screen that looks like Figure 9.10.

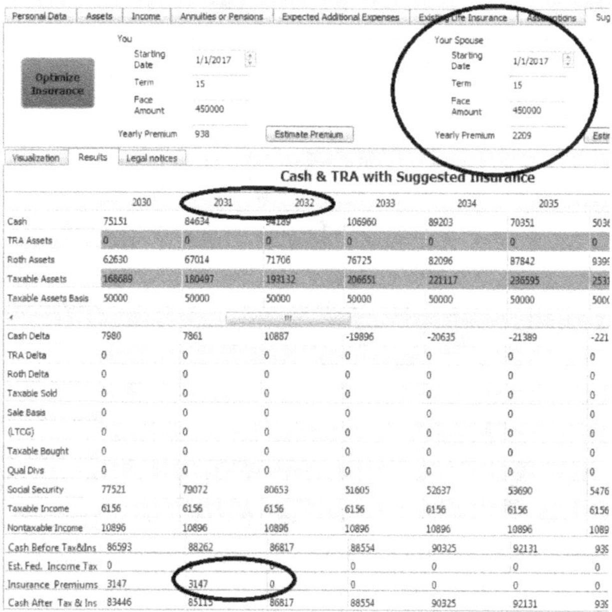

Figure 9.10: The Rhino Retirement Analyzer with the spousal suggested insurance and the insurance premiums for years 2031 and 2032 highlighted

"As you can see, the starting date for both your and Jim's suggested insurance is 1/1/2017 and they have a term of 15 years, which means they would expire at the beginning of 2032. That's why the insurance premiums near the bottom of the screen disappear in 2032. Any questions about this?"

Jane says, "Yes. Why does the insurance start in the past? We don't have it yet, and it's not January any more. Shouldn't it start in the future, maybe June 15th so that we have time to get the applications in and have them approved?"

Selecting the Starting Date for Life Insurance

Bob replies, “Yes, that is a good point. I can change those dates and rerun it to see if it makes any significant difference. Let’s see.” He changes the insurance dates to June 15th and clicks the “Optimize Insurance” button. (See Figure 9.11)

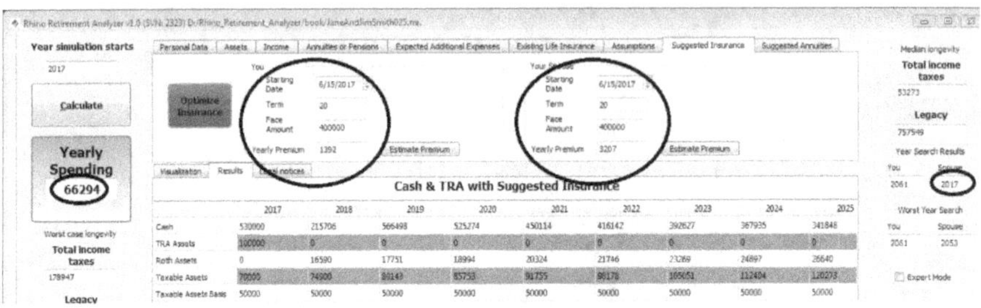

Figure 9.11: The Rhino Retirement Analyzer with an insurance starting date of 6/15/2017 and highlighting on the ‘Yearly Spending’, term, and insurance face amounts and premiums

Bob continues, “Hmm, interesting. It increased the term to 20 years and reduced the face amount slightly to $400,000. That increased the premium, but also increased sustainable spending by about $1500. I think what happened is that the amount of your premium was limited by its percentage of your overall cash flow, and since you now have more potential cash flow with your higher asset level, the program recommended a longer insurance term to increase sustainable spending”.

“By the way, I see that a side effect of this change is that the worst death year for Jim is now 2017; that sort of change can happen with even a small difference in the input data.”

“We can go back and check what the optimizer does before and after adding the $500,000 to your assets, if you want me to do that.”

Jane says, “No, I don't think that will be necessary at this point. We can decide on the term later, right?”

Bob replies, “Yes, if the insurance company approves you for the face amount that we applied for, they should accept any term that they will write for people your age, and of course reducing the face amount would be possible as well. But since you bring that up, I should check to see what happens if we make the starting date May 31 instead of June 15. The insurance company I am using goes by ‘age last birthday’, which means that it would consider both of you a year older if you purchase the insurance on June 15 because both of you were born on June 1. Let's see what that does." He changes the date and clicks the "Optimize Insurance" button, resulting in a screen that looks like Figure 9.12.

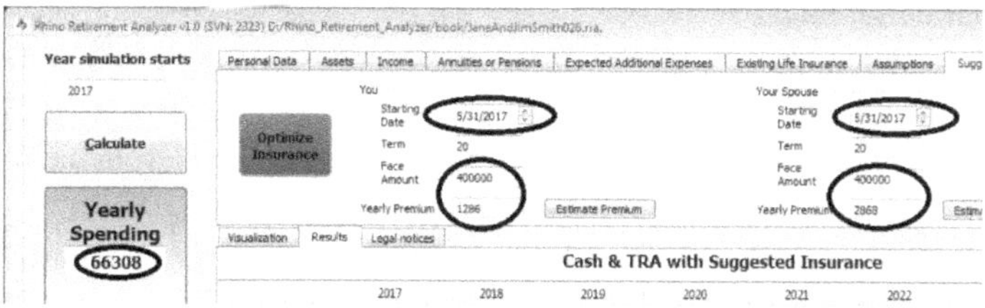

Figure 9.12: The Rhino Retirement Analyzer with an insurance starting date of 5/31/2017 and highlighting on the Yearly Spending, insurance starting dates, face amounts, and premiums

Bob continues, "That saves you over $400 a year compared to waiting until June 15th to buy the policies. That's because you are still a year younger for insurance purposes at the end of May than you will be a few days later. Since it also has almost no effect on the sustainable spending, perhaps we should try to get the policies dated before that birthday so that you can get the lower rates. Any more questions?"

Jane says, "I don't have a question, but I have made a decision. We'll buy the insurance and the annuity."

Bob replies, "Great! Let's fill out the paperwork for both of those so we can get the process started with the insurance companies. How about you, June?"

June answers, "I'll have to think about the annuity. That's not as urgent because we already have the insurance."

Bob continues by saying, "Thanks both of you for all of the time you've spent with me. Any other questions on the whole process?"

Jane says, "Actually I do have one more question now that you mention all of the time we have spent. I assume that you will be compensated as a result of our buying the insurance and the annuities, as I doubt this is a hobby for you. Can you explain how that works?"

Bob replies, "Sure. The life insurance company pays a commission which amounts to roughly the whole first year's premium, about $4,000 in the case of the policies for you and Jim. I don't get all of that, since some of it must go to my 'general agent' who takes care of dealing with the insurance company so I can concentrate on my clients. I'll get about 80% of that amount, or about $3,200."

"Now for the annuity, the commission is about 3% of the premium, depending on exactly which policy you buy, and I get most of that. So that would amount to about $10,000 if you buy the $340,000 annuity. Any other questions on this?"

Jane shakes her head "no", but June says, "Does your commission on the annuity affect how much it pays?"

Bob says, "Sure, because that money has to come from the premium that the client pays. But the amount that the annuity pays is the amount that the program shows, because the commission is already included in the quotations from immediateannuities.com. Anything else before we wrap this up?"

Jane replies, "So we aren't going to cover the Expert Mode in any detail? I know you showed us some of those features, but I'm sure there are other things it allows you to do."

Bob says, "I can send you some documentation on how the other features work, including a command-line interface to the program and its scripting language for batch processing. How's that?"

Jane agrees, so Bob shuts down the program and starts going over the forms for the insurance applications with her.

---

i The IRS has a service to calculate the taxable amount for situations where it's too complicated for them to give the formula on their website.

Appendix A
Reference Manual for the Gui Interface of the Rhino Retirement Analyzer V1.0, Basic Mode

The Rhino Retirement Analyzer is a complex program with a number of screens and options controlling its operation. As with any such program, in order to use it effectively you will need a step-by-step explanation of what each screen is for and how to use it. That is the purpose of this appendix.

The Opening Screen

Figure A.1 shows the screen that you will see when first opening the program. It is ready for you to enter the data needed to calculate sustainable spending. In this appendix, we will cover the basic mode functionality of each of the input tabs in detail, including how the data on each tab is used in the sustainable spending calculations.[i]

Important note: the results shown in this appendix are **for illustrative purposes only**. It is very likely that when you run the actual program that you have downloaded, the answers will be different. This is due to changing tax laws, brackets, and so on, as well as modifications to the program's algorithms.

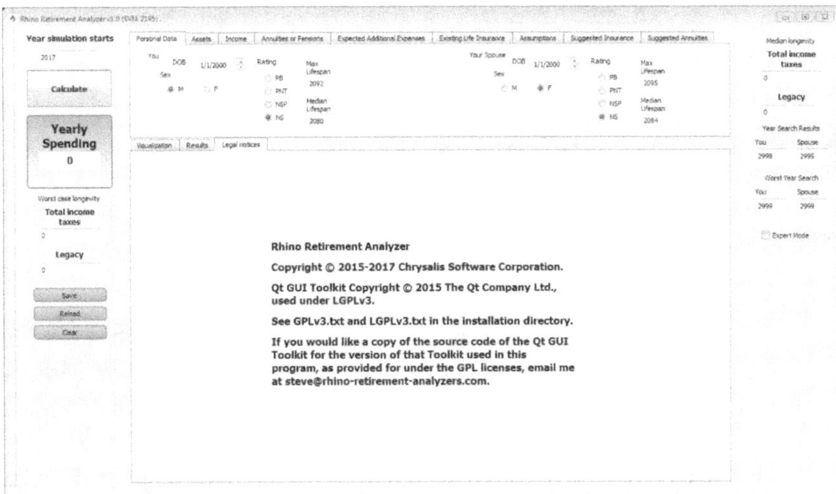

Figure A.1: The opening screen

DOI 10.1515/9781501506185-010

The Personal Data Tab

The first input tab is the Personal Data tab, shown in Figure A.2.

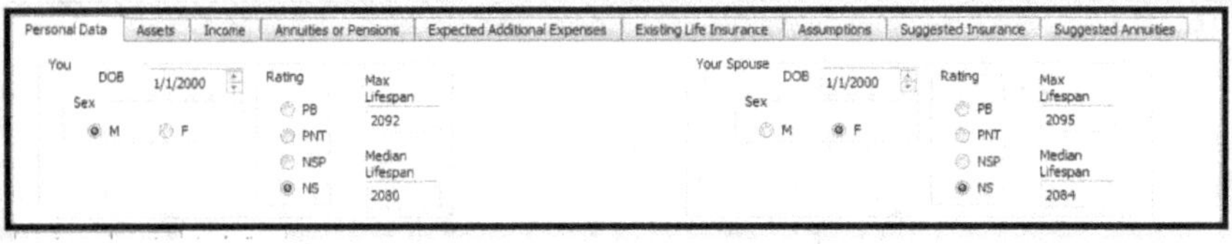

Figure A.2: The Personal Data tab

This tab contains two sets of data, one for the client ("You") and one for the client's spouse ("Your Spouse"). Each of these sets of data has identical content, so we will discuss only the first set.[ii]

Let's go over each field in turn, starting with DOB in the upper left. (See Figure A.3)

DOB

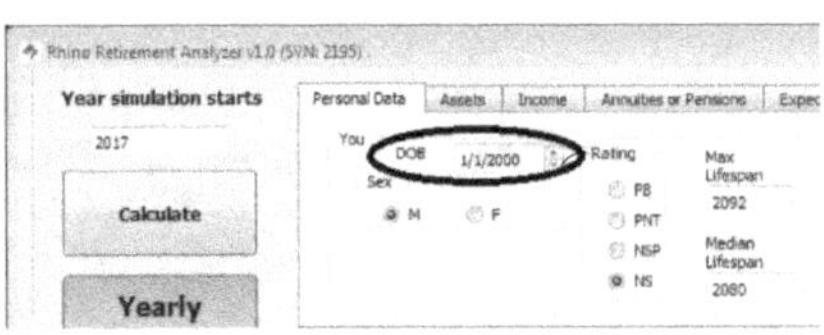

Figure A.3: The Personal Data tab with the first client's DOB field highlighted

Definition: The date of birth of the first client.

Uses in the program:

1. Calculating estimates for the client's median and maximum lifespan (the Median Lifespan and Max Lifespan output fields), in conjunction with the Rating input field and the Sex field. These estimates are used to determine how many years the clients' assets must last.
2. Contributes to the estimation of insurance premiums, shown on the Existing Life Insurance and Suggested Insurance tabs.

3. Calculating the client's FRA (Social Security Full Retirement Age) date, shown on the Income tab. The FRA date is used to adjust the expected Social Security payment for the client based on the SSA's rules for early or late payments.
4. Estimating the taxable portion of annuity payments, shown on the Annuities or Pensions tab.

The next field is Sex. (See Figure A.4)

Sex

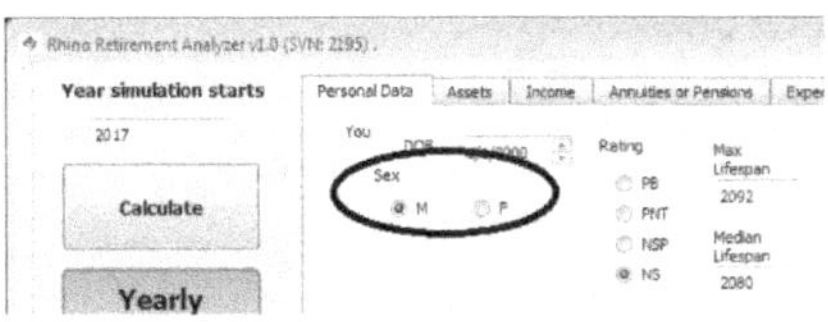

Figure A.4: The Personal Data tab with the first client's Sex field highlighted

Definition: The sex of the first client.

Uses in the program:
1. Contributes to the calculation of lifespan estimates, along with the DOB and Rating fields.
2. Contributes to the estimation of insurance premiums, shown on the Existing Life Insurance and Suggested Insurance tabs.

The next field is Rating. (See Figure A.5)

Rating

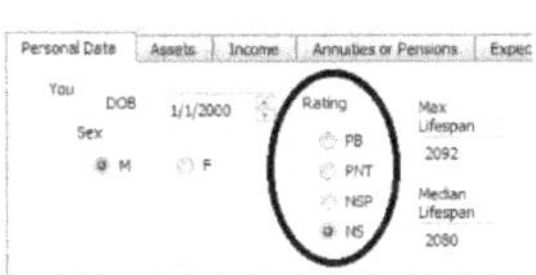

Figure A.5: The Personal Data tab with the first client's Rating field highlighted

Definition: The estimated life insurance company rating for the first client.[iii]

Possible values:[iv]
- PB (Preferred Best), the highest rating (lowest risk)
- PNT (Preferred Non-Tobacco), the second highest rating
- NSP (Non-Smoker Plus), third highest rating
- NS (Non-Smoker), fourth highest rating.

Uses in the program:
1. Contributes to the calculation of lifespan estimates, along with the DOB and Sex fields.
2. Contributes to the estimation of insurance premiums, shown on the Existing Life Insurance and Suggested Insurance tabs.

The next field is Max Lifespan. (See Figure A.6)

Max Lifespan

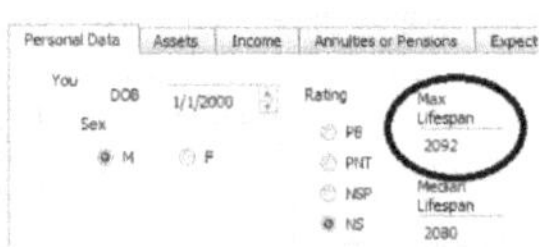

Figure A.6: The Personal Data tab with the first client's Max Lifespan field highlighted

Definition: The estimated 90th percentile life expectancy of the first client from the present year, based on the client's DOB, Sex, and Rating. In other words, starting from the current year, the program estimates that 90% of people with the given DOB, Sex, and Rating will have died by the end of the calendar year shown in this field.

Uses in the program: The later of the two Max Lifespan values is used to limit the terminating date for any simulation. So, if we were running a simulation, starting in the year 2017, for a couple consisting of one male and one female, both born on 1/1/2000, and both having an NS (standard) rating, the program would stop the simulation no later than 2095.[v]

The next field is Median Lifespan. (See Figure A.7)

Median Lifespan

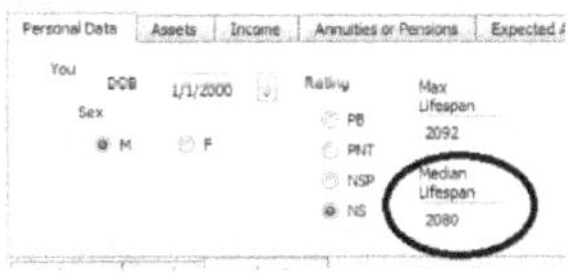

Figure A.7: The Personal Data tab with the first client's Median Lifespan field highlighted

Definition: The estimated 50th percentile life expectancy of the first client from the present year, based on the client's DOB, Sex, and Rating. In other words, starting from the current year, the program estimates that 50% of people with the given DOB, Sex, and Rating will have died by the end of the calendar year shown in this field.

Uses in the program: Contributes to the calculation of the results shown in the "Median Longevity" box in the upper right of the screen. The "Total income taxes" and "Legacy" numbers represent estimates of the total income taxes and the total assets they would leave to their heirs if each spouse died at his or her median longevity.[vi] (See Figure A.8)

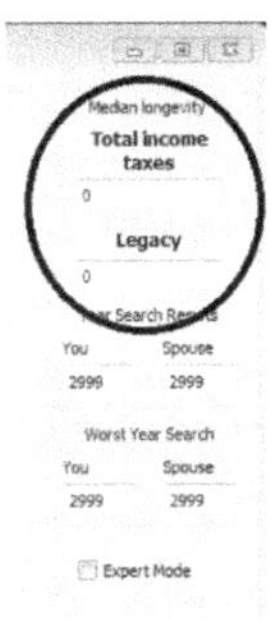

Figure A.8: The Median Longevity output data highlighted

Entering Some Reasonable Data for the Personal Tab

In order for us to be able to compute some reasonable results, we will need reasonable data. Let's start by entering values for DOB and ratings for both clients on the Personal tab. (See Figure A.9)

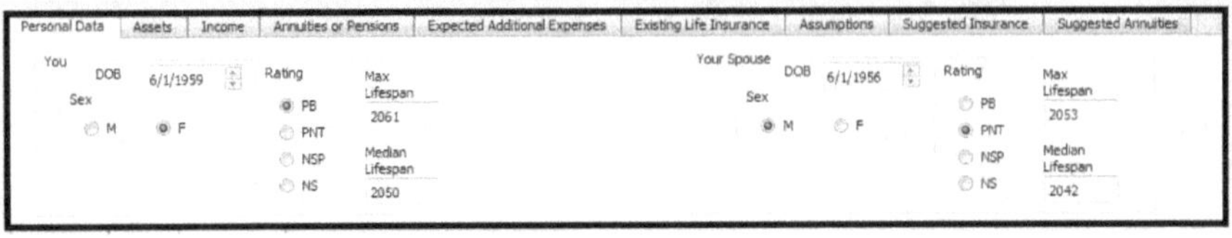

Figure A.9: The Personal tab with data that we will use to compute some reasonable results

The Assets Tab

Next let's take a look at the Assets tab. (See Figure A.10)

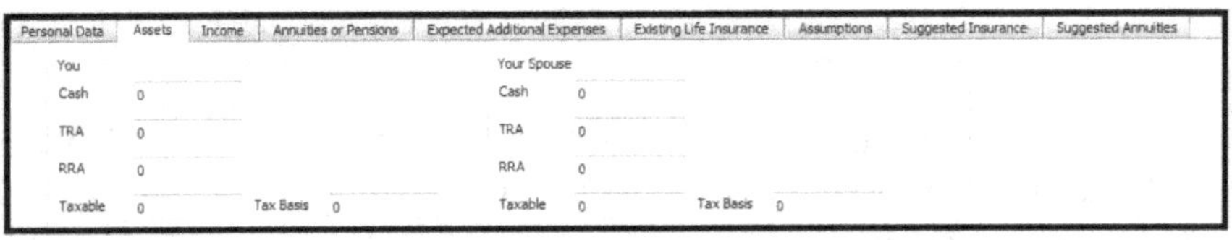

Figure A.10: The Assets tab

As with the Personal tab, this tab contains two sets of data, one for the client ("You") and one for the client's spouse ("Your Spouse"). Each of these sets of data has identical content, so we will discuss only the first set.

Let's go over each field in turn, starting with Cash in the upper left. (See Figure A.11)

Cash

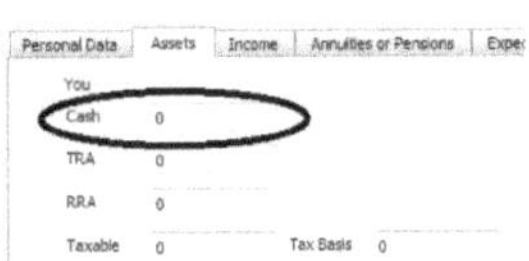

Figure A.11: The Assets tab screen with the first client's Cash field highlighted

Definition: The first client's holding of dollar assets that do not fluctuate with the market, e.g., checking and savings accounts and CDs. These assets are projected to collect interest according to the entry for Cash Nominal Return on the Assumptions tab.

Use in the program: Contributes to the calculation of sustainable spending.

The next field is TRA. (See Figure A.12)

TRA

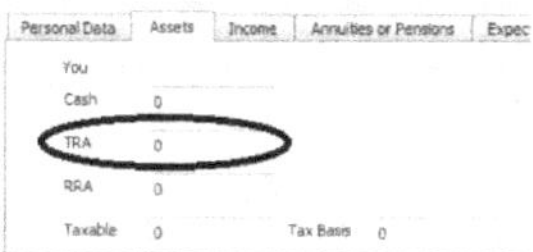

Figure A.12: The Assets tab with the first client's TRA field highlighted

Definition: The first client's holding of assets in traditional retirement accounts.[vii]

Use in the program: Contributes pre-tax assets to the calculation of sustainable spending.

The next field is RRA. (See Figure A.13)

RRA

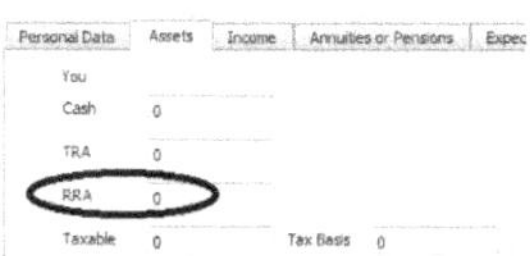

Figure A.13: The Assets tab with the first client's RRA field highlighted

Definition: The first client's holding of assets in Roth retirement accounts.

Use in the program: Contributes post-tax assets to the calculation of sustainable spending.[viii]

The next field is Taxable. (See Figure A.14)

Taxable

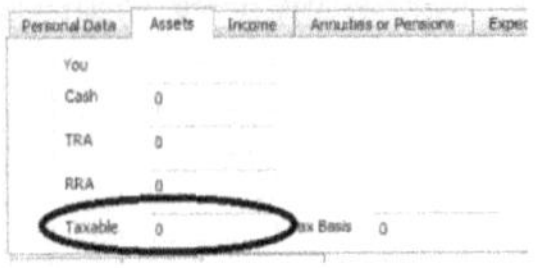

Figure A.14: The Assets tab with the first client's Taxable field highlighted

Definition: The first client's total assets in taxable accounts.

Use in the program: Contributes assets having a tax basis to the calculation of sustainable spending. This includes any assets outside retirement accounts that can generate capital gains or losses, e.g., stock and bond accounts. It does not include cash or savings accounts, which do not generate capital gains, nor does it include assets in retirement accounts, which also do not generate capital gains.

The next field is Tax Basis. (See Figure A.15)

Tax Basis

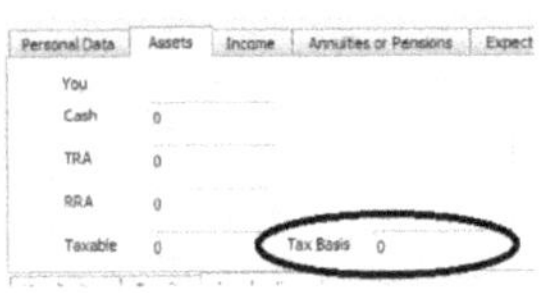

Figure A.15: The Assets tab with the first client's Tax Basis field highlighted

Definition: The first client's tax basis for assets in taxable accounts. This is the amount that is deducted from a sale of the assets before calculating capital gains. For example, let's say you buy a stock for $10,000 and sell it for $12,000. In that case, your tax basis is $10,000, which means you don't pay capital gains taxes on the whole $12,000, just on the $2,000 amount in excess of your tax basis.

Use in the program: Used to calculate capital gains when selling assets in the client's taxable account

Entering Some Reasonable Data for the Assets Tab

Let's enter values for the assets and tax basis of both clients. (See Figure A.16)

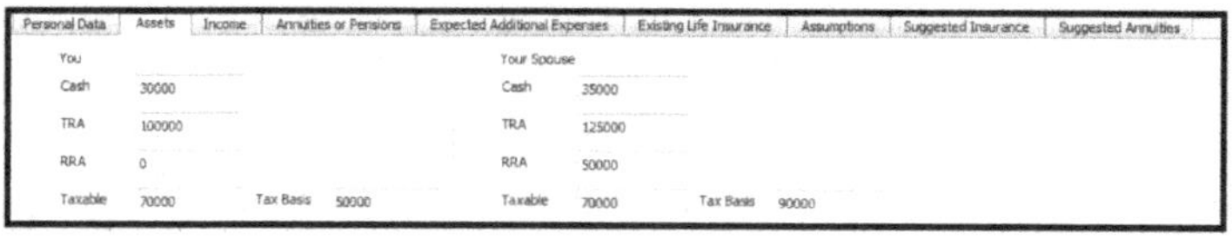

Figure A.16: The Assets tab with data that we will use to compute some reasonable results

Now that we have the Personal tab and the Assets tab filled in, we can calculate a very preliminary spending estimate by clicking the Calculate button. Of course, this won't include Social Security or any other income source, so it is far from complete. What it shows is how much money the example couple could spend from assets every year without running out of money before the second spouse dies in 2061 (90th percentile longevity, as shown in Figure A.9), assuming no income taxation (given no income), no inflation and no return on assets. (See Figure A.17)

Figure A.17: The first estimate of yearly sustainable spending based solely on entries on the Personal and Assets tabs

The Income Tab

The next input tab is the Income tab, shown in Figure A.18.

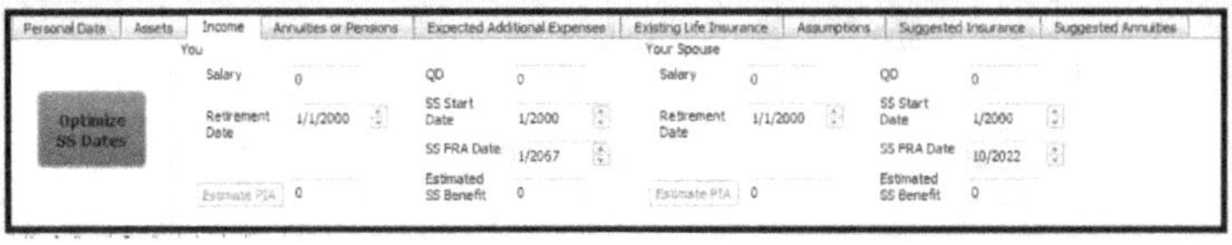

Figure A.18: The Income tab

As with the previous tabs, this tab contains two sets of data, one for the client ("You") and one for the client's spouse ("Your Spouse"). Each of these sets of data has identical content, so we will discuss only the first set.

Let's go over each data field in turn, starting with Salary in the upper left. (See Figure A.19)

Salary

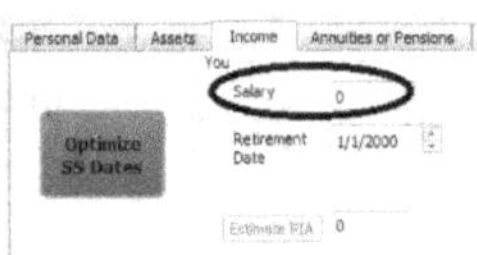

Figure A.19: The Income tab with the first client's Salary field highlighted

Definition: The current yearly salary of the first client, or the last salary if the first client is already retired, no matter how long ago he or she retired.[ix]

Uses in the program:

1. Contributes to calculations of income and income taxes.
2. Used in the PIA (Primary Insurance Amount) calculation (See description of Estimate PIA button below).

The next field is Retirement Date.(See Figure A.20)

Retirement Date

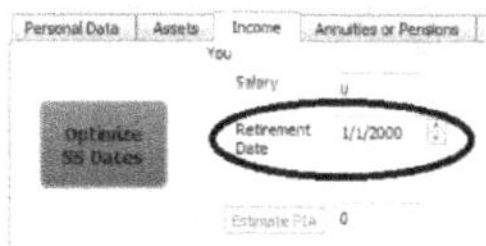

Figure A.20: The Income tab with the first client's Retirement Date field highlighted

Definition: The date when the first client expects to retire (or did retire, if the date is in the past) from the job that provides the salary listed in that client's Salary field.

Use in the program: Indicates when to stop including the salary income of this client in the calculations, assuming that the client is alive at retirement.[x]

The next field is QD. (See Figure A.21)

QD

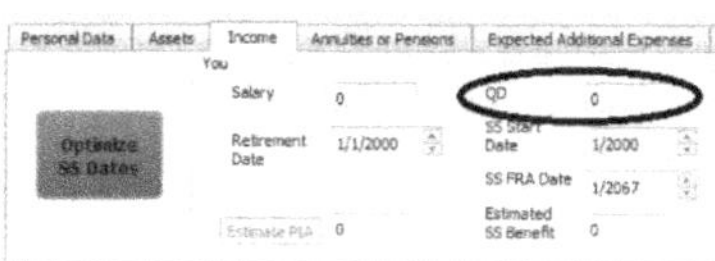

Figure A.21: The Income tab with the first client's QD field highlighted

Definition: The first client's yearly qualified dividends, i.e., those that qualify for capital gains taxation rules under the current income tax code as of this writing.[xi]

Use in the program: These qualified dividends will add to yearly spending until the death of the second spouse.

Note that these dividends must be from stocks that are *not* included in the Taxable field on the Assets tab, as the stocks in that Taxable account will be sold off over time to pay living expenses and therefore would not be able to generate a fixed amount of qualified dividends. The assumption is that stocks used to generate qualified dividends are intended to be left to heirs and are therefore not included in salable assets.

The next field is SS Start Date. (See Figure A.22)

SS Start Date

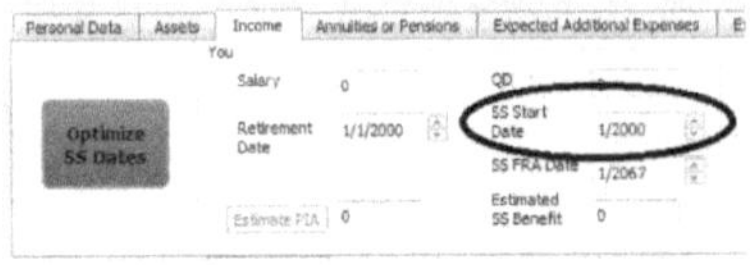

Figure A.22: The Income tab with the first client's SS Start Date field highlighted

Definition: The first client's actual (if in the past) or expected Social Security start date. In the latter case, this is the date when the client *expects* to start, not necessarily the best date when he or she *should* start.

Uses in the program:
1. Used in conjunction with the client's PIA (Primary Insurance Amount) and FRA (Full Retirement Age) to compute the estimated Social Security benefit that this client will receive, assuming that the client has not yet started to collect Social Security.
2. Used to determine the contribution of this client's Social Security payments to the couple's sustainable spending.
3. Used to determine the survivor's benefit if this client dies before the other client.

The next field is SS FRA Date. (See Figure A.23)

SS FRA Date

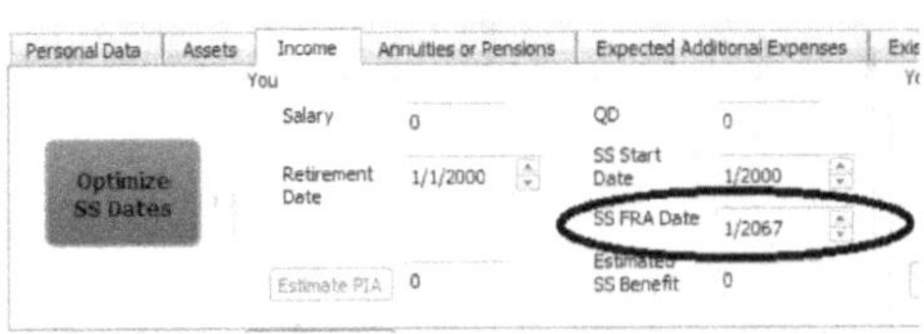

Figure A.23: The Income tab with the first client's SS FRA Date field highlighted

Definition: This is the date that the Social Security Administration considers "Full Retirement Age", or FRA, for someone born on the date specified by the

DOB entry on the Personal tab. Benefits started at FRA are equal to the Social Security Primary Insurance Amount (PIA), rather than being reduced due to early claiming or increased due to late claiming. This is an output-only field that cannot be changed by the user, because it is defined by the SSA's rules.

Use in the program: The SS FRA Date is used to adjust payments starting at any date other than at the client's FRA, based on SSA's rules for early or late claiming of benefits.

The next field is the button labeled Estimate PIA. (See Figure A.24)

Estimate PIA

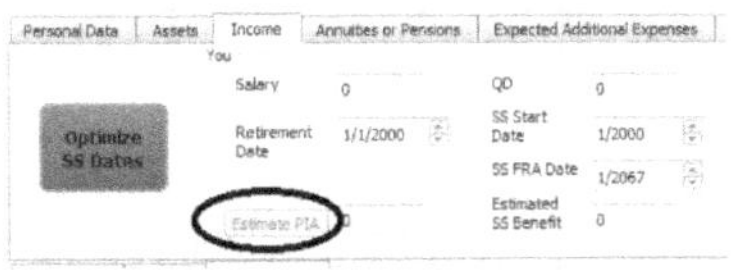

Figure A.24: The Income tab with the first client's Estimate PIA button highlighted

Definition: This button, when enabled, will make a rough estimate of the first client's PIA (Primary Insurance Amount) based on the Salary field, on the assumption that your current (or last) salary is representative of your top 35 years of earnings.

Note that this estimate tends to be too optimistic for most people's situations, but fortunately you can get a much more accurate estimate from the Social Security Administration by going to https://www.ssa.gov/planners/benefitcalculators.html and picking one of their online or downloadable calculators. Of course, most people approaching retirement age will already have been notified what their PIA is. If you know the correct number, enter it in the PIA field, which is the unlabeled field immediately following the Estimate PIA button. (See Figure A.25)

PIA

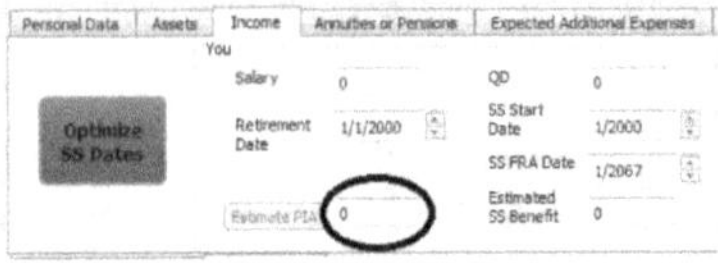

Figure A.25: The Income tab with the first client's PIA field highlighted

Definition: This is the first client's Primary Insurance Amount (PIA), which is the amount that the client would receive every month (before adjustment for inflation) if the client retired at Full Retirement Age (FRA).

Use in the program: The PIA contributes to the calculation of the actual amounts received by both the first client and the spouse both during life and after the death of the first spouse to die. For example, if one spouse dies, the other spouse may be able to collect more by taking the survivor's benefit than by continuing with his or her personally earned benefit. The program takes this and several other effects into consideration when calculating the maximum sustainable spending.

The final field in the first client's data on this tab is the Estimated SS Benefit field. (See Figure A.26)

Estimated SS Benefit

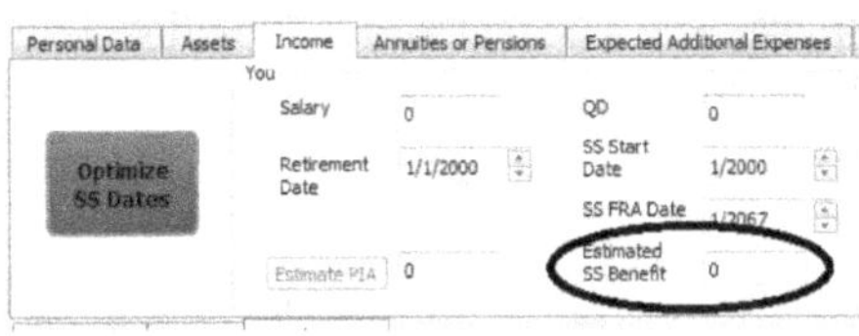

Figure A.26: The Income tab with the first client's Estimated SS Benefit field highlighted

Definition: This is the first client's estimated Social Security benefit, assuming that the PIA and SS Start Date have been entered correctly.[xii]

Use in the program: Contributes to the calculation of sustainable spending. While both spouses are alive, both SS benefits are used; after one spouse dies, the survivor's benefit is estimated according to the SSA's rules for survivor benefits. This usually results in a significant reduction in income to the survivor, which is why life insurance can be useful in mitigating the risk of early death of one spouse near or during retirement.

Entering Some Reasonable Data for the Income Tab

Let's enter values for the Salary, Retirement Date, QD, SS Start date, and estimated PIA for both clients. (See Figure A.27)

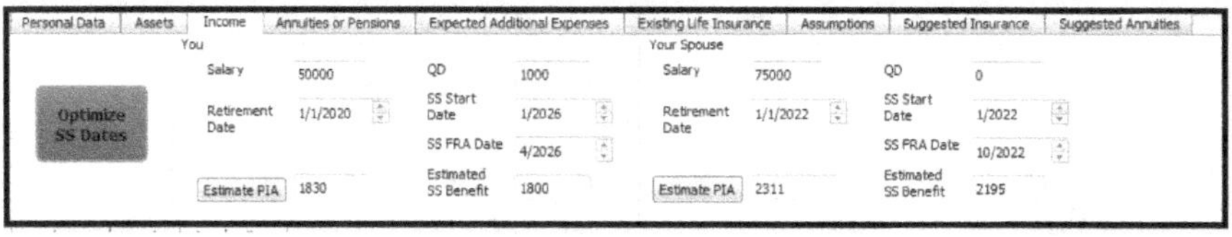

Figure A.27: The Income tab with entries for Salary, Retirement Date, QD, SS Start date, and estimated PIA for each client

What sustainable yearly spending does this produce? Let's click the Calculate button and find out. (See Figure A.28)

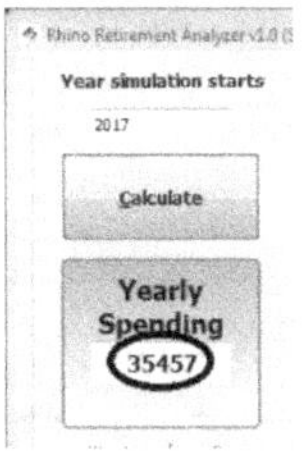

Figure A.28: An estimate of yearly sustainable spending based on entries on the Personal, Assets, and Income tabs

Now, does this represent the best sustainable spending with everything we have entered so far?

That's a trick question. The answer is "Yes", if we assume that the dates that the clients plan to start receiving SS are set in stone. But what if we use the

Optimize SS Dates button to check whether there are any better dates? (See Figure A.29)

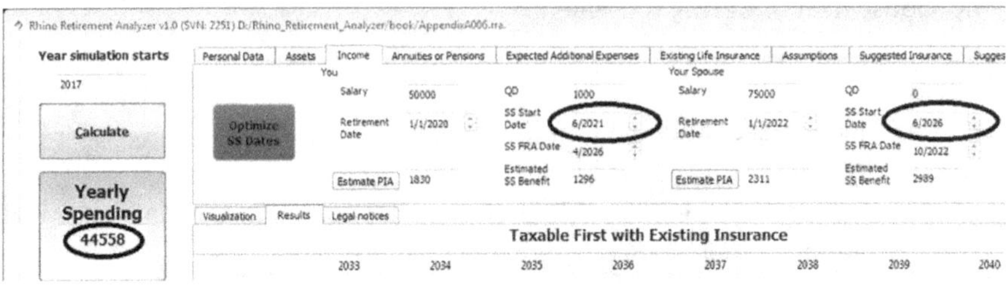

Figure A.29: An estimate of yearly sustainable spending based entries on the Personal, Assets, and Income tabs, after running the SS date optimizer

That increases yearly sustainable spending by over $9,000, which is a significant increase of about 25% over the base amount of $35457. How does it do that?

By starting the Social Security payments of the younger and lower-paid spouse first, whereas the higher-paid and older spouse postpones receiving payments until age 70, to get the maximum payment for the younger spouse if she is widowed.[xiii]

But interestingly, this works even though the worst case scenario is for the older, higher paid spouse to die immediately. That's because the younger spouse still collects her own benefit for the years until her FRA, which is in April 2026.

The Annuities or Pensions Tab

The next input tab is the Annuities or Pensions tab, shown in Figure A.30.

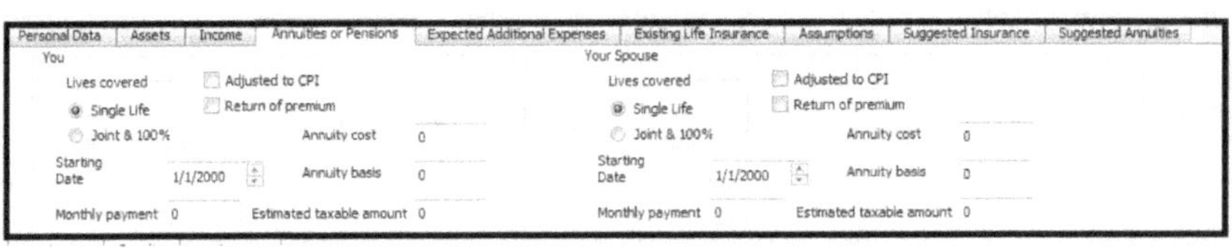

Figure A.30: The Annuities or Pensions tab highlighted

As with the previous tabs, this tab contains two sets of data, one for the client ("You") and one for the client's spouse ("Your Spouse"). Each of these sets of data has identical content, so we will discuss only the first set.

Let's go over each data field in turn, starting with the Lives Covered box. (See Figure A.31)

Lives Covered

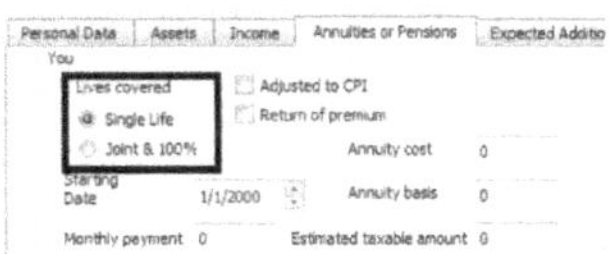

Figure A.31: The Annuities or Pensions tab with the first client's Lives Covered box highlighted

Definition: Specifies whether the annuity is for the life of the first client only and will cease at that client's death ("Single Life"), or will pay the same amount as long as either client is alive ("Joint & 100%").[xiv]

Use in the program: Contributes to the calculation of sustainable spending, because single life annuities can not be relied on to the end of the second client's life, whereas joint & 100% annuities can be.

The next field is the Adjusted to CPI checkbox. (See Figure A.32)

Adjusted to CPI

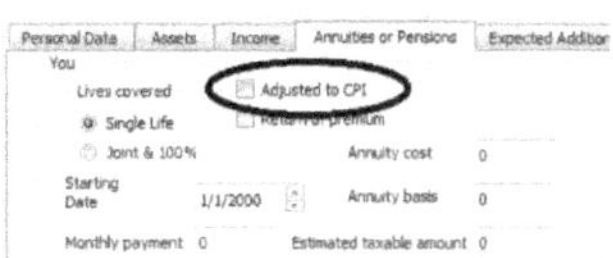

Figure A.32: The Annuities or Pensions tab with the first client's Adjusted to CPI checkbox highlighted

Definition: Specifies whether the annuity payment is adjusted according to the Consumer Price Index inflation index. This is specified in the annuity contract.

Use in the program: Used to determine whether to increase annuity payments in line with the inflation adjustment on the Assumptions tab; if the box is not checked, the annuity payment is in nominal dollars, i.e., is not adjusted for inflation.

The next field is the Return of Premium checkbox. (See Figure A.33)

Return of Premium

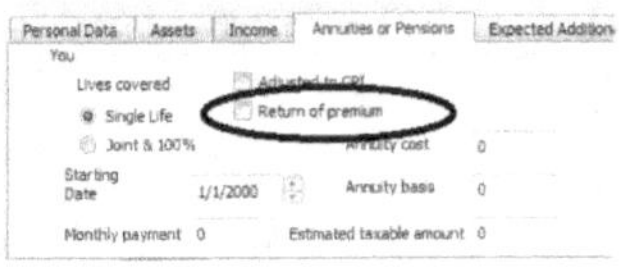

Figure A.33: The Annuities or Pensions tab with the first client's Return of Premium checkbox highlighted

Definition: Specifies whether the insurance company will pay the remainder (if any) of the annuity premium to the heirs of the annuitant(s), as specified in the contract provisions of the annuity.

Use in the program: Used to determine whether a relatively early death of the annuitant(s) will cause a payment to the survivor (or heirs, if it is a joint annuity); if the box is not checked, no such payment will be made.

The next field is Annuity Cost. (See Figure A.34)

Annuity Cost

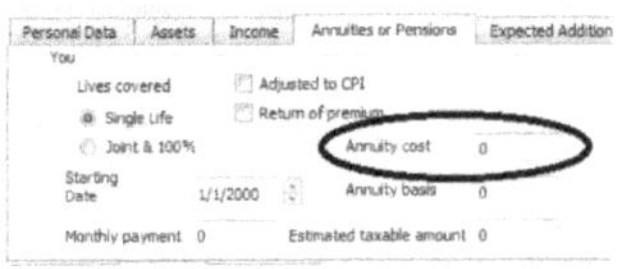

Figure A.34: The Annuities or Pensions tab with the first client's Annuity Cost field highlighted

Definition: Specifies the cost of the annuity.

Use in the program: Used to determine how much remaining premium would be returned via the "Return of premium" feature, if that applies to this annuity.

The next field is the Annuity Basis checkbox. (See Figure A.35)

Annuity Basis

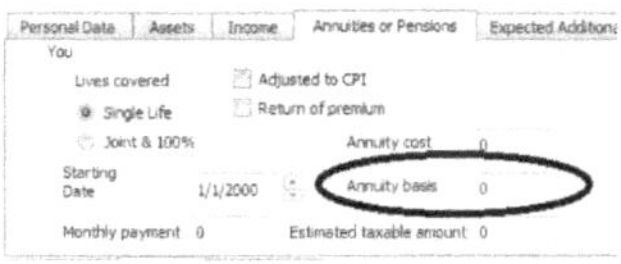

Figure A.35: The Annuities or Pensions tab with the first client's Annuity Basis field highlighted

Definition: Specifies the tax basis of the annuity, which is the amount paid for the annuity if it was paid for with after-tax money. In general, the tax basis for an annuity that is distributed from a traditional retirement account will be different from the amount paid to purchase that annuity. The plan administrator should provide that information when distributing the annuity.

Use in the program: Contributes to calculation of the date that the annuity payments become fully taxable. This will happen as soon as the whole basis has been returned to the annuitant.

The next field is Starting Date. (See Figure A.36)

Starting Date

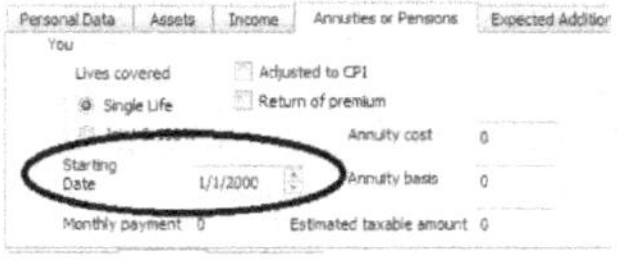

Figure A.36: The Annuities or Pensions tab with the first client's Starting Date field highlighted

Definition: Specifies the starting date of the annuity.

Uses in the program:

1. Contributes to the calculation of income for the future.
2. Contributes to the calculation of the remaining principal for the return of premium feature.[xv]
3. Contributes to the calculation of the remaining basis, which determines when the annuity payments become fully taxable. This will happen as soon as the whole basis has been returned to the annuitant.[xvi]

The next field is Monthly payment. (See Figure A.37)

Monthly Payment

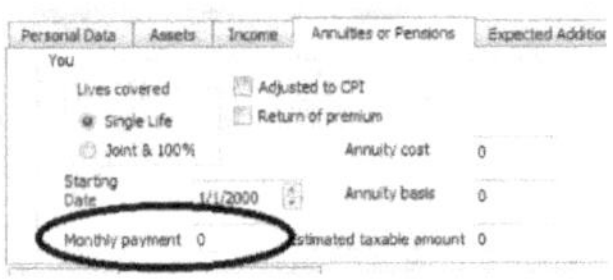

Figure A.37: The Annuities or Pensions tab with the first client's Monthly payment field highlighted

Definition: Specifies the initial monthly payment of the annuity.[xvii]

Uses in the program:
1. Contributes to the calculation of income for the future.
2. Contributes to the calculation of the remaining principal for the return of premium feature.[xviii]
3. Contributes to the calculation of the remaining basis, which determines when the annuity payments become fully taxable. This will happen as soon as the whole basis has been returned to the annuitant.[xix]

The next field is Estimated taxable amount. (See Figure A.38)

Estimated Taxable Amount

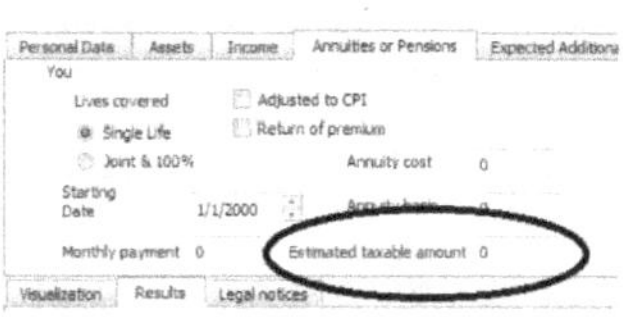

Figure A.38: The Annuities or Pensions tab with the first client's Estimated taxable amount field highlighted

Definition: Specifies the estimated taxable amount of the annuity payment.

Use in the program: Contributes to the calculation of the remaining basis, which determines when the annuity payments become fully taxable. This will happen as soon as the whole basis has been returned to the annuitant.[xx]

Note that this field is initially calculated according to rules in the program. However, if you have better information, such as provided in quotes from immediateannuities.com, you can type it in to override the calculated value.

Entering Some Reasonable Data for the Annuities or Pensions Tab

Let's enter values for the annuities of both clients. (See Figure A.39)

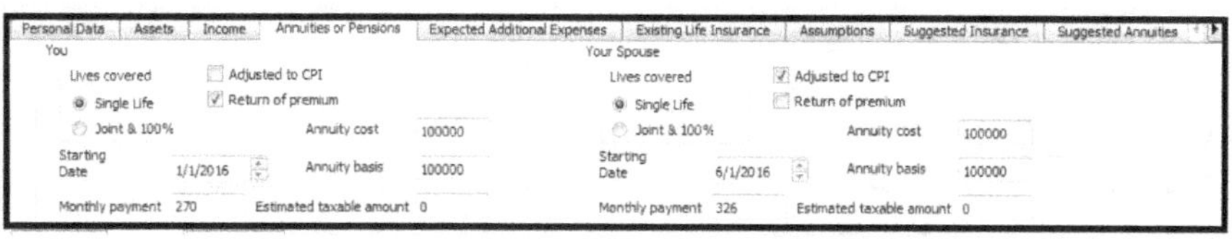

Figure A.39: The Annuities or Pensions tab with data that we will use to compute some reasonable results

What sustainable yearly spending does this produce? Let's click the Calculate button and find out. (See Figure A.40)

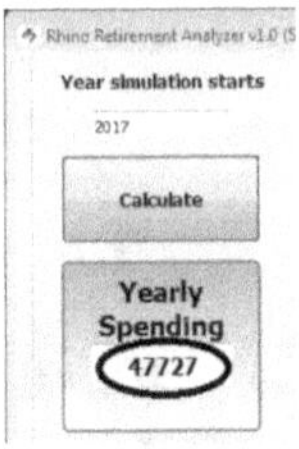

Figure A.40: An estimate of yearly sustainable spending based on entries on the Personal, Assets, Income, and Annuities or Pensions tabs

In this case, the spouse's annuity doesn't contribute anything to the sustainable spending. That is because if he dies right away (his worst death year), the remainder of the money put into his annuity is lost due to its lack of the "return of premium" feature; if it had such a feature then his dying right away would at least leave something to support his wife's spending. This may affect how much life insurance he should have; we'll see when we get to the insurance optimizer on the "Suggested Insurance" tab.

The Expected Additional Expenses Tab

The next input tab is the Expected Additional Expenses tab, shown in Figure A.41.

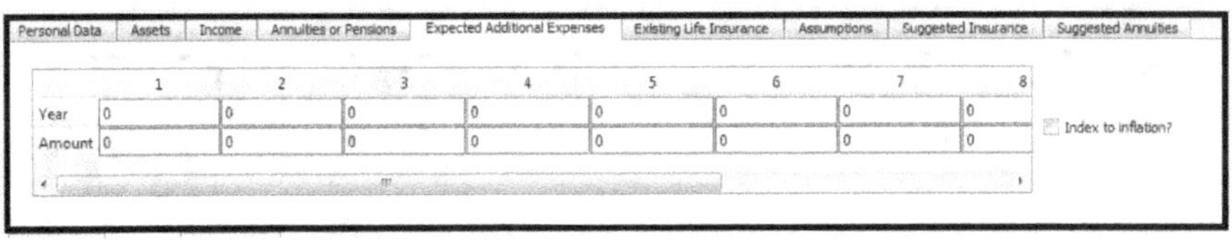

Figure A.41: The Expected Additional Expenses tab

Unlike the previous tabs, this tab contains only one set of data, not a set for each client.

The main feature of this tab is a two-row spreadsheet with the years in which the additional expenses occur on the top row and the amount of those additional expenses on the bottom row.

Expected Additional Expenses Spreadsheet

Definition: Specifies up to ten years' worth of expected additional expenses by the year they are expected to occur and the amount of the expected expense.

Use in the program: Contributes to the calculation of sustainable spending by requesting additional spending in the specified years, thus reducing resources available for sustainable spending.

The other feature on this tab is the "Index to inflation?" checkbox.

Index to Inflation?

Definition: Specifies whether these expenses should be inflated according to the inflation assumption on the Assumptions tab.

Use in the program: Contributes to the calculation of sustainable spending by determining whether the listed expenses should be increased according to the inflation assumption.

Entering Some Data for the Expected Additional Expenses Tab

Let's enter values for two years of additional expenses and check the "Index to inflation?" box.[xxi]

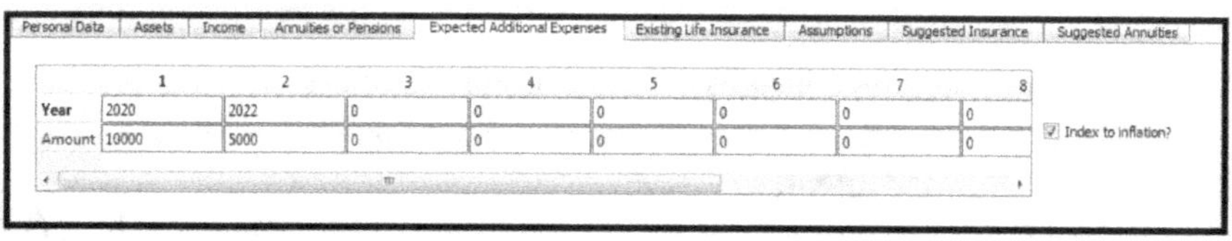

Figure A.42: The Expected Additional Expenses tab with some entries on the Expected Additional Expenses tab and the checkbox checked

What sustainable yearly spending does this produce? Let's click the Calculate button and find out. (See Figure A.43)

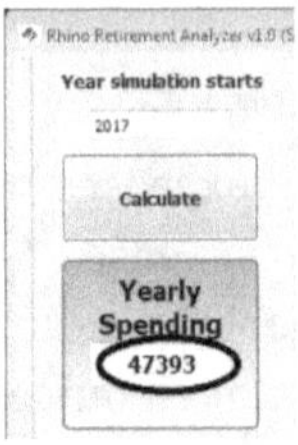

Figure A.43: An estimate of yearly sustainable spending based on entries on the Personal, Assets, Income, Annuities or Pensions, and Expected Addition Expenses tabs

That decreases sustainable spending by about $400/year.

The Existing Life Insurance Tab

The next input tab is the Existing Life Insurance tab, shown in Figure A.44.

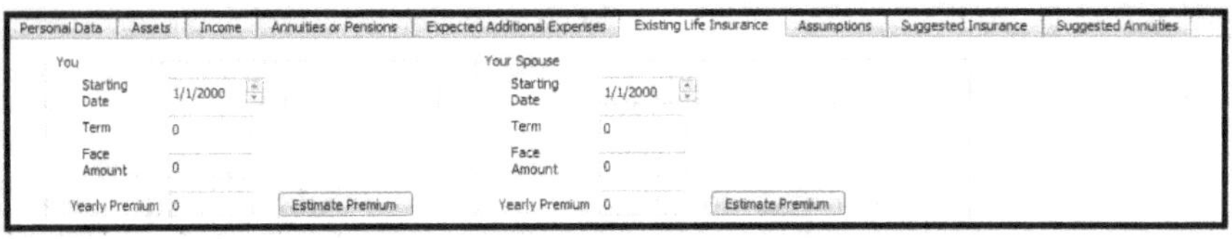

Figure A.44: The Existing Life Insurance tab

As with most of the previous tabs, this tab contains two sets of data, one for the client ("You") and one for the client's spouse ("Your Spouse"). Each of these sets of data has identical content, so we will discuss only the first set.

Let's go over each data field in turn, starting with the Starting Date box. (See Figure A.45)

Starting Date

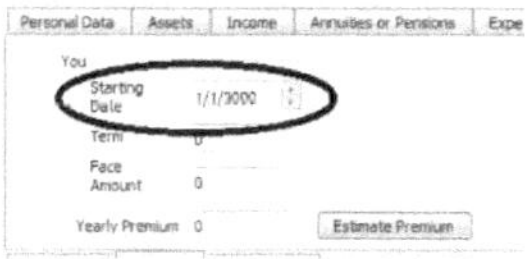

Figure A.45: The Existing Life Insurance tab with the first client's Starting Date field highlighted

Definition: Specifies the starting date for the first client's existing life insurance policy.[xxii]

Use in the program: Contributes to the calculation of sustainable spending by considering an insurance policy payout's ability to mitigate a reduction in income caused by early death of the client.

The next field is Term. (See Figure A.46)

Term

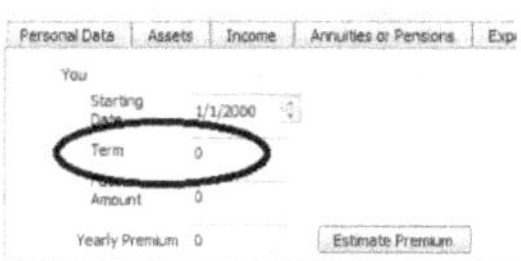

Figure A.46: The Existing Life Insurance tab with the first client's Term field highlighted

Definition: Specifies the term of the first client's existing life insurance policy, beginning at the Starting Date.[xxiii]

Use in the program: Contributes to the calculation of sustainable spending by considering an insurance policy payout's ability to mitigate a reduction in income caused by death of the client while the policy is in force.

The next field is Face Amount. (See Figure A.47)

Face Amount

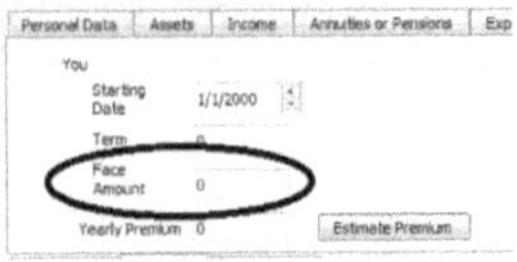

Figure A.47: The Existing Life Insurance tab with the first client's Face Amount field highlighted

Definition: Specifies the face amount that would be paid out if the first client dies while the policy is in force.

Use in the program: Contributes to the calculation of sustainable spending by considering an insurance policy payout's ability to mitigate a reduction in income caused by death of the client while the policy is in force.

The next field is Yearly Premium. (See Figure A.48)

Yearly Premium

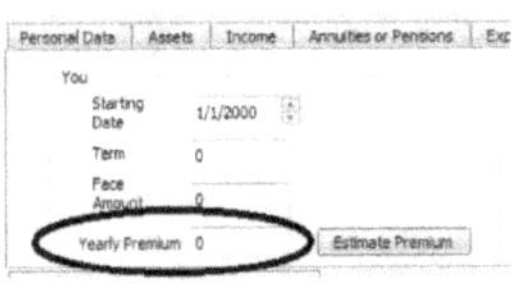

Figure A.48: The Existing Life Insurance tab with the first client's Yearly Premium field highlighted

Definition: Specifies the yearly premium for the first client's policy.

Use in the program: Contributes to the calculation of sustainable spending by deducting the insurance premium from the cash available for spending until the term expires, the client dies, or the spouse dies, whichever comes first.[xxiv]

Of course most of the time, the premium will be known, as the policy is in force. However, in the event that it is not known, you can press the Estimate Premium button to estimate it by using the premiums built into the program. (See Figure A.49)

Estimate Premium

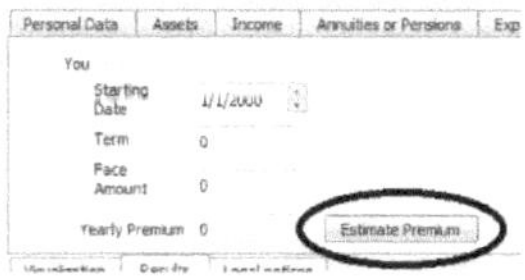

Figure A.49: The Existing Life Insurance tab with the first client's Estimate Premium button highlighted

Definition: Estimates the yearly premium for the first client's policy, using the rates built into the program.

Use in the program: To estimate the premium if it is not known.[xxv]

Entering Some Reasonable Data for the Existing Life Insurance Tab

Let's enter starting dates, terms, and face amounts for both clients, then use the Estimate Premium button for each client to populate the corresponding Yearly Premium fields. (See Figure A.50)

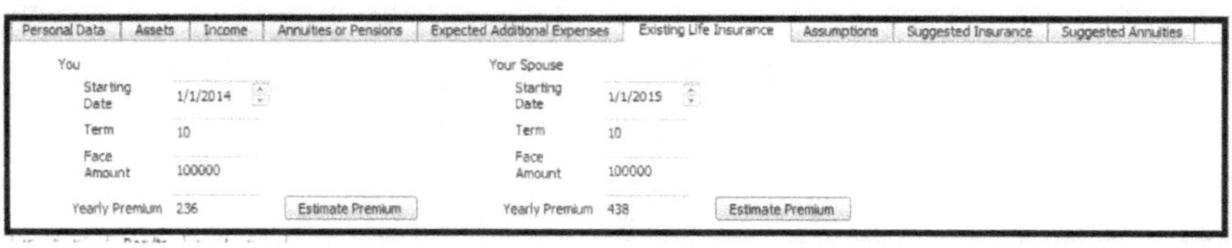

Figure A.50: The Existing Life Insurance tab with data entered for both clients and the premiums estimated by using the Estimate Premium buttons

How will this affect the sustainable spending? Let's press the Calculate button and find out. (See Figure A.51)

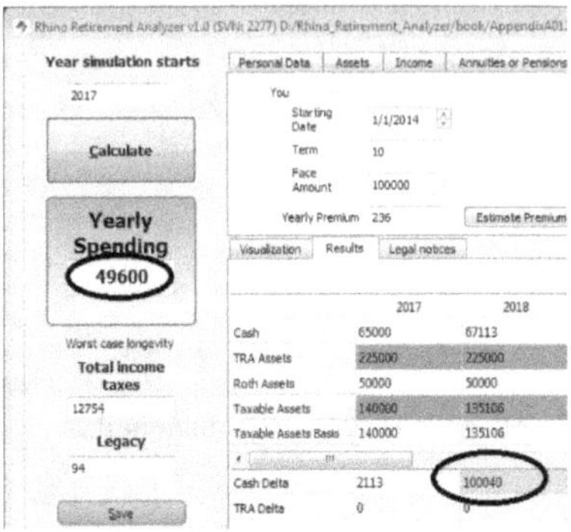

Figure A.51: The new sustainable spending and the insurance payout, with 100K of 10-year term insurance for both spouses

That improves the sustainable spending by about $2000/year, with an insurance payout after the death of the second client in 2017.[xxvi]

The Assumptions Tab

The next input tab is the Assumptions tab shown in Figure A.52.

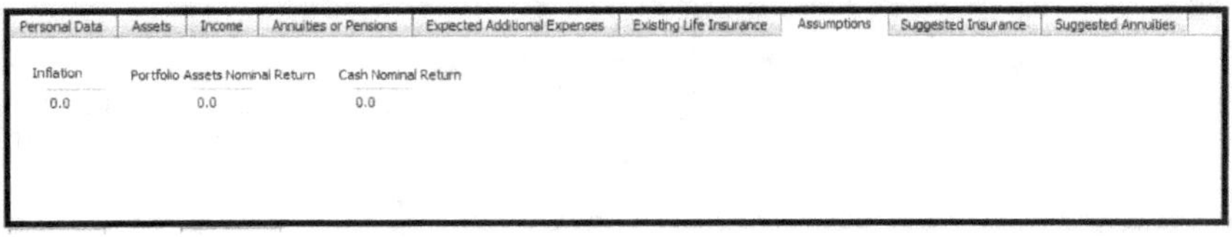

Figure A.52: The Assumptions tab

Let's go over each data field in turn, starting with Inflation. (See Figure A.53)

Inflation

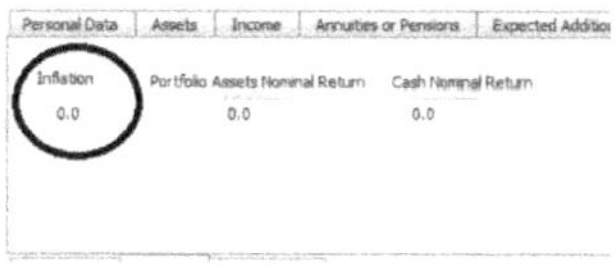

Figure A.53: The Assumptions tab with the Inflation field highlighted

Definition: The assumed rate of inflation for each year of the simulation.[xxvii]

Use in the program: Applied to all inflation-adjusted values in the program, including Social Security payments, tax brackets, inflation-adjusted expected additional expenses and inflation-adjusted annuities. It is *not* applied to clients' salary payments, because not all salaries keep pace with inflation.

The next field is Portfolio Assets Nominal Return. (See Figure A.54)

Portfolio Assets Nominal Return

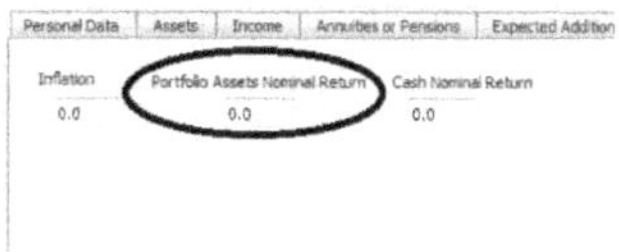

Figure A.54: The Assumptions tab with the Portfolio Assets Nominal Return field highlighted

Definition: The assumed rate of return for portfolio assets, i.e., all assets except for cash, for each year of the simulation.

Use in the program: Applied to assets in each account type (TRA, Roth, or Taxable) each year, before withdrawing money from the account in question.

The next field is Cash Nominal Return. (See Figure A.55)

Cash Nominal Return

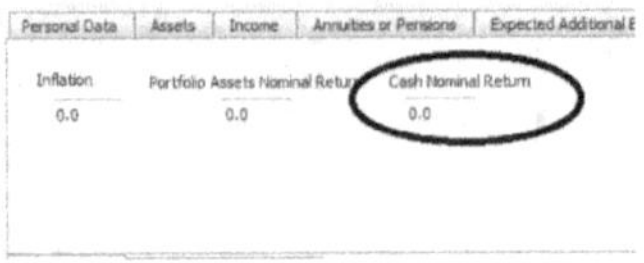

Figure A.55: The Assumptions tab with the Cash Nominal Return field highlighted

Definition: The assumed rate of return for cash assets for each year of the simulation.

Use in the program: Applied to cash each year, before withdrawing cash for spending.

Entering Some Reasonable Data for the Assumptions Tab

Let's enter projections for Inflation, Portfolio Assets Nominal Return, and Cash Nominal Return. (See Figure A.56)

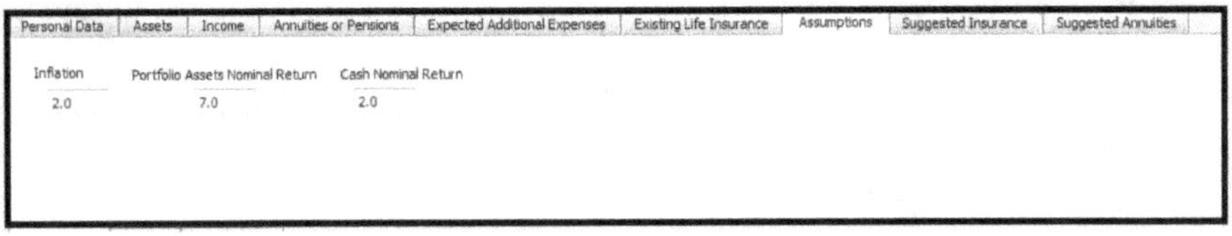

Figure A.56: The Assumptions tab with data entered for Inflation, Portfolio Assets Nominal Return, and Cash Nominal Return

What effect will that have on the sustainable spending? Let's press the Calculate button and find out. (See Figure A.57)

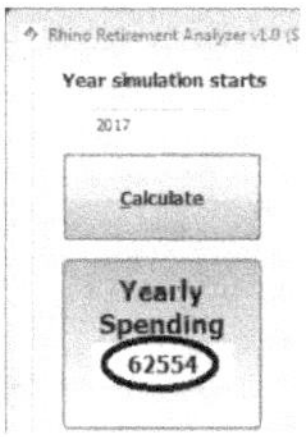

Figure A.57: The new sustainable spending with assumptions set to 2% Inflation, 7% Portfolio Assets Nominal Return, and 2% Cash Nominal Return

That increased projected sustainable spending by about $13,000/year over the default assumptions of 0% for inflation and returns. Of course, no one knows what will actually happen, but these assumptions are fairly representative of projections made for long-term investment planning as of this writing.[xxviii]

The Suggested Insurance Tab

The next input tab is the Suggested Insurance tab, shown in Figure A.58.

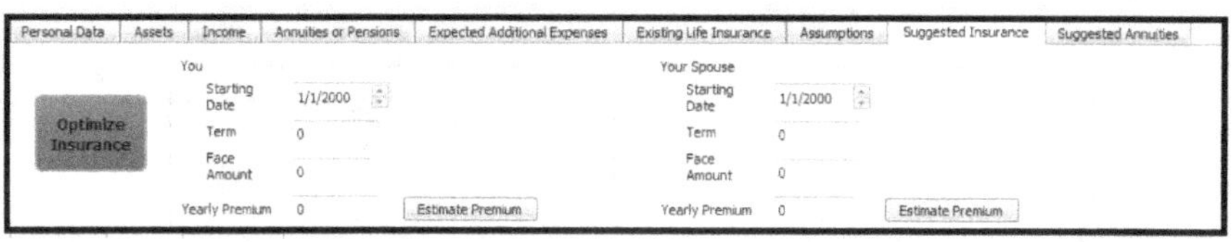

Figure A.58: The Suggested Insurance tab

This tab is different from the others we have seen previously, because it is normally populated by the program rather than having to enter the data manually.

Note that it is possible to enter data here manually if you want to check the expected results of adding a specific insurance policy that you already have the specifications for.

This is most likely to be useful when you are using the free version of the program, which has generic premiums, to get a general recommendation. Then once you have the recommendation for the amount and term of insurance, you put in your actual premiums to get a more accurate projection of costs.

Let's click the "Optimize Insurance" button to see what the program recommends. (See Figure A.59)

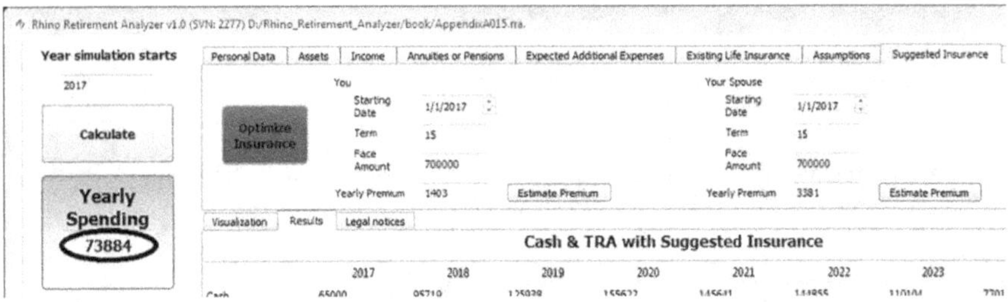

Figure A.59: The new sustainable spending with suggested insurance

That suggested insurance of $700,000 of 15-year term adds over $10,000/year to sustainable spending, after deducting the insurance premiums.

The Suggested Annuities Tab

The next input tab is the Suggested Annuities tab, shown in Figure A.60.

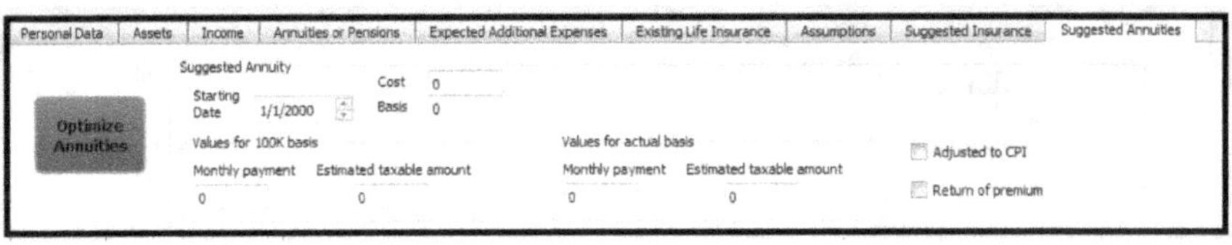

Figure A.60: The Suggested Annuities tab

This tab is used to enter data for a suggested joint and 100% annuity with payments to begin on a date in the future. Because annuity rates vary so frequently, and because variations in rates have so much effect on the price of a given payment amount, it doesn't make sense for the program to have stored rates for annuities as it does with term insurance. Thus, the starting date, amount of the monthly payment per $100K, and the taxable amount of that payment[xxix] must be entered here for the program to have enough information to compute the effects of purchasing an annuity.

Let's go over each data field, beginning with Starting Date. (See Figure A.61)

Starting Date

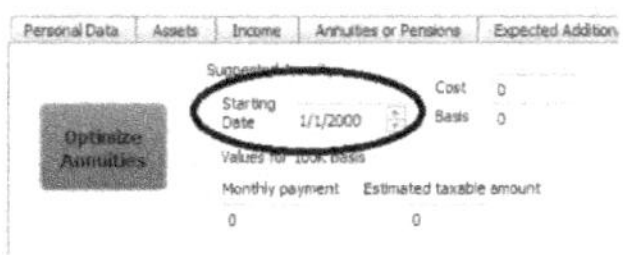

Figure A.61: The Suggested Annuities tab with the Starting Date field highlighted

Definition: This is the user-specified starting date for a joint & 100% annuity that the program will attempt to optimize.

Use in the program:
1. Contributes to the calculation of income for the future.
2. Contributes to the calculation of the remaining principal for the return of premium feature.
3. Contributes to the calculation of the remaining basis, which determines when the annuity payments become fully taxable. This will happen as soon as the whole basis has been returned to the annuitant.

The next data set is the Values for 100K basis box. (See Figure A.62)

Values for 100K Basis

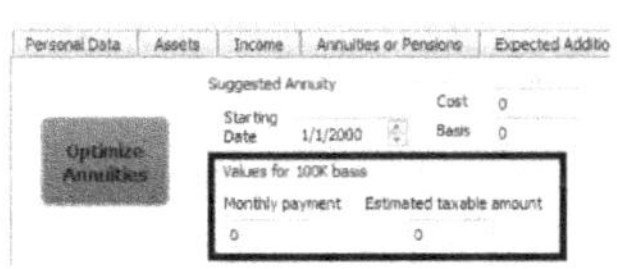

Figure A.62: The Suggested Annuities tab with the Values for 100K basis box highlighted

Definition: Specifies the initial monthly payment and estimated taxable amount for every 100K of premium for the annuity.

Use in the program: Serves as the source of data for calculating the effect of different amounts of premium used to purchase a joint annuity.

1. Contributes to the calculation of income for the future.
2. Contributes to the calculation of the remaining principal for the return of premium feature.
3. Contributes to the calculation of the remaining basis, which determines when the annuity payments become fully taxable. This will happen as soon as the whole basis has been returned to the annuitant.

The first field in this box is Monthly payment. (See Figure A.63)

Monthly Payment

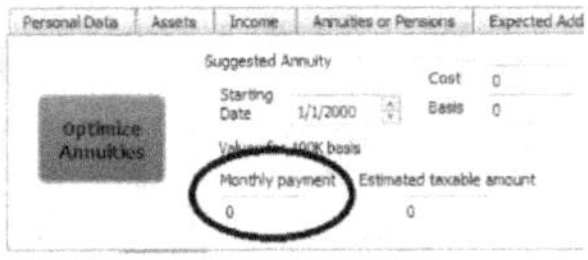

Figure A.63: The Suggested Annuities tab with the Monthly payment field in the Values for 100K basis box highlighted

Definition: Specifies the initial monthly payment that the insurance company will pay to the annuitant for each 100K of purchase premium.

Uses in the program:
1. Contributes to the calculation of income for the future.
2. Contributes to the calculation of the remaining principal for the return of premium feature.
3. Contributes to the calculation of the remaining basis, which determines when the annuity payments become fully taxable. This will happen as soon as the whole basis has been returned to the annuitant.

The next field in this box is Estimated taxable amount. (See Figure A.64)

Estimated Taxable Amount

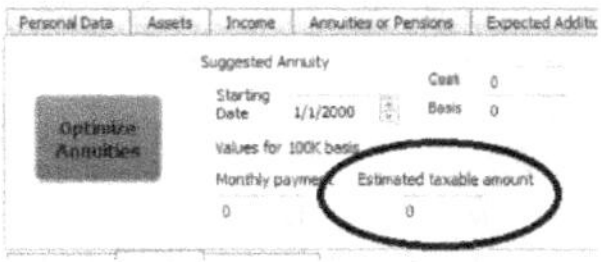

Figure A.64: The Suggested Annuities tab with the Estimated taxable amount field in the Values for 100K basis box highlighted

Definition: Specifies the estimated taxable amount of the annuity payment for each 100K of purchase premium.

Use in the program: Contributes to the calculation of the remaining basis, which determines when the annuity payments become fully taxable. This will happen as soon as the whole basis has been returned to the annuitant.

Note that this field is initially calculated according to rules in the program. However, if you have better information, such as provided in quotes from immediateannuities.com, you can type it in to override the calculated value.

The next field we will cover is the Adjusted to CPI checkbox. (See Figure A.65)

Adjusted to CPI

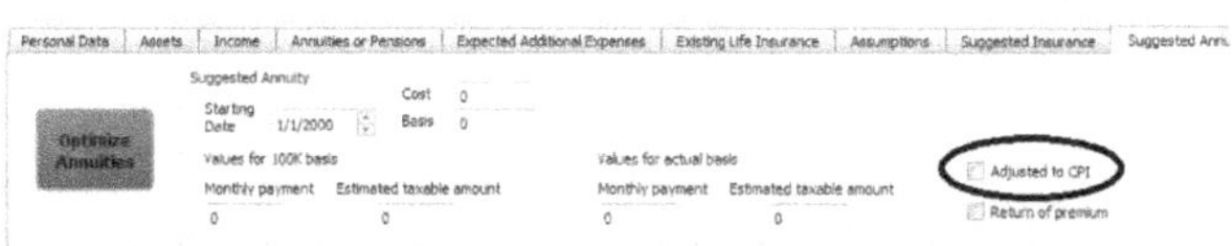

Figure A.65: The Suggested Annuities tab with the Adjusted to CPI checkbox highlighted

Definition: Specifies whether the annuity payment is adjusted according to the Consumer Price Index inflation index.

Use in the program: Used to determine whether to increase annuity payments in line with the inflation adjustment on the Assumptions tab; if the box is not checked, the annuity payment is in nominal dollars, i.e., is not adjusted for inflation.

The next field is the Return of Premium checkbox. (See Figure A.66)

Return of Premium

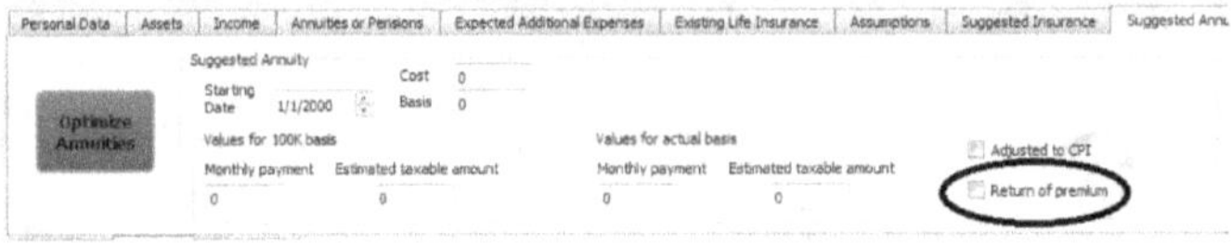

Figure A.66: The Suggested Annuities tab with the Return of Premium checkbox highlighted

Definition: Specifies whether the insurance company will pay the remainder (if any) of the annuity premium to the heirs of the annuitants.

Use in the program: Used to determine whether a relatively early death of the annuitants will cause a payment to their heirs; if the box is not checked, no such payment will be made.

The rest of the fields on the Suggested Annuities tab are filled in by the program when the "Optimize Annuities" button is pressed, although the Cost and Basis fields can be updated by the user. Let's fill in the entries in the Starting Date field and the Values for 100K basis box. (See Figure A.67)

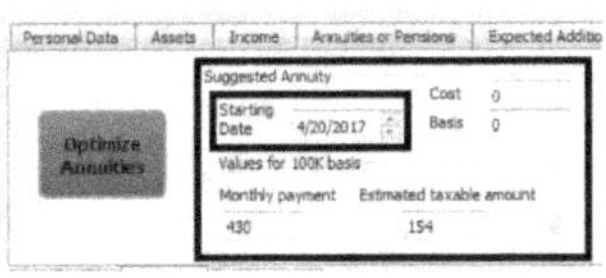

Figure A.67: The Suggested Annuities tab with entries in the Starting Date field and the Values for 100K basis box.

Now let's press the Optimize Annuities button and see what the program suggests for an annuity. (See Figure A.68)

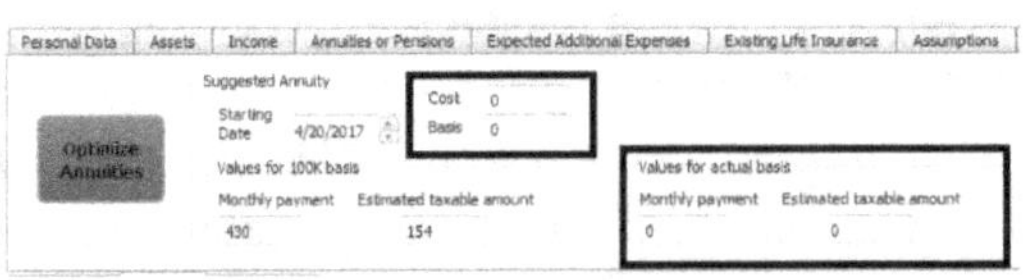

Figure A.68: The Suggested Annuities tab after pressing the Optimize Annuities button

In this case, with the couple's assets and given the assumptions of 2% inflation and cash nominal returns and 7% portfolio asset returns, buying an annuity doesn't increase sustainable spending in the worst case death year scenario, so the program doesn't recommend one.

Other Features of the GUI Main Screen

There are several features of the GUI main screen that we haven't covered yet. Let's start with the screen header, at the top of the screen. (See Figure A.69)

Figure A.69: The Rhino screen header

The first part of the screen header is the program name and version number. In this case, that is "Rhino Retirement Analyzer v1.0".

The next part of the screen header is the program revision ID, which in this case is "SVN: 2295". The number "2295" indicates the exact revision of the source code used to produce the executable that is running. The reason that the program displays this information is to improve customer support by making it easier for tech support personnel to reproduce any issue that the customer might find.[xxx]

The final part of the screen header is the full path to the parameter file that was most recently used to save the parameters that the program is using for its calculations. If these parameters haven't been saved, then this part of the screen header will be blank.

The next feature is the Calculate button. (See Figure A.70)

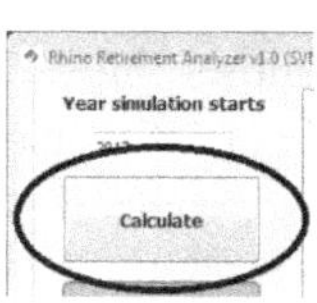

Figure A.70: The Calculate button

The Calculate button executes a search for the highest sustainable spending, given all of the specified data and options. As the search proceeds, you will see changing numbers in the result fields: Yearly Spending, the Worst case longevity box, the Median longevity box, the Year Search Results box, and the Worst Year Search box. (See Figure A.71)

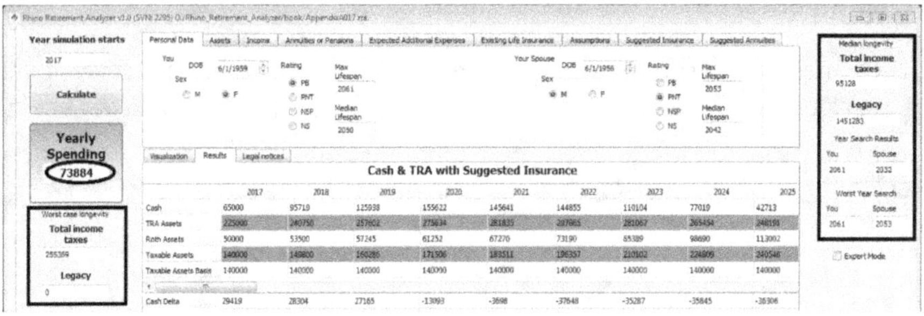

Figure A.71: The Yearly Spending field, the Worst case longevity box, the Median longevity box, the Year Search Results box, and the Worst Year Search box

The Yearly Spending field, as we have discussed at length, indicates the maximum sustainable spending in the worst-case death year scenario, i.e., deaths in those years indicated in the Year Search Results box at the end of the calculation.

The Total income taxes entry in the Worst case longevity box shows the estimated total federal income taxes in the event of that worst-case death scenario, given all of the other assumptions about inflation, returns, and the like.

The Legacy entry in the Worst case longevity box shows how much money will be left to heirs after the second death in the worst-case death year scenario, assuming that the couple spends the maximum sustainable amount shown in the Yearly Spending field. This will generally be a very small number because the Yearly Spending calculation is intended to maximize sustainable spending during the couple's lives and therefore will consume all or nearly all of their resources in that situation.

The Total income taxes entry in the Median longevity box shows the estimated total federal income taxes in the event of both spouses living to their median longevity, shown in the Median Lifespan field for each spouse, given all of the other assumptions about inflation, returns, and the like.

The Legacy entry in the Median longevity box shows how much money will be left to heirs after the second death in the event of both spouses living to their median longevity, assuming that the couple spends the maximum sustainable amount shown in the Yearly Spending field. This will often be a substantial number because the Yearly Spending calculation is intended to maximize sustainable spending in the worst case death year scenario, and therefore will leave a significant amount of resources if they die at times that put less stress on those resources, assuming that the return and inflation assumptions are fairly accurate. However, this outcome also depends on exactly how the resources are deployed, e.g., if most of the assets have been used to purchase life annuities without return-of-premium provisions, there may not be much left for heirs regardless of when each spouse dies.

Saving, Reloading, and Clearing Data

Rhino provides functionality to save, reload, and clear the data used in its calculations. These features are controlled by the buttons in the middle of the left side of the main screen. (See Figure A.72)

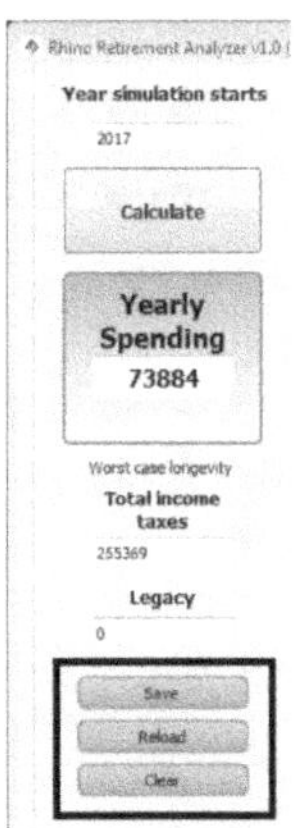

Figure A.72: The Save, Reload, and Clear buttons

Pressing the Save button displays a standard file save dialog, which enables the user to save a copy of the current program parameters needed to reproduce the scenarios shown on the screen, in a file with an extension of .rra (**R**hino **R**etirement **A**nalyzer). If the file has been previously saved, the default name will be the same as the current name, which as previously mentioned is shown at the top of the screen after the program revision number. In this case, the name of the file is AppendixA017.rra, and the file save dialog looks something like Figure A.73.

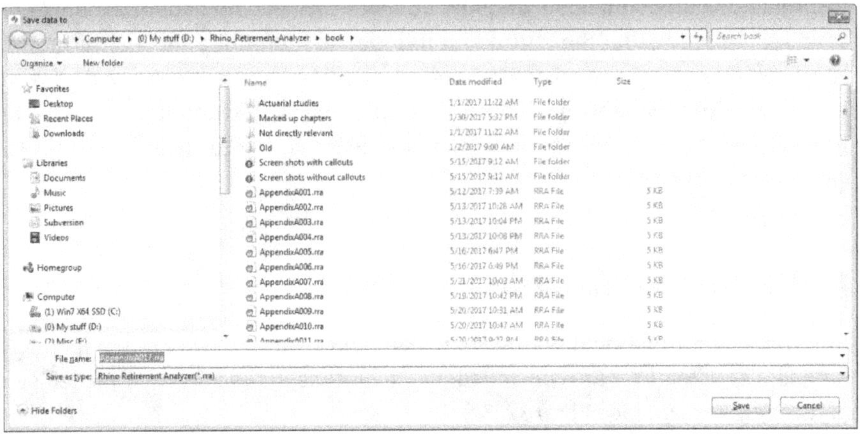

Figure A.73: The Save dialog

Pressing the Reload button displays a standard file open dialog allowing the user to choose a parameter file. (See Figure A.74)

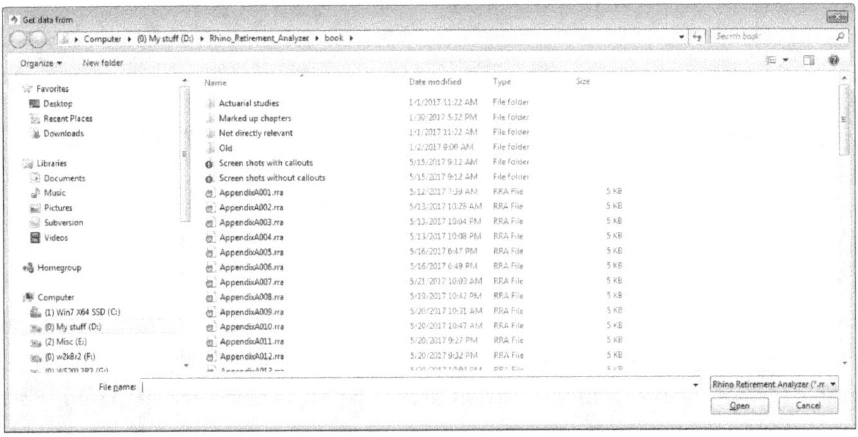

Figure A.74: The Reload dialog

Finally, the Clear button clears out the current data so that the user can start a new session with fresh information, just as if the program were being launched for the first time. (See Figure A.75)

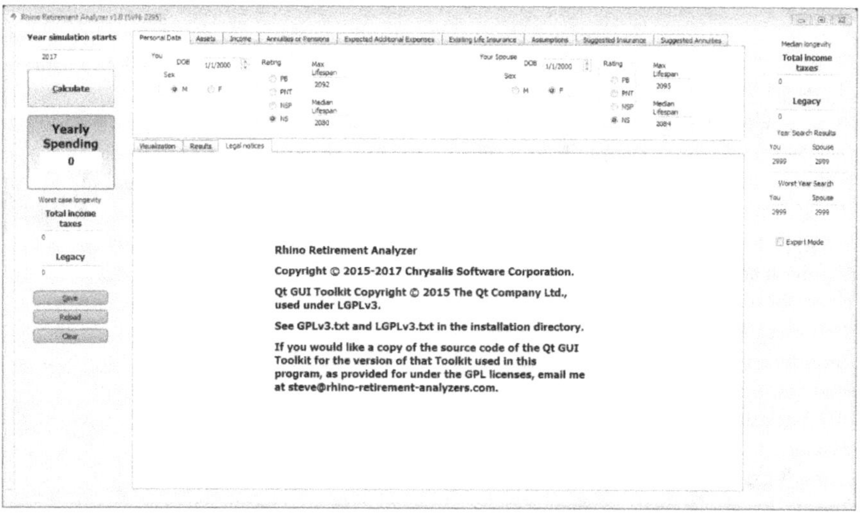

Figure A.75: The screen after pressing the Clear button

Now that we have covered all of the basic mode functionality, in Appendix B we will cover "Expert Mode".

---

[i] We will cover "Expert Mode" functionality in Appendix B.

[ii] Note that the program doesn't require one spouse to be male and the other female. The initial setting is for the first client to be male and the second female, but the sexes of the spouses are independently selectable, so same-sex couples are fully accommodated.

[iii] Note that the ratings shown are those in the current version of the program that can be downloaded from the website at no charge. Customized versions of the program will probably have different names for the ratings, and possibly fewer different ratings.

[iv] Note that the last of these is a standard rating, whereas all the others are preferred ratings. While it would in theory be possible to use the program with substandard ratings, the costs of insurance for such ratings would almost certainly not be cost-effective, so the current version of the program does not accommodate such ratings.

[v] In fact, the current version of the program won't run a simulation for more than 50 years. That is more than enough for retirees or near-retirees, who won't have a life expectancy of more than 50 years.

[vi] Note that the results for "Total income taxes" and "Legacy" in the "Worst case longevity" box do not assume the spouses' maximum lifespans as the corresponding results in the "Median case longevity" box do with the median lifespans. This is because the worst case is the case that produces the lowest sustainable spending, not the case where the spouses both live the longest time.
[vii] Note that the program assumes that all TRA assets have a tax basis of zero, i.e., that all contributions were deductible pre-tax contributions. Thus, all withdrawals are calculated as being taxed at the client's marginal rate.
[viii] Note that the program assumes that the Roth account will have been open for five years by the time any earnings are withdrawn, as required for those earnings not to be taxed.
[ix] Note that yearly salary values in the simulations are *not* adjusted for inflation, to keep the results conservative.
[x] Obviously if the retirement date is in the past, the client would still have been alive then, but it will often be in the future with the client's actual data.
[xi] September 2017.
[xii] The Social Security benefit can also be entered directly if you don't want to use the Social Security optimizer that is triggered by clicking the Optimize SS Dates button. In that case, you don't need to fill in the PIA.
[xiii] Having the older and higher paid spouse wait until the latest possible time to claim benefits is one of the suggestions commonly made by retirement advisors. However, this program doesn't *assume* that is the best solution, but rather *calculates* which claiming dates allow for the maximum sustainable spending in the particular case of a specific couple.
[xiv] There are other types of annuity that pay lesser amounts after the death of the first annuitant, or after the death of either annuitant, but "Single Life" and "Joint & 100%" are the only types that the current version of the program can handle.
[xv] Note that since many existing annuities have already begun payments by the time the simulation begins, some of the premium will already have been returned by the time the simulation begins. The program takes account of this when calculating how much premium, if any, would be returned at death.
[xvi] As with the return of premium feature, some of an existing annuity's basis may have already been returned by the time the simulation begins. The program takes account of this when calculating the remaining non-taxable amounts.
[xvii] For an annuity with the "adjusted to CPI" feature, the payment shown in the first year of the simulation will already have been adjusted by assumed inflation from the starting date of the annuity. This is an approximation that is necessary to calculate the return of premium and non-taxable income amounts before the simulation begins.
[xviii] Note that since many existing annuities have already begun payments by the time the simulation begins, some of the premium will already have been returned by the time the simulation begins. The program takes account of this when calculating how much premium, if any, would be returned at death.
[xix] As with the return of premium feature, some of an existing annuity's basis may have already been returned by the time the simulation begins. The program takes account of this when calculating the remaining non-taxable amounts.
[xx] As with the return of premium feature, some of an existing annuity's basis may have already been returned by the time the simulation begins. The program takes account of this when calculating the remaining non-taxable amounts.

[xxi] Note that we haven't set an inflation assumption yet, so checking the checkbox won't affect the results at present. However, it will when we set the inflation adjustment.

[xxii] Of course it is possible for a client to have more than one existing life insurance policy, but most clients who have multiple life insurance policies have probably been extensively counseled on their need for life insurance and are less likely to need more. For this reason, the free version of the program handles only one existing policy per client.

However, it would be quite feasible to add the ability to handle multiple policies to the program as a customization, if desired.

[xxiii] If the policy is a whole life policy, you can enter "99" for the term, so that the program will assume that the policy will remain in force during the entire simulation.

[xxiv] Of course the client can keep the policy in force after the spouse dies, assuming that the term has not expired. However, the program's goal is to maximize sustainable spending, and once the spouse dies the policy is no longer needed to mitigate the loss of income to the spouse. Thus, the program assumes that the policy will be dropped at that point.

[xxv] Note that not all terms, ages, and face amounts can be estimated using this button. It is provided only as a convenience.

[xxvi] Insurance payouts are always shown in the year after the event that caused the payout, because the death is (arbitrarily) projected to happen at the end of the year.

[xxvii] Note that for existing inflation-adjusted annuities, the same inflation rate is applied to payments starting from the beginning of the annuity.

[xxviii] See https://portfoliosolutions.com/latest-learnings/blog/30-year-risk-and-return-forecast-2016.

[xxix] The program will estimate the taxable amount so that it will have something to work with if that information is not available from the initial annuity quotation. Of course, the actual taxable amount should be known before purchasing the annuity, but an approximate taxable amount generally doesn't affect the sustainable spending significantly.

[xxx] Obviously, tech support for the free version of the program will be limited by available resources. Paid versions include enhanced support, and enhanced support for the free version can be purchased on the program's web site, rhino-retirement-analyzers.com.

Appendix B
Reference Manual for the GUI for the Rhino Retirement Analyzer v1.0, Expert Mode

The Expert mode of the Rhino Retirement Analyzer provides a number of options that are useful in exploring alternatives to the results calculated by the automated features. For example, after calculating the worst-case scenario for death dates of the two spouses, clients often ask how things would turn out if those death dates were different. The Expert mode allows you to specify different death years and see how those scenarios would play out. Similarly, you can show your client what could happen if they spent more (or less) than what the program calculates as their sustainable spending rate.

This appendix describes the Expert mode features in detail.

The Expert Mode Checkbox

Figure B.1 shows the location of the Expert Mode checkbox on the right side of the screen.

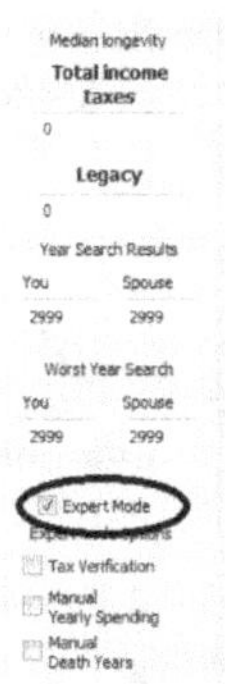

Figure B.1: The location of the Expert Mode check box on the right side of the screen

The first Expert Mode option is Tax Verification. (See Figure B.2)

DOI 10.1515/9781501506185-011

Tax Verification

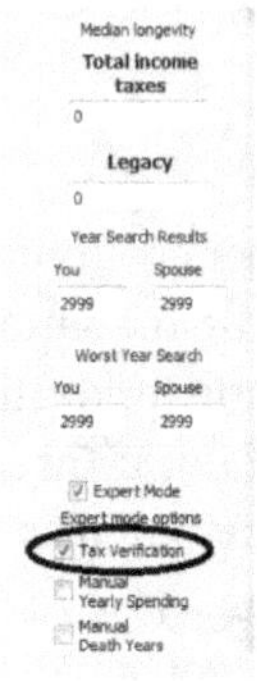

Figure B.2: Expert Mode controls with the Tax Verification checkbox checked

Definition: Causes tax brackets and other quantities that are normally inflation-adjusted to remain at the original values

Use in program: Allows comparison of tax calculations with the results of tax-preparation programs

The results of tax preparation programs apply only to the year for which they are published, e.g., the "2015 filing year edition" of a tax preparation program will use the tax brackets, deductions, exemptions, and so on that were in effect for 2015. This is what such programs are intended for, so the results are perfectly appropriate for these programs.

Rhino also contains official IRS tax brackets, deductions, and so on for a particular ("base") year, but in addition, it needs to calculate estimates for *future* tax liabilities. This requires adjusting these values according to projected inflation, so that its tax calculations will correspond to the results that would be obtained in each future year according to that projected inflation rate.

But in order to see whether Rhino's tax estimates are close to the results of a tax preparation program, we need to suppress these inflation effects so that Rhino will calculate taxes as though every year had the same brackets, deductions, and so on as the base year. This is the main purpose of the Tax Verification checkbox and its associated Expert Mode tab, the Tax Test tab. (See Figure B.3)[i]

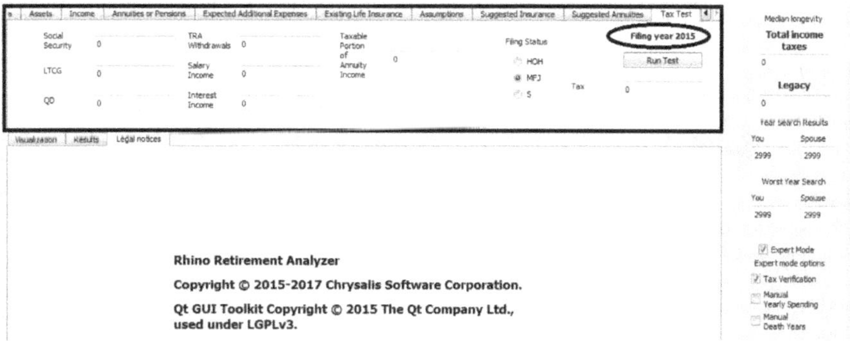

Figure B.3: The Expert Mode screen with highlighting on the Tax Test tab and the filing year for which it is intended

Let's take a look at an example. First, Figure B.4 shows the Income tab for a couple who have a combined salary income of $125,000 and an income from qualified dividends of $1,000.

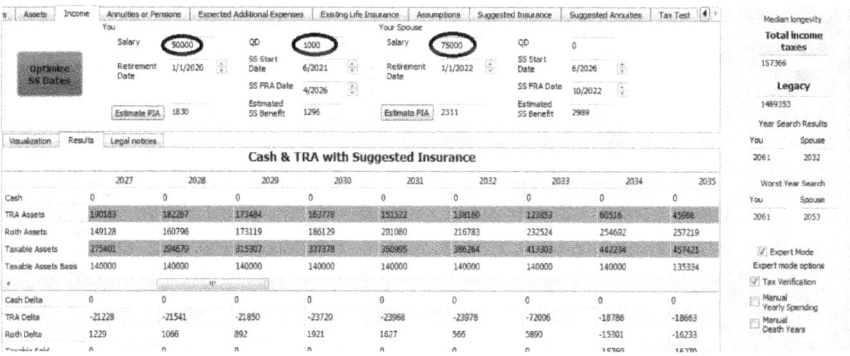

Figure B.4: The Expert Mode screen showing the Income tab with a total salary income of $125,000 and a qualified dividend income of $1,000.

Now let's go back to the Tax tab and enter those values for salary and qualified dividend income, along with the $1,300 interest income that they would receive on their $65,000 in cash at a 2% interest rate, then push the Run Test button. (See Figure B.5)

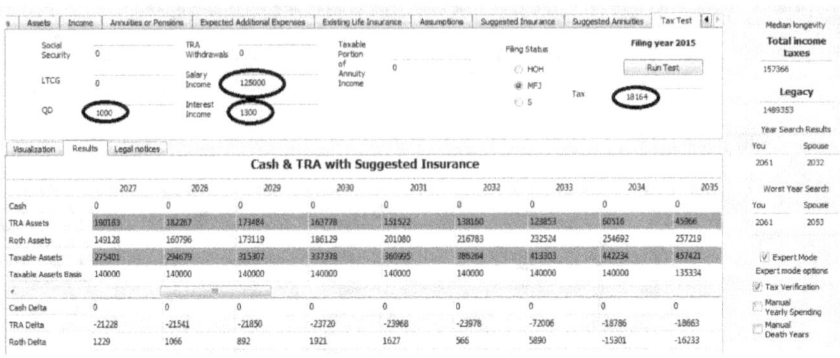

Figure B.5: The Expert Mode screen showing the estimated income tax on the Tax Test tab using Tax Verification, with a total salary income of $125,000, a qualified dividend income of $1,000, and interest of $1,300.

As you can see, the tax test feature estimates the federal income tax as $18,164. How does this compare with the results of a tax preparation program for the same filing year (2015), given the same inputs? (See Figure B.6)

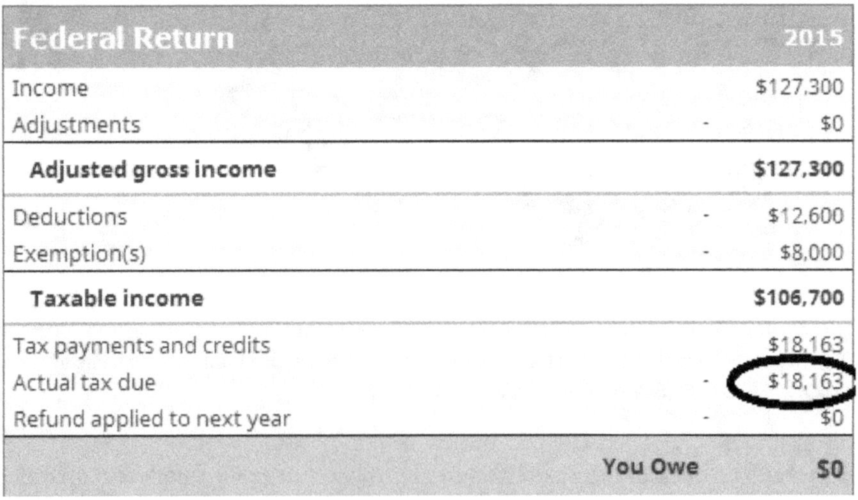

Figure B.6: The results of a tax preparation program given the same inputs as the Rhino Tax Test calculator

The Rhino tax calculator is $1 off from the tax preparation program's results. That is certainly close enough for projections 30 years or more into the future, when we will be very fortunate to have the outcomes match our projections within 10%!

The next expert mode feature is Manual Yearly Spending. (See Figure B.7)

Manual Yearly Spending

Figure B.7: Expert Mode controls with the Manual Yearly Spending checkbox checked

As we have already seen, the Rhino Retirement Analyzer, in its basic mode, calculates the maximum sustainable spending level automatically. However, the client often wishes to know what would happen in the event that he or she spent more (or less) than the automatically determined maximum sustainable spending level. Another use for this option is to illustrate what would happen if the assumptions are too generous (or too stingy). We will take a look at both of these uses for this option as soon as we discuss the effects on the GUI of turning the option on.

First, let us look at the change in the graphical user interface as a result of clicking the Manual Yearly Spending checkbox. (See Figure B.8)

The Asset Depletion Box

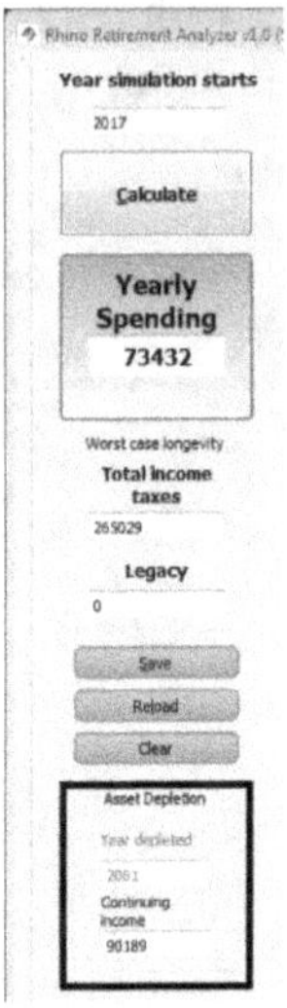

Figure B.8: The change in the GUI with the Manual Yearly Spending checkbox checked"

The only change to the GUI caused by checking the Manual Yearly Spending checkbox is that the Asset Depletion box is now visible in the lower left of the screen. The first field in that box is Year depleted. (See Figure B.9)

Year Depleted

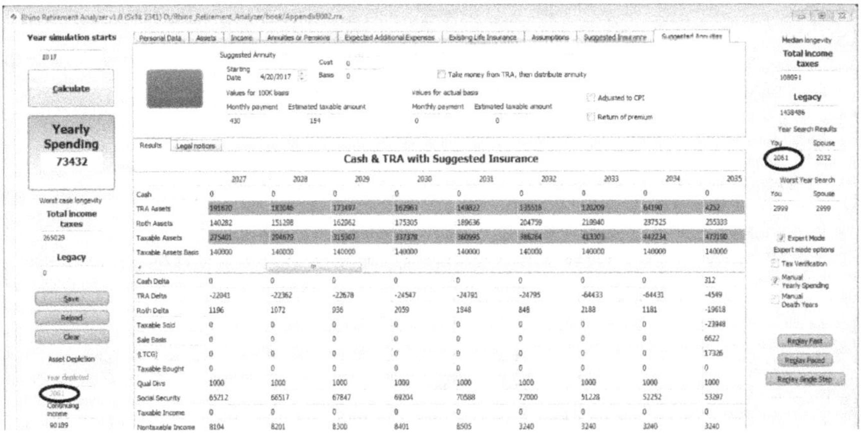

Figure B.9: The Expert Mode screen showing Year depleted

Year depleted, as the name suggests, indicates the year when remaining assets will be insufficient to continue the sustainable Yearly Spending amount previously calculated. Until you change the Yearly Spending from the automatically calculated value, the year shown in Year depleted will be the last year that either of the spouses is alive, as shown in the Figure. That is because the sustainable Yearly Spending amount is calculated to use up the assets in the year of the later death.

The other value in the Asset Depletion box is Continuing income, which is the amount of income that will continue after the assets are depleted. In this case that figure is $90,189 per year. (See Figure B.10)

Continuing Income

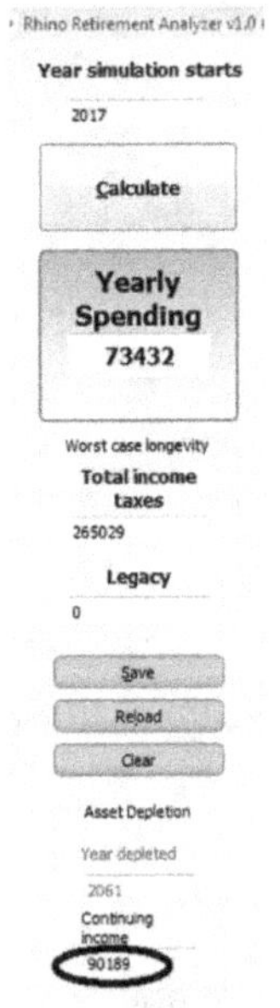

Figure B.10: The Asset Depletion box showing Continuing income

Increasing Yearly Spending

The first use of setting manual yearly spending amounts is to see what would happen with higher yearly spending. Obviously, higher yearly spending amounts will cause asset depletion to occur more rapidly, but the question is how much more rapidly. For example, if we increase Yearly Spending to $80,000, the result might look like Figure B.11.

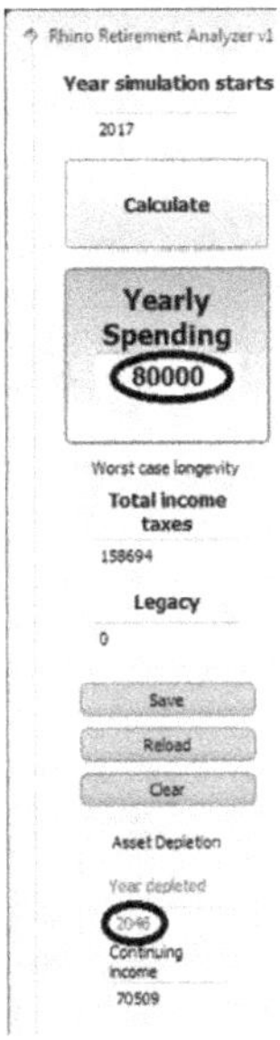

Figure B.11: The Asset Depletion box showing that the Year depleted is earlier when spending is increased

Checking the Results of More Conservative Return Assumptions

Another use of the manual yearly spending feature is to see what would happen if we spent the amount that was projected using more aggressive assumptions on returns and inflation, but the actual results for returns and inflation are less favorable. For example, let's suppose that we estimate sustainable spending using inflation of 2%, cash returns of 2%, and asset returns of 7%, as shown in Figure B.12.

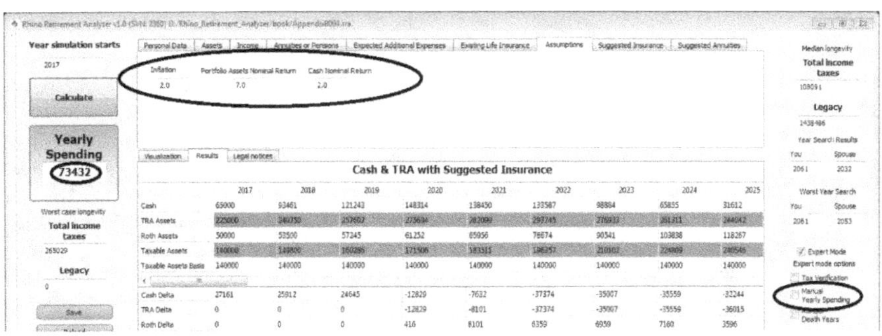

Figure B.12: An example of calculated sustainable spending with our assumptions set to Inflation at 2%, Cash Nominal Return at 2%, and Portfolio Assets Nominal Return at 7%

Now let's set the Inflation, Portfolio Assets Nominal Return, and Cash Nominal Return assumptions to 0%, click the Manual Yearly Spending checkbox, then click the Calculate button. The result will look like Figure B.13.

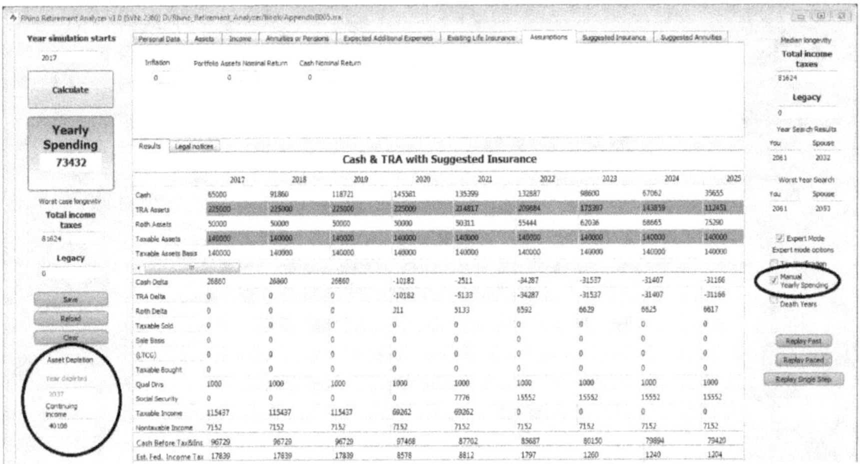

Figure B.13: An example of the result of spending the same amount as previously calculated, when the assumptions have been changed to more conservative assumptions. In this case, they would deplete their assets in 2037, with continuing income of $40,108/year after that point.

The next expert mode feature is Manual Death Years. (See Figure B.14)

Manual Death Years

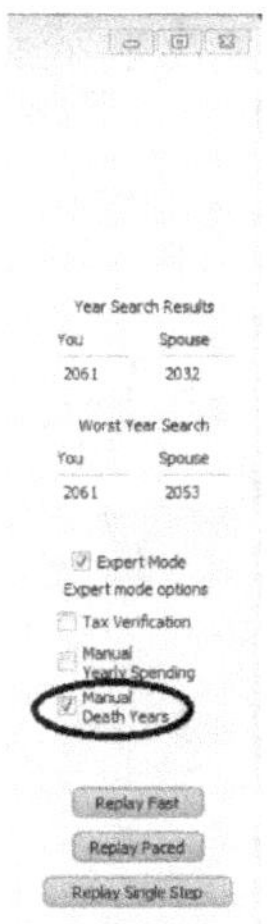

Figure B.14: Expert Mode controls with the Manual Death Years checkbox checked

As we have already seen, the Rhino Retirement Analyzer, in its basic mode, calculates the maximum sustainable spending level, assuming that both spouses die at times that put the maximum strain on their assets. However, the client often wishes to know what would happen in the event that they die at different times than those worst possible times. This option allows the user to illustrate results with different death dates.

First, let's look at the change in the graphical user interface as a result of clicking the Manual Death Years checkbox. (See Figure B.15)

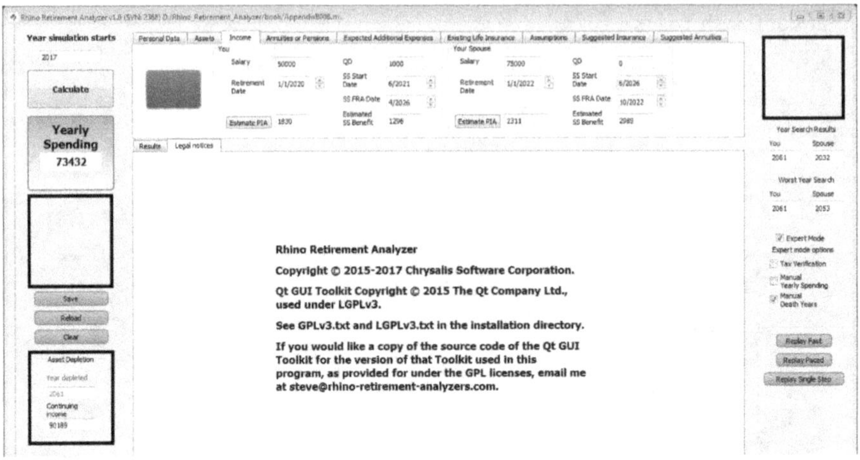

Figure B.15: The Expert Mode screen showing the changes in the GUI with the Manual Death Years checkbox checked

The changes in the GUI are that the median longevity and worst-case longevity boxes are no longer visible, because they are irrelevant when you are specifying death years manually, and as with the Manual Yearly Spending option, the Asset Depletion box is shown.

Now let's see what happens if we specify different death years from those selected by the program, which in this case are 2061 for the client and 2032 for the spouse. Probably the most common use of this option will be to answer the question "What if we both live to our median lifespans?", so those are the years we will choose. (See Figure B.16)

Checking the Results of Manually Specified Death Years

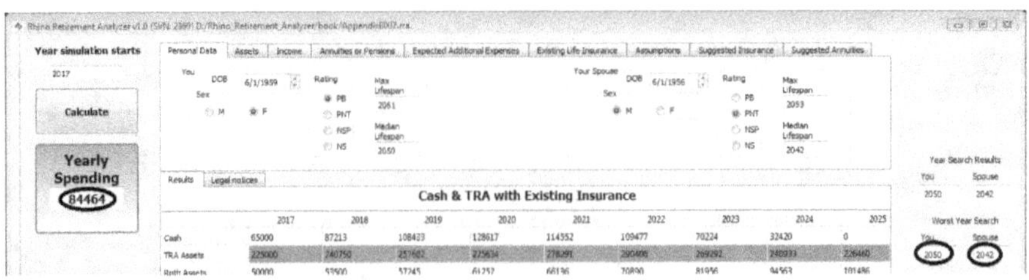

Figure B.16: The Expert Mode screen showing that the Yearly Spending is higher when median lifespan is chosen for the manual death years

Note that the sustainable yearly spending would be about $10,000 higher if we knew that both spouses would die at the median lifespan. Of course, it is to be expected that sustainable yearly spending would be higher if the spouses did not die at the worst possible time, but it is convenient to be able to investigate the magnitude of the difference.

Also note that the Asset Depletion box shows the later of the two years of death, as we have told the program to use up all the assets by that year. (See Figure B.17)

Assets Depleted in the Later of the Two Death Years

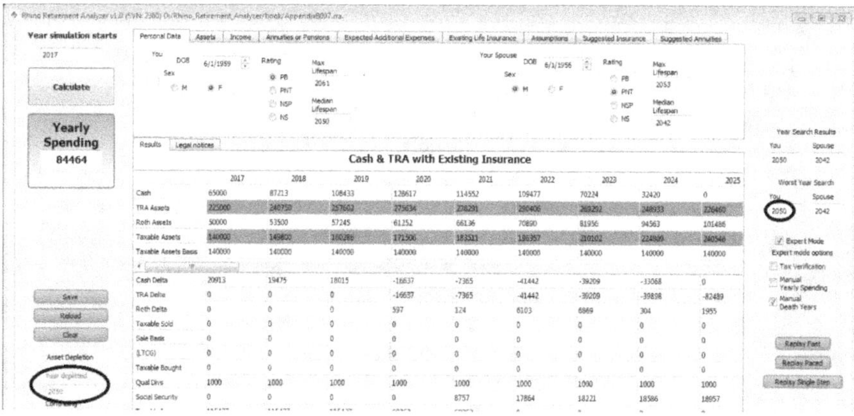

Figure B.17: The Expert Mode screen showing the assets being depleted in 2050, as that is the later of the two manually selected death years

Also note that it is possible to combine manual yearly spending and manual death years, if you have a need to do so.

---

[i] The Tax Test tab shows the filing year for which the taxes should be compared. Use of a tax preparation program for a different filing year will probably not produce the same results.

Appendix C Tutorial for the Scripting Language and Command-Line Interface of the Rhino Retirement Analyzer v1.0

The features explained in this appendix are very helpful if you need to rerun existing scenarios for training or demonstration purposes, or in the event that you run into a bug in the program. However, for day-to-day use of the program, you can ignore them.

Why does the Rhino Retirement Analyzer Need a Command-Line Interface and a Scripting Language?

Complex programs such as the Rhino Retirement Analyzer are subject to what is colloquially referred to as "software rot".[i] Of course software does not actually rot or decay; if you run the same program under the same conditions, assuming it is a deterministic program that doesn't make use of random numbers, you should always get the same results.

However, it is very unusual for a complex program to remain the same for any extended period of time, especially a program that employs tax calculations, which are subject to change at the whim of Congress as well as statutory changes such as tax bracket adjustments for inflation that cannot be known in advance.

Another reason to make changes in a program that might change the results is to add features to that program, which can happen hundreds or thousands of times during the lifespan of a complex program.

And of course every complex program will have bugs that will need to be fixed. Fixing one bug can introduce another one. Even if this doesn't happen, any change to the algorithm may affect the results, so that the program now produces a different answer for the same inputs. Some of these changes are intended, but unintentional or unexpected changes may also result from a seemingly "safe" change.

As a result, a wise programmer will provide a way to run "regression tests" on such a program. Regression tests are tests intended to ensure that changes made to a program do not result in unexpected changes in the program's output.

While it would, *in theory*, be possible to run regression tests via a GUI, doing so is infeasible for any significant amount of testing. The effort required to run even one test via the GUI is significant, and errors will inevitably creep into the

DOI 10.1515/9781501506185

testing effort itself. Since dozens or hundreds of tests will be required to have any reasonable chance of catching most errors introduced into a program as complex as this one, a way of running tests without user interaction is required. This means that we need a scripting language that can exercise the program automatically, and that can be invoked from the command line, generally via a batch file.

Once you have such a scripting language, it can be used for other purposes, such as reproducing bugs (often the hardest part of debugging) and for training, via a visual replay operation that shows the steps that the program goes through during its operation. The Rhino scripting language supports both of these additional applications as well as the batch mode of operation, as we will see later.

The `rra` File Type: Initializing the Program with Previously Saved Data

By far the most common use of the Rhino scripting language is to initialize the program with data that was previously saved, for which we use the `rra` file type.

Let's look at an example of how that works from the command line.

A Command-Line Example

The simplest command-line example that uses the scripting language is to provide only the name of a script file as the argument. (See Figure C.1)

Figure C.1: Starting Rhino from the command line with an `rra` script file called `JaneAndJimSmith023.rra`

If you run this command, the resulting Rhino GUI window will look like Figure C.2.[ii]

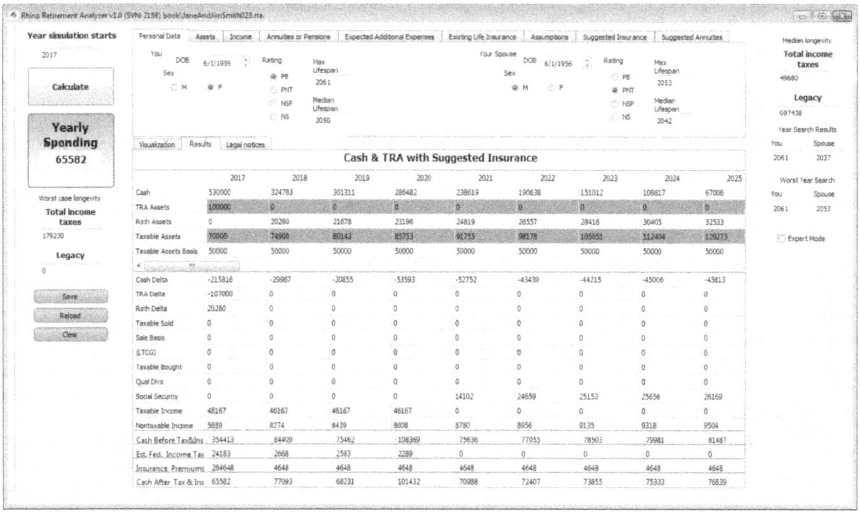

Figure C.2: The Rhino GUI window resulting from starting Rhino from the command line with a script file called `JaneAndJimSmith023.rra`

As you may have noticed, the program takes a few seconds to get to the final state you see in Figure C.2. What is it doing during that time?

It is initializing variables based on the `JaneAndJimSmith023.rra` script file, then executing commands in that script file. Figure C.3 shows that entire script file. We'll go over it in pieces as shown in subsequent figures.

A Sample rra Script File

```
1024
F0,FileType,rra
R0,RevisionNumber,2158
A0,AssetNominalReturn,7.000000
A0,BestLegacy,0
A0,BestMethod,3
A0,BestMethodWithExistingInsurance,3
A0,BestMethodWithSuggestedInsurance,3
A0,BestYearlySpendingWithExistingInsurance,56266
A0,BestYearlySpendingWithSuggestedInsurance,65582
A0,CalculationTime,0
A0,CashNominalReturn,2.000000
```

```
A0,DistributeAnnuity,F
A0,ExpectedExpenseAmounts,10000,30000,0,0,0,0,0,0,0,0,
A0,ExpectedExpenseYears,2018,2020,0,0,0,0,0,0,0,0,
A0,ExpertMode,F
A0,FileNameForOutputOfSpecifiedVariablesInCSVFormat,
A0,HOH,F
A0,InflateExpectedExpenses,T
A0,Inflation,2.000000
A0,LTCG,0
A0,LegacyMode,F
A0,MFJ,T
A0,QDForTest,0
A0,SSIncome,0
A0,SalaryIncome,0
A0,SelfCalculatedInsurance,1434,20,450000,Wed May 31
2017
A0,SelfExistingInsurance,0,0,0,Sat Jan 1 2000
A0,Self_AnnuityBasis,0
A0,Self_AnnuityCost,0
A0,Self_AnnuityInflationAdjusted,F
A0,Self_AnnuityIsJointAnd100,F
A0,Self_AnnuityIsSingleLife,T
A0,Self_AnnuityMonthlyPaymentPer100KCost,0
A0,Self_AnnuityReturnOfPremium,F
A0,Self_AnnuityStartDate,Sat Jan 1 2000
A0,Self_Cash,530000
A0,Self_DOB,Mon Jun 1 1959
A0,Self_EstimatedTaxablePortionOfMonthlyPayment,0
A0,Self_EstimatedTaxablePortionOfMonthlyPaymentPer100K
Spent,0
A0,Self_Female,T
A0,Self_LatestDeathEstimate,2061
A0,Self_LifeAnnuityIncome,0
A0,Self_Male,F
A0,Self_MedianDeathEstimate,2050
A0,Self_PIA,2526
A0,Self_QD,0
A0,Self_RRAAssets,0
A0,Self_RatingBest,T
A0,Self_RatingFourthBest,F
A0,Self_RatingSecondBest,F
A0,Self_RatingThirdBest,F
```

```
A0,Self_RetirementDate,Sat Jan 1 2000
A0,Self_SSBenefit,1789
A0,Self_Salary,50000
A0,Self_SocSecStartDate,Tue Jun 1 2021
A0,Self_TRAAssets,100000
A0,Self_TaxableAssets,70000
A0,Self_TaxableBasis,50000
A0,SimulationStartingYear,2017
A0,Single,F
A0,SpouseCalculatedInsurance,3214,20,450000,Wed May 31
2017
A0,SpouseExistingInsurance,0,0,0,Sat Jan 1 2000
A0,Spouse_AnnuityBasis,0
A0,Spouse_AnnuityCost,0
A0,Spouse_AnnuityInflationAdjusted,F
A0,Spouse_AnnuityIsJointAnd100,F
A0,Spouse_AnnuityIsSingleLife,T
A0,Spouse_AnnuityMonthlyPaymentPer100KCost,0
A0,Spouse_AnnuityReturnOfPremium,F
A0,Spouse_AnnuityStartDate,Sat Jan 1 2000
A0,Spouse_Cash,0
A0,Spouse_DOB,Fri Jun 1 1956
A0,Spouse_EstimatedTaxablePortionOfMonthlyPayment,0
A0,Spouse_EstimatedTaxablePortionOfMonthlyPaymentPer10
0KSpent,0
A0,Spouse_Female,F
A0,Spouse_LatestDeathEstimate,2053
A0,Spouse_LifeAnnuityIncome,0
A0,Spouse_Male,T
A0,Spouse_MedianDeathEstimate,2042
A0,Spouse_PIA,2509
A0,Spouse_QD,0
A0,Spouse_RRAAssets,0
A0,Spouse_RatingBest,F
A0,Spouse_RatingFourthBest,F
A0,Spouse_RatingSecondBest,T
A0,Spouse_RatingThirdBest,F
A0,Spouse_RetirementDate,Fri Jan 1 2021
A0,Spouse_SSBenefit,3212
A0,Spouse_Salary,50000
A0,Spouse_SocSecStartDate,Wed Apr 1 2026
A0,Spouse_TRAAssets,0
```

```
A0,Spouse_TaxableAssets,0
A0,Spouse_TaxableBasis,0
A0,State,
A0,SuggestedAnnuity_AnnuityBasis,260000
A0,SuggestedAnnuity_AnnuityCost,260000
A0,SuggestedAnnuity_AnnuityInflationAdjusted,T
A0,SuggestedAnnuity_AnnuityIsJointAnd100,F
A0,SuggestedAnnuity_AnnuityIsSingleLife,T
A0,SuggestedAnnuity_AnnuityMonthlyPaymentPer100KCost,2
60
A0,SuggestedAnnuity_AnnuityReturnOfPremium,F
A0,SuggestedAnnuity_AnnuityStartDate,Thu Apr 20 2017
A0,SuggestedAnnuity_Cash,0
A0,SuggestedAnnuity_DOB,Sat Jan 1 2000
A0,SuggestedAnnuity_EstimatedTaxablePortionOfMonthlyPa
yment,0
A0,SuggestedAnnuity_EstimatedTaxablePortionOfMonthlyPa
ymentPer100KSpent,0
A0,SuggestedAnnuity_Female,F
A0,SuggestedAnnuity_LatestDeathEstimate,2092
A0,SuggestedAnnuity_LifeAnnuityIncome,676
A0,SuggestedAnnuity_Male,T
A0,SuggestedAnnuity_MedianDeathEstimate,2080
A0,SuggestedAnnuity_PIA,0
A0,SuggestedAnnuity_QD,0
A0,SuggestedAnnuity_RRAAssets,0
A0,SuggestedAnnuity_RatingBest,F
A0,SuggestedAnnuity_RatingFourthBest,T
A0,SuggestedAnnuity_RatingSecondBest,F
A0,SuggestedAnnuity_RatingThirdBest,F
A0,SuggestedAnnuity_RetirementDate,Sat Jan 1 2000
A0,SuggestedAnnuity_SSBenefit,0
A0,SuggestedAnnuity_Salary,0
A0,SuggestedAnnuity_SocSecStartDate,Sat Jan 1 2000
A0,SuggestedAnnuity_TRAAssets,0
A0,SuggestedAnnuity_TaxableAssets,0
A0,SuggestedAnnuity_TaxableBasis,0
A0,TRAWithdrawals,0
A0,TestTime,0
A0,UseManualDeathYears,F
A0,UseManualYearlySpending,F
A0,VerificationMode,F
```

```
A0,YearlySpending,65582
S0,Recalculate,
S0,ExecuteBestMethodCalculation,
```

Figure C.3: The Rhino script file JaneAndJimSmith023.rra

There are three parts of an rra script file: the file header, the variable assignment section, and the function execution section. Let's start the analysis with the file header, as shown in Figure C.4.

A Sample File Header

```
1024
F0,FileType,rra
R0,RevisionNumber,2158
```

Figure C.4: The file header in the Rhino script file JaneAndJimSmith023.rra

The first line of the file header, in this case 1024, tells Rhino the "file version" of this file. This file version number is modified whenever there is a change in the file layout that the program has to take account of when decoding the file contents. This prevents the program from being confused by an unexpected difference in the file layout, so that backward compatibility to earlier file layouts can be maintained to the greatest feasible extent. When there are incompatibilities, this version number allows the program to diagnose and report them in a reasonable manner rather than by simply being unable to read the file.

Now that the program knows the file version, it can decode a more specific set of scripting commands, so each line in the rest of the file has a specific layout. With file versions 1023 and 1024, the file versions supported as of this writing, each scripting command has the following format:

1. A command type letter, which can currently be A, B, C, F, M, R, or S;[iii]
2. A non-negative number;[iv]
3. A comma;
4. The command name;
5. A comma;
6. Any arguments that this specific command needs, separated by commas.

The second line of the file header, in this case F0,FileType,rra, is a "file type" command, as indicated by the command type letter F. The number, 0 in this case, is ignored for this command type. The command name argument is `FileType`, which is redundant in this case because the command type letter `F` indicates the same thing. It tells the program what type of script file this is, which can affect the detailed file decoding.[v] In this case, the file type is `rra`, short for "Rhino Retirement Analyzer file".

The third line of the file header, in this case `R0,RevisionNumber,2158`, indicates the exact revision number of the Rhino Retirement Analyzer program that recorded this script file. This can be very useful to a developer who is trying to reproduce a bug or other result of running the program, because that information can be used by the developer to recreate an equivalent version of the executable program at any time in the future.

The Variable Assignment Portion of the Sample Script File

As we have already seen, there are quite a few variable assignments in an `rra` script file. We will go over an example of each type of assignment rather than explaining every assignment in detail here.[vi] Let's start with the assignment for `AssetNominalReturn`, shown in Figure C.5.

```
A0,AssetNominalReturn,7.000000
```

Figure C.5: An assignment to the `AssetNominalReturn` variable

This assignment command, like all assignment commands, starts with the command letter `A`. As indicated previously, the `0` following the command letter is ignored when loading an `rra` file. After the separating comma, we have the name of the variable, in this case `AssetNominalReturn`, then another separating comma, and finally the value to be assigned to the variable, namely `7.000000`.[vii]

So the effect of this variable assignment command is to set the value for `AssetNominalReturn` to `7.000000`. Let's look at the GUI representation of this value to check that it has been assigned the correct value. (See Figure C.6)

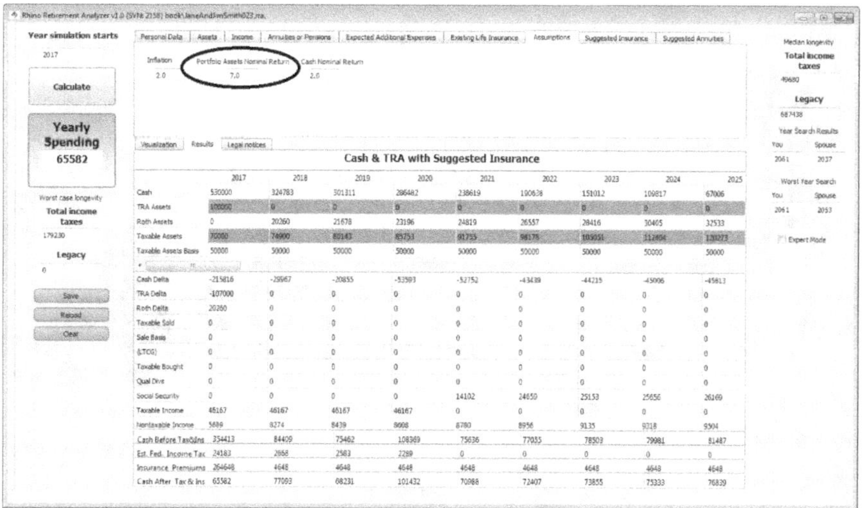

Figure C.6: The representation of the `AssetNominalReturn` variable in the GUI

You may notice that the value in the file has 6 zeroes after the decimal place, whereas the value in the GUI has only one. This is because the GUI representation of floating point numbers is controlled by formatting in the program. In the case of the variables representing our assumptions for returns and inflation, there wouldn't be much point in specifying a highly precise number, given that we would be lucky to get the first digit right.

The next line we will examine, `ExpectedExpenseAmounts,10000, 30000,0,0,0,0,0,0,0,0,` is an assignment to an integer vector called `ExpectedExpenseAmounts`. This variable corresponds to the amounts on the second line of the "Expected Additional Expenses" tab, as shown in Figure C.7.

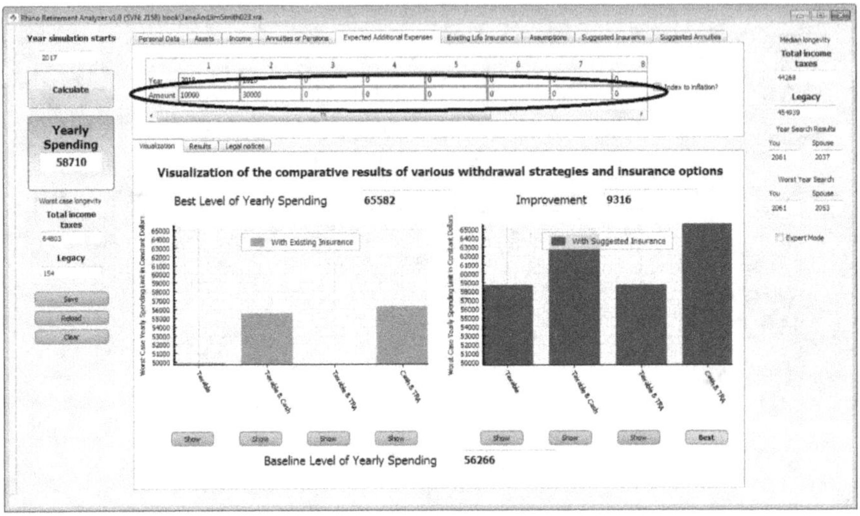

Figure C.7: The representation of the `ExpectedExpenseAmounts` variable in the GUI

Next we have an assignment to a Boolean variable called InflateExpectedExpenses: `A0, InflateExpectedExpenses, T`. This corresponds to the checkbox in the GUI shown in Figure C.8.

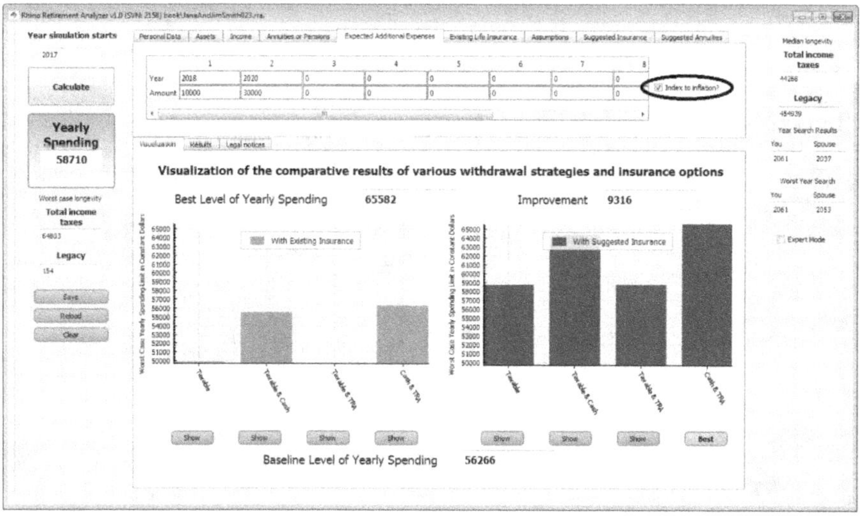

Figure C.8: The representation of the `InflateExpectedExpenses` variable as shown in the GUI

Values for this type of variable can be either `T` or `F`, for what I hope are obvious reasons.

The next line we will look at is `A0,SelfCalculatedInsurance, 1434,20,450000,Wed May 31 2017`. This variable, `SelfCalculated Insurance`, represents an insurance policy, as follows:

`1434` = the yearly premium

`20`= the term of the policy, in years

`450000`= the face amount of the policy

`Wed May 31 2017` = the starting effective date of the policy.

The GUI representation of this variable is as shown in Figure C.9.

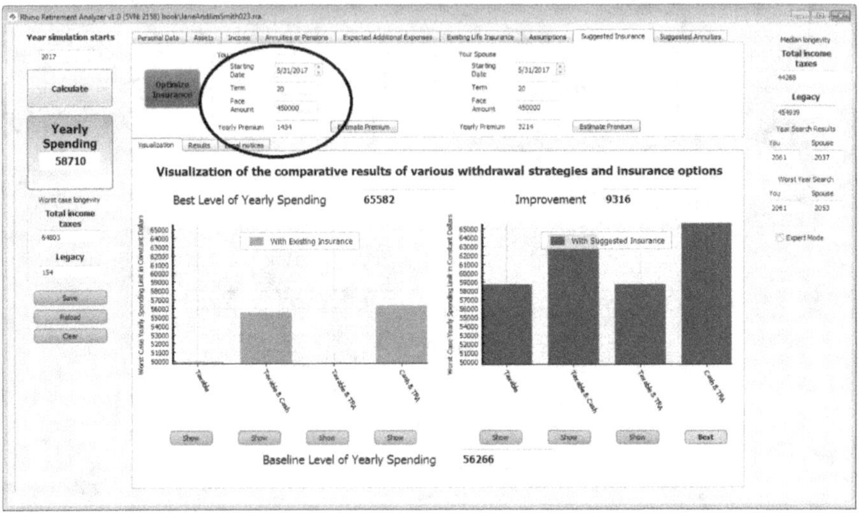

Figure C.9: The representation of the SelfCalculatedInsurance variable in the GUI

Next we have A0,Self_Cash,530000 which represents the amount of cash that the first client has in his or her portfolio. This is an integer variable, as indicated by the lack of a decimal point in the value. Figure C.10 shows the GUI representation of this variable.

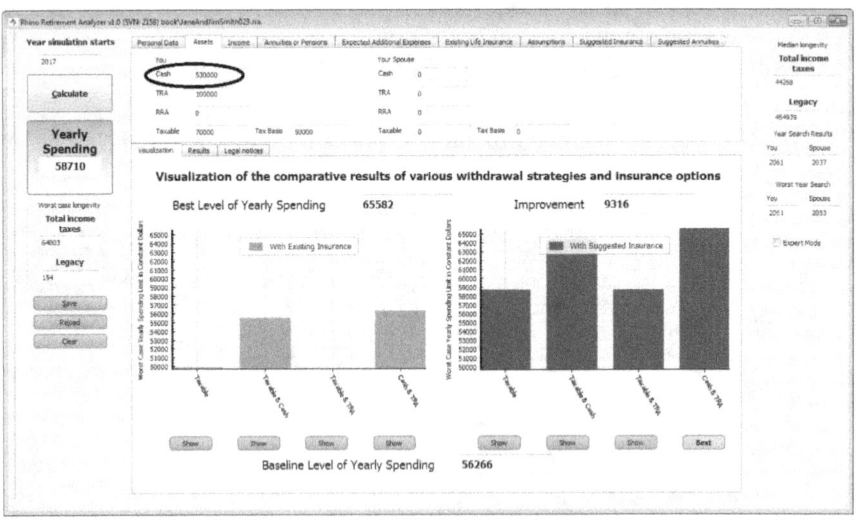

Figure C.10: The representation of the Self_Cash variable in the GUI

The last variable assignment we will look at is `A0,Self_DOB,Mon Jun 1 1959`, which represents a date variable corresponding to the date of birth of the first client.[viii] Figure C.11 shows how that variable is represented in the GUI.

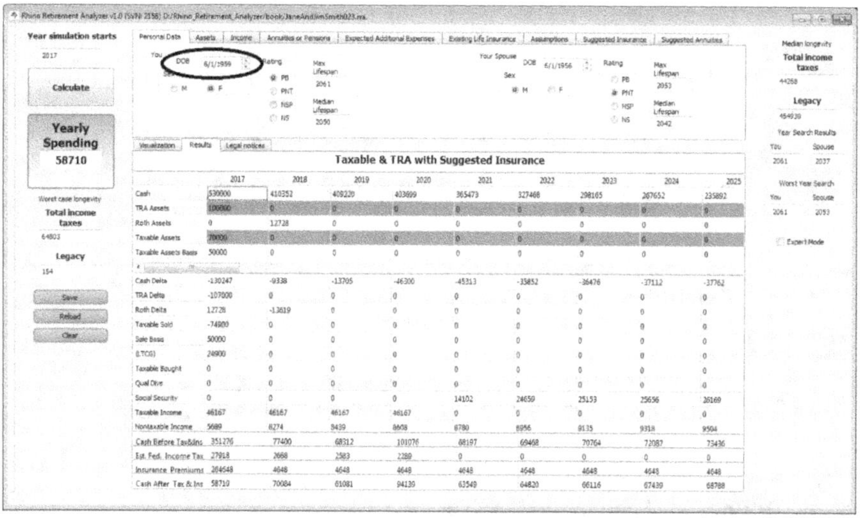

Figure C.11: The representation of the `Self_DOB` variable in the GUI

The Function Execution Portion of the Sample `rra` File

The last portion of an `rra` file is the function execution portion. This portion is the same in all `rra` files in currently supported file formats. It consists of the lines

```
S0,Recalculate,
S0,ExecuteBestMethodCalculation,
```

These lines cause the execution of functions in the program. The first of these lines, `S0,Recalculate,` executes the same operation as the `Calculate` button in the GUI, namely to update the calculation results according to the current variable values. The second of these lines, `S0,ExecuteBestMethodCalculation,` causes the GUI to display the results of whatever withdrawal strategy and insurance selection produces the best result. This is equivalent to clicking the "Best" button shown in Figure C.12.

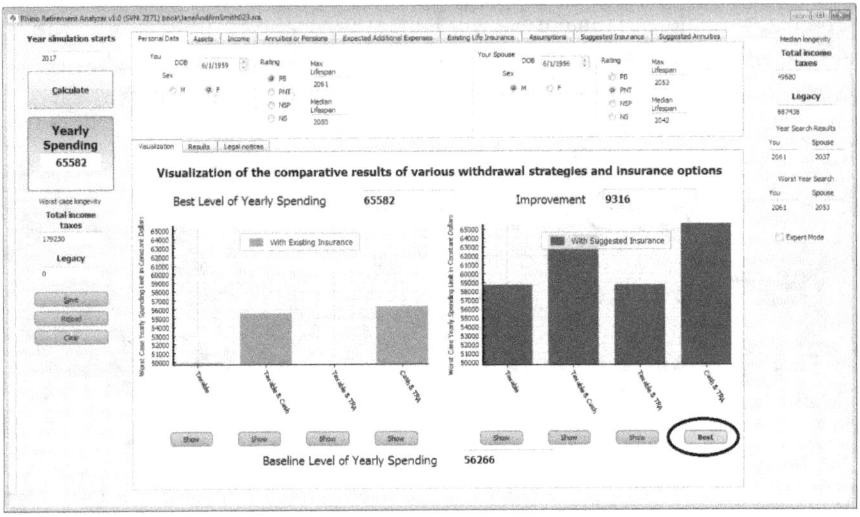

Figure C.12: The GUI button that requests display of the best result

Other Options for Command-Line Use

There are a number of other options available from the command line, which are detailed in the online documentation for the program. However, we can cover the most commonly used options used in testing here. These are the `BatchProcessingMode` option and the `SaveCSVFile` option, both of which are Boolean flag variables.

As an example, let's use the following command line, which should be all on one line, but is broken up to fit on this page:

```
rhino "book\JaneAndJimSmith023.rra"
BatchProcessingMode,T SaveCSVFile,T
```

1. `BatchProcessingMode`
   This option is set to `F` by default, which means that the program will present the GUI for user interaction. Setting it to `T` tells the program to load and execute the script file without showing the GUI.

   Since our sample command line invocation includes the argument `BatchProcessingMode,T,` the program will load and execute the script file, then exit without showing the GUI.
2. `SaveCSVFile`

This option is used in conjunction with the `BatchProcessingMode` option, and is also set to `F` by default. This means that when the program exits after loading and executing the script file, it will not produce the .csv output file. The .csv output file is generally used to verify that the program is still producing the same output as it did previously. Setting this variable to `T` tells the program to save the .csv file with a name corresponding to the script file's name.

Since our sample command line invocation includes `SaveCSVFile,T,` after the end of execution of the script file the program will save the .csv file `book\JaneAndJimSmith023.csv`.

So, the net effect of executing that command line invocation of Rhino will be to load and execute the script file called `book\JaneAndJimSmith023.rra` without showing the GUI, then saving the output file called `book\JaneAndJimSmith023.csv`.

The `rrr` File Type: Recording a Run of the Program for Later Replaying

The other type of scripting file used with the Rhino Retirement Analyzer is a recording of a run of the program, for later replay.

Figure C.13 shows several portions of an `rrr` file called `timingtest.rrr`, recorded during the self-test that the program runs every time it starts up.

```
1024
F0,FileType,rrr
R0,RevisionNumber,2193
...
S0,UpdateYearHeadersSlot,
...
A0,YearlySpending,91490
M0,YearlySpending,83697
...
```

Figure C.13: An example `rrr` file called `timingtest.rrr`

Let's start with the header, which, as before, consists of the first three lines of the file.

```
1024
F0,FileType,rrr
R0,RevisionNumber,2193
```

Figure C.14: The first three lines of the sample .rrr file

As before, the file version number is 1024, which is an arbitrary number assigned by the program to the specific layout of this file. The program uses this first line to determine whether it knows how to process this particular version of this type of file.

The second line, `F0,FileType,rrr,` tells the program the type of this file. This file is an `rrr` file, which is a Rhino Retirement Analyzer 'recording and replay' file.

The third line specifies the revision number of the program that recorded it, to allow that revision of the program to be recreated for later debugging and analysis if a problem should be detected.

The remainder of the file consists mostly of a number of variable assignment commands just like the ones in the .rra file with function commands interspersed where they occurred during the run of the program. The first of these function commands is

```
S0,UpdateYearHeadersSlot,
```

This tells the program to update the year numbers displayed on the screen so that they start with the simulation starting year (2017 in this case).

Another type of command is the `M` command, which indicates that we are modifying the same variable as we did in the previous command. An example of such a sequence is: [ix]

```
A0,YearlySpending,91490
M0,YearlySpending,83697
```

So the format of the .rrr file is quite similar to the .rra format. Why do we need the .rrr file type?

Uses for the .rrr File Type

There are several uses for this file type:

1. Regression tests
   I have already mentioned this use of these files, but perhaps haven't made it clear that they provide the ability, via a batch file, to rerun saved sessions. This is used to ensure that these sessions still produce the same results as they did previously. The ability to rerun these sessions makes program changes much less risky than they would be without a way to detect a regression (defined as something that used to work but no longer does).

2. Training
   With the single-step and paced replay features in the GUI, an instructor can show one or more students the exact sequence of operations used in a particular run of the program. The instructor can also check the student's work by rerunning test sessions that they have recorded.
3. Demonstration
   This is similar to the training use, except that the audience is potential users rather than existing students. It is very common to make mistakes during demonstrations that prevent the demonstrator from displaying the product in its best light. By using .rrr files to record the steps of a demo in advance, this risk can be mitigated.

---

[i] See https://infogalactic.com/info/Software_rot

[ii] There may be slight differences in the GUI window you will see if you execute this command, due to changes in the program between the time this book was written and the version that you have downloaded from the web site.

[iii] See the online documentation for a definition of the meanings of all of the different command type letters. In this document we will see how A, F, M, R, and S are used.

[iv] This number will always be 0 in an `rra` file, and will be ignored when processing the file. It is present for compatibility with the `rrr` file type, to be discussed later.

[v] With the current version of the program, the file type does not affect decoding, but this line must be present to validate the script file.

[vi] See the online documentation for the complete list of variables that can be assigned in a script file for the current version of the program, the format for each variable type, and the corresponding GUI entity for each variable.

[vii] All user-accessible floating point variables in the current version of the program are `floats` rather than `doubles`, which is why there are 7 significant digits in the value.

[viii] It would be very inconvenient to be required to include the day of the week when entering a date in a script file. However, that isn't necessary because I have included the ability for the program to read dates with just the month, day and year. So in this example of the date of birth, you could change the assignment statement to "`A0,Self_DOB,Jun  1  1959`", and it would still work in the same way. In other words, the day is included in the output but isn't required for input.

[ix] The distinction between the A and M command letters is not meaningful in the current version of the program. However, it is recorded so that the program could change the timing of the replay to be faster if we are modifying the same variable several times in a row, e.g., when typing in a value of 100000, the same variable might take on values 1, 10, 100, 1000, 10000, and 100000 consecutively.

Appendix D
The Market for Retirement Spending Optimization

Does the Public Know that Retirement Spending Optimization is a Problem?

According to a chart labeled "Importance of selected factors in Social Security claiming decisions" from a report recently prepared by AARP[i], 55% of those surveyed said that "Maximizing amount of money that spouse receives after their death" was "very important", and 28% said it was "somewhat important".

This indicates that the problem of retirement spending optimization is not a secret to many people in this age group. But how big a group is it? Obviously this is key to understanding the market potential for selling life insurance for such optimization.

Here are a few facts that suggest that the size of this market is very large.
- There are ~75 million Baby Boomers, of whom roughly 2/3 are married (source: http://usatoday30.usatoday.com/news/nation/census/2009-11-10-topblline10_ST_N.htm).[ii]
- Thus, there are ~25 million married Baby Boomer couples.
- Assume 8 million of these couples are both insurable at standard rates or above.
- If the average premium per couple is $2000/year, the total potential premium would be $2000 * 8 million, or ~$16 billion/year.
- If 10% would buy the insurance, we get $16 billion * 10%, or ~$1.6 billion in annual premium.

This suggests that the market for life insurance to help prevent a large drop in retirement income to a widowed spouse due to the loss of the second Social Security benefit should be fairly significant.

---

[i] "Perspective of Future Social Security Beneficiaries Ages 45-64: Detailed Findings", downloaded from http://www.aarp.org/content/dam/aarp/research/surveys_statistics/econ/2015/perspectives-future-beneficiaries-res-econ.pdf

[ii] Of course not everyone in the AARP survey is technically a Baby Boomer, as that encompasses people born from 1946 through 1965, meaning that age 50 was the cutoff when

DOI 10.1515/9781501506185-013

---

that survey was done in 2015. But most of them are, and the results are unlikely to be affected too much by including a few people under 50.

Appendix E
The Genesis of the Rhino Retirement Analyzer (and this Book)

A few years ago, as I was contemplating retirement, I perused a lot of financial advice for people in my situation. One of the mainstays of personal financial retirement advice is that you should always take money out of your accounts "in a tax-efficient manner". While this is obviously true, merely telling people to do something doesn't give them the tools they need to follow that advice. After a fairly thorough search of available resources, I couldn't find anything that even claimed to allow a layman to convert this general recommendation into actionable advice.

Fortunately, I'm a software developer with some knowledge of financial matters, so I decided to take a crack at that problem myself, on the theory that if I needed such a tool, others would need it as well.

However, as I began the development process, it became clear that the scope of the project was far beyond my original conception. Once I decided to add analysis of the effects of term life insurance, I discovered how significant those effects could be. At that point, I decided to become a life insurance agent, so that I could help married couples in or near retirement avoid that worst-case scenario of one spouse dying early in retirement and leaving the survivor (usually the widow) a long time at a very low standard of living due to the loss of the second Social Security payment.

Then I got an email from the editor of some of my previous books (on computer programming) asking if I had any ideas for writing another book. I suggested a book on what I had found out about retirement income security. After some discussion, he agreed that a book on this topic would fit into the product line of his new publisher. This book is the result of that agreement.

So what does the resulting program, now called the Rhino Retirement Analyzer, do?

A General Description of the Current Version of the Program

The Rhino Retirement Analyzer is a program that estimates the sustainable spending level for a married couple and the surviving spouse after the first spouse dies. It relies on a number of assumptions about federal income taxes, Social Security rules, and other financial variables that can and will change, so

DOI 10.1515/9781501506185-014

the results are and *must be* estimates, not actual results that can be relied on as calculated. Of course, the same caveats apply to *any* forecasting or estimating method that attempts to model future events, as no one knows what the actual laws and regulations will be in the future, nor does anyone know exactly when he or she will die.

However, the fact that we don't know exactly how the future will play out does not mean that estimating future events has no value. On the contrary, without trying to estimate future results, we are flying completely blind. The Rhino Retirement Analyzer provides a view of what **might** happen, which is the best anyone can do. Its results, while not guaranteed, are very helpful in determining whether one's retirement plans are feasible or must be scaled back if one wants a high probability of having sufficient retirement savings to sustain planned spending.

In the event that you are a licensed insurance agent who would be interested in a custom version of the program described in this book (the Rhino Retirement Analyzer), please contact me at steve@steveheller.org for a quotation on such customization. If, on the other hand, you are a financial planner *without* an insurance license, you may be interested in the fact that at this writing, I have licenses to sell life insurance and fixed annuities in the following states: AZ, CA, FL, IA, OH, MI, PA, VA, and TX. I'd be happy to help your clients in those states insure their retirement income.

Appendix F
What is Included, What is Excluded, and Known Limitations of the Program

Financial planning, especially tax planning, is a very complex subject. Accordingly, no single program can encompass every possible scenario or effect. This appendix explains which factors are and are not included in the calculations and results provided by the Rhino Retirement Analyzer.

Factors that are Included in the Rhino Retirement Analyzer Calculations

Taxes

The tax calculations of the Rhino Retirement Analyzer include the following considerations:

1. FICA taxes, including Medicare contributions and OASDI.
2. Capital gains, including the special treatment of capital gains and qualified dividends in the 10% and 15% brackets, and the maximum $3000 capital loss that can be deducted from income.
3. Filing status, which starts out as married filing jointly and changes to single after the death of one spouse.
4. Standard deductions, exemptions (including the over 65 special exemptions), and tax brackets.
5. The special tax treatment of Social Security income.
6. Increases in OASDI limits, income tax brackets, exemptions, and the standard deduction according to projected inflation.
7. RMD calculations for withdrawals from retirement accounts.
8. Calculations of taxes based on withdrawing money from various accounts in different orders, including taxable first, taxable and cash first, taxable and traditional retirement accounts first, and cash and traditional retirement accounts first.
9. The effects of Roth accounts, including the possibility of adding withdrawals from traditional retirement accounts that are not needed in the current year. This excludes RMD's, as required by IRS regulations.
10. The partially nontaxable tax treatment of annuity payments when not all of the basis has been recovered.

DOI 10.1515/9781501506185-015

11. Estimates of the taxable portion of annuity payments for either one or two life annuities, if the actual taxable portions are not known.

Social Security

The Social Security calculations of the Rhino Retirement Analyzer include the following considerations:

1. Calculation of full retirement age.
2. Adjustments of payments based on starting date relative to full retirement age.
3. The ability for a widow (or widower) to switch to the higher of the two benefits at his or her full retirement age.
4. The special tax treatment of Social Security payments.
5. A very rough estimate of the "primary insurance amount" used by the Social Security Administration to calculate benefits, based on the most recent year's salary of the client. This should be used only when no other estimate is available.

Insurance Analysis

The insurance analysis of the Rhino Retirement Analyzer includes the consideration of insurance ratings of standard or above. The free version includes four ratings, with representative rates obtained from web sources.

Annuities and Pensions

The annuities and pensions calculations of the Rhino Retirement Analyzer include the following options:

1. Single life or joint and 100% to survivor options.
2. Return of premium option.
3. Inflation adjustment option.
4. Immediate or deferred fixed annuities.
5. Cost and basis entries for calculating the return of premium benefit and the taxability of payments.

Assumptions

The assumptions of future rates of return and rates of inflation used in the Rhino Retirement are applied on a yearly basis at constant rates. The rates of return are applied to assets in the various investment accounts included in the calculations, and the inflation rate is applied to Social Security benefits and tax brackets, deductions, and exemptions, but not to salary.

Lifespan Estimates

The estimates of median and maximum longevity are computed according to Social Security Administration tables, modified by insurance ratings.

Factors that are Not Included in the Rhino Retirement Analyzer Calculations

Taxes

1. The "Net investment income tax".
2. AMT calculations.
3. State and local income taxes.
4. The "Married filing separately" filing status.
5. The 20% capital gains tax bracket.
6. Itemized deductions.
7. Income-based limitations on the standard deduction and exemptions.
8. The penalty for taking money out of retirement accounts before age 59 ½.
9. Taxes incurred by taking money out of Roth accounts less than five years after opening the first Roth account.

Social Security

1. The possibility of taking Social Security as early as age 60 if you are a widow or widower.
2. Automatic calculations of the spousal benefit that can top up the benefit of a very low paid worker.

Assumptions

The assumptions of future rates of return and rates of inflation used in the Rhino Retirement Analyzer are applied on a yearly basis without variation. For this reason, conservative rates of return should be used, as "sequence of return risk" is not considered.

Pensions and Annuities

Only fixed pensions and annuities, not ones indexed to or dependent on market conditions, are considered. CPI adjustments are included, however.

Known Limitations of the Program

1. The Rhino Retirement Analyzer is intended for use with clients whose income is less than the amount that causes reductions in deductions, exemptions and so on, and who are not subject to AMT calculations or the net investment income tax. It can still be used in those situations, but the calculations will be less accurate.
2. State and local income taxes are not included in the calculations. This is impossible because such taxes are deductible only if the taxpayer itemized deductions, and the program uses the standard deduction.
3. Estate tax calculations are not included in computing the legacy left after the second spouse dies.

Disclaimer and Caveats

Of course, I cannot guarantee that the Rhino Retirement Analyzer's results are correct even to the extent that the future unfolds as the scenarios calculated by the program suggest. Every complex program will have bugs of various levels of seriousness. Although I have made every reasonable attempt to debug and validate the results of this program, any reliance on the results of the program are at the risk of the user. As always when making financial decisions, do your own diligence and consult whatever financial experts you consider knowledgeable and reliable. You can also validate the tax calculations of the program by comparing them with a commercial tax preparation program; there is a validation mode that allows such comparison for future dates by eliminating the inflation adjustments to tax brackets and the like.

Index

V

W, X

Y, Z

www.ingramcontent.com/pod-product-compliance
Lightning Source LLC
LaVergne TN
LVHW022209200926
848481LV00006B/1910

* 9 7 8 1 5 0 1 5 1 5 1 2 5 *